Resolving Homosexual Problems

A Guide for LDS Men

by
Jason Park

with a Foreword by
A. Dean Byrd, Ph.D.

CENTURY PUBLISHING
SALT LAKE CITY, UTAH
1997

Resolving Homosexual Problems: A Guide for LDS Men

ISBN 0–941846–06–7
Library of Congress Catalog Card Number: 97–67741

Printed in the United States of America.

Dedicated
to those who believe that the
homosexual attractions within them
can be changed

To my dear friends Buzz, Todd, and Warren

To my friend Alan
who died before he could
find his way out of homosexual problems

My thanks to Dr. A. Dean Byrd
for his help in reviewing this book

Contents

Foreword

by A. Dean Byrd, Ph.D.

". . . and the truth shall make you free" (John 8:32).

Jason Park's journey out of homosexuality is reminiscent of the journeys made by many other men. Like many others, the trip was well worth the effort. Weaving his personal story throughout the book, Jason offers timely counsel both psychological and spiritual. He identifies critical periods of development as well as critical interventions for those who struggle with unwanted homosexual attractions. The lighthouse of the gospel is ever present and offers a constant source of hope.

To the astute reader, Jason's inherent goodness is present from the very beginning. He's a man of integrity who has Christlike concern for those who struggle with homosexual difficulties. His empathy is not vicarious. He has been there. From his own experience he reaches out to others and bids them to "Come unto Christ." His life is a testimony of the power of the Savior's healing love.

I have read many manuscripts in recent months on the topic of homosexuality. There are few of the manuscripts that I would endorse. Jason's book is one of them. For the lay and professional alike, the book will make a difference if you let its message enter your heart: change is possible. The truth will set you free.

Dr. A. Dean Byrd
Salt Lake City, Utah

Introduction

This book is written to you if you are an LDS man who wants to follow Christ and you want to learn how to resolve your homosexual feelings. You may have tried in the past to get rid of your homosexual feelings, with varying degrees of success. You may be further confused by the notion that homosexuality is inborn and unchangeable. If your past efforts have failed, and if it really is unchangeable, why try to overcome it? But if you embrace homosexuality, what about the gospel, your family, and eternal life? There are answers to this dilemma.

This book presents an understanding of homosexuality in the gospel context and provides practical solutions to resolve the personal problems you face. There is hope. I know there are solutions because I have experienced them in my own life. And for every person like me who has written a book, there are hundreds more who have found the same success I have, and thousands more who have achieved at least some success. I write this book in behalf of those hundreds and thousands of people who have experienced real change in their lives.

Although homosexuality has been around for centuries, this book and others like it represent a pioneering effort. Pioneers are those who do something to make the way easier for those who follow. The psychological community is still plowing new ground when it comes to homosexuality, still looking for answers, while the pro-gay movement tries to stop them. We in the LDS community need to move forward. This book is an attempt to show how the psychological know-how can be applied in harmony with gospel truths to help LDS men. Some of the theories, approaches, and ideas may also be helpful to women who struggle with lesbianism and some may not. More research needs to be done on women's issues to better determine causes and solutions.

This book is only a guide. It is impossible in a book this size to give an exhaustive description of the problems or to make more than just a few suggestions of possible solutions. Throughout this book, I give examples of how people have dealt with particular issues. In all cases, these examples involve real people and real events, although many of the names have been changed to protect identities. And by the way, Jason Park is my pen name. Since I've left homosexuality behind, I would rather not expose myself or my family to publicity by using my real name.

You may also wish to get a copy of the book *Helping LDS Men Resolve Their Homosexual Problems: A Guide for Family, Friends, and Church Leaders*, which I have written as a companion to this book to help others understand what you are working through and how they can support you in the process.

Chapter One

What Is Homosexuality?

This chapter defines homosexuality, including attractions, identity, and behavior. The chapter then presents LDS doctrines concerning homosexuality, including the distinction between homosexual thoughts and behavior, and the importance of overcoming both. Finally, it offers correct information about homosexual problems.

Description

Homosexual problems include erotic thoughts, feelings, and behaviors directed toward the same gender. The psychological community uses the term *homosexuality* to refer to the entire complex that includes attractions, feelings, desires, sexual behavior, identity, and all its associated aspects, such as problems with masculinity, self-perception, emotional dependencies, and relationship issues.

These problems should not be confused with a healthy emotional and social interest in persons of the same gender. Homo*emotional* and homo*social* interests are healthy as long as they are not excessive and do not develop an erotic dimension. When same-gender interests are eroticized, they become homo*sexual*.

I use the term *homosexual* as an adjective to describe a person's feelings, thoughts, or behavior, but not as a noun to describe the person. The terms *gay* (referring to men) and *lesbian* (referring to women) include not only personal feelings and behaviors, but also describe a political, cultural, and social identity.

Homosexuality may include sexual feelings or attractions without sexual behavior or it may include complete emotional and sexual involvement. It cannot be identified simply by the presence or absence of outward sexual behavior.

Attractions

Homosexual attractions develop over time and almost always without any conscious choice. At some point in your life, you realized that you are sexually attracted to other men.* These attractions can be a major source of frustration, because in spite of your best efforts to get rid of them, you continue to have compelling sexual thoughts toward other men. These inner attractions may be intense and may consume a great deal of your thoughts and energy. If the sexual attractions are not resolved, they can grow into obsessions that interfere with your ability to function at work and at home, and can be destructive spiritually. Homosexual attractions are usually more compelling than attractions toward the opposite sex because they spring from more than sexual desires—they are attempts to fill unmet emotional and social needs.

Many men report they first noticed these attractions before puberty—before they felt or understood sexual feelings. The feelings were not inherently sexual, but at some point became eroticized. The needs involved are normal social and emotional needs that everyone has, but have become confused and sexualized toward the same gender. The attractions are actually attempts to meet the emotional and identity needs that have not yet been met in your life. As a child, some part of your normal developmental process was stopped and interfered with your ability to develop a heterosexual orientation. Ironically, sexual intimacy will not fill the needs. They should not be ignored (the conservative mistake) nor eroticized (the liberal mistake), but should be filled through legitimate, nonsexual means. Here, then, is the irony. Homosexuality itself has little to do with sex; the needs are not homo*sexual*, but homo*emotional*.

Identity

Many men with homosexual attractions report they felt "different" as boys but didn't know why. For them, the pain of growing up with homosexual attractions was not so much the pain of being attracted to boys, but the feelings of being different. If this describes you, these feelings of being different may have become self-fulfilling prophecies as you separated yourself from the very boys you needed to bond with.

---

* As explained in the introduction, the focus of this book is on male homosexual problems. Although much of the information in this book can also be helpful to women who have lesbian issues, don't assume that all the theories or strategies presented in this book will work for them.

You may have longed to feel you were on par with other boys, but this longing only widened the gulf between you and the rest of the guys. Feeling different may have created a mindset that influenced your self-perception and development. When other children sensed this hesitancy, they may have attacked it, confirming that you were different. Thus, you withdrew from other boys to defend yourself from the pain.

You knew your attractions were not right because of the "fag" jokes you heard, so you learned to keep the feelings to yourself, creating further problems of isolation and secrecy, which are powerful forces that keep homosexual problems from being resolved. When the rest of your male friends seemed normally attracted to females, you may have wondered why you were abnormally attracted to males. Knowing that these attractions were in conflict with your religious beliefs and society's norms, you realized that your innermost feelings were wrong and since you didn't choose to have these feelings, you may have wondered if there was something inherently wrong with you. This may have created an internal struggle as you desperately tried to understand the unnatural feelings and make sense of them in terms of your own internal values and religious beliefs.

Our identity is an accumulation of self-perceptions. Some people believe they were born with homosexual feelings which are part of their core identity. If you have accepted a homosexual identity, it has far-reaching implications and can profoundly influence how you think and act. Part of your challenge in resolving homosexual issues will be to correct misperceptions about yourself.

Behavior

Homosexual attractions can be strong if you entertain sexual fantasies. Because of the intensity of these sexual desires, you may have participated in sexual activities to fill the void you feel. However, this causes further confusion, leading you to believe that your needs are sexual rather than emotional. In a desperate attempt to satisfy these building tensions, you may have become involved in sexual activities that provide a temporary gratification of the sex drive, but leave you with deeper feelings of emptiness, loneliness and frustration. Rather than satisfying the real needs for acceptance and companionship, the sexual behavior only intensifies the needs. One of the greatest tragedies of homosexuality is the unawareness in most men that their needs are emotional. All they know is that they are sexually attracted to other men and they seek sexual contacts, which ironically do not fill their need for love from a friend.

Not all men find themselves involved in sexual behavior. Some men have participated in only limited behavior and others have remained chaste in spite of their intense attractions. If you have not become involved in homosexual behavior, congratulations! Your journey out of homosexuality will be much easier because of it.

Homosexuality is symptomatic of other problems

One of the reasons homosexual problems are difficult to address is that they are not the real problem. Focusing too much on homosexual problems can actually be misleading, since they are symptoms of deeper struggles, such as rejection, envy, abuse, self-perception, gender identity, distrust, or fear. However, it may be difficult to recognize this because you may be a master at hiding the real issues in your life. You may hide things from others and even from yourself. Many of these issues are common and others vary from person to person. Once you identify the causes of your painful hunger you can learn ways to feed the hunger in appropriate, nonsexual ways. Once you resolve the underlying problems, you will find that the homosexual problems resolve themselves.

Why is homosexuality a problem?

Your sexual *attraction* toward other men distorts healthy, loving relationships and can steer you away from the blessings that can be found in marriage and family relationships. It diverts capable priesthood holders from the roles of husband and father. Homosexual *behavior* is of particular concern because it violates God's commandments and blocks your eternal progress.

Gospel teachings regarding homosexuality

God created us as male or female (see Genesis 1:27). He wants men and women to join with each other under the covenant of marriage to procreate and fulfill their eternal destiny. In His eternal plan, there are no classifications of *homosexuals*, *bisexuals*, or *heterosexuals*. We are all on this earth having a human experience with various challenges to overcome so we can become the true men, women, priesthood holders, wives, husbands, mothers, and fathers that God wishes us to be.

Homosexual feelings

A 1991 letter issued by the First Presidency to all members of the Church stated, "there is a distinction between [1] immoral thoughts and feelings and [2] participating in either immoral heterosexual or any homosexual behavior."[1] The feelings that trigger your homosexual attractions emerged through no fault of your own. Since you made no conscious choice for them, you should not feel guilty for having them. However, you can choose how to respond to the attractions and should not deliberately feed the feelings by fantasizing and turning them into lustful thoughts. The First Presidency letter continued, "However, such thoughts and feelings, regardless of their causes, can and should be overcome. . . ."[2] You are responsible for your agency in the thoughts you entertain. In an article in the *Ensign* magazine about same-gender attraction, Elder Dallin H. Oaks clarified that "although immoral thoughts are less serious than immoral behavior, such thoughts also need to be resisted and repented of because we know that 'our thoughts will also condemn us' (Alma 12:14). Immoral thoughts (and the less serious feelings that lead to them) can bring about behavior that is sinful."[3]

Homosexual behavior

The scriptures are clear in condemning homosexual practices. We read in Romans, "For this cause God gave them up unto *vile* affections: for even their women did *change* the *natural* use into that which is *against nature*: And likewise also the men, leaving the *natural* use of the woman, burned in their *lust* one toward another; *men with men* working that which is *unseemly*, and receiving in themselves that recompense of their *error* which was meet" (Romans 1:26–27; emphasis added).

President Gordon B. Hinckley stated, "Prophets of God have repeatedly taught through the ages that practices of homosexual relations, fornication, and adultery are grievous sins. Sexual relations outside the bonds of marriage are forbidden by the Lord."[4] The First

Presidency declared, "The Lord's law of moral conduct is abstinence outside of lawful marriage and fidelity within marriage. Sexual relations are proper only between husband and wife appropriately expressed within the bonds of marriage. Any other sexual contact, including fornication, adultery, and homosexual and lesbian behavior, is sinful."[5]

Overcome thoughts and behavior

The 1991 letter from the First Presidency further stated, "We commend and encourage those who are overcoming inappropriate thoughts and feelings. We plead with those involved in such behavior to forsake it. We love them and pray for them. We are confident that through repentance and obtaining needed help, they can experience the peace that comes from conforming their lives to God's teachings."[6] President Gordon B. Hinckley said, "Our hearts reach out to those who struggle with feelings of affinity for the same gender. We remember you before the Lord, we sympathize with you, we regard you as our brothers and our sisters. However, we cannot condone immoral practices on your part any more than we can condone immoral practices on the part of others."[7]

Elder Dallin H. Oaks said, "The struggles of those who are troubled by same-sex attraction are not unique. There are many kinds of temptations, sexual and otherwise. The duty to resist sin applies to all of them."[8]

"Church leaders are sometimes asked whether there is any place in The Church of Jesus Christ of Latter-day Saints for persons with homosexual or lesbian susceptibilities or feelings. Of course there is. The degree of difficulty and the pattern necessary to forgo behavior and to control thoughts will be different with different individuals, but the message of hope and the hand of fellowship offered by the Church is the same for all who strive."[9] Elder Oaks further explained that "all should understand that persons (and their family members) struggling with the burden of same-sex attraction are in special need of the love and encouragement that is a clear responsibility of Church members, who have signified by covenant their willingness 'to bear one another's burdens' (Mosiah 18:8) 'and so fulfil the law of Christ' (Gal. 6:2)."[10]

How many people have homosexual problems?

Pro-gay advocates claim that 10% of the population has a homosexual orientation. More conservative estimates place the figure at 1–3%. However, estimates are problematic not only because it is hard to get accurate information, but also because it is difficult to define what homosexuality is. Do you include in the numbers everyone who has had a homosexual thought, or just those who have had a homosexual experience? How many experiences or thoughts qualify? Some people are reluctant to admit homosexual experiences, while others exaggerate the numbers. Further, since it is to the political advantage of those who seek to normalize homosexuality to establish the practice as widespread, you must be cautious about the studies that are reported.

Kinsey research

Alfred C. Kinsey conducted research on human sexuality in the late 1940s and early 1950s and published his findings in *Sexual Behavior in the Human Male*[11] and *Sexual Behavior in the Human Female*.[12] Kinsey ranked his findings on a seven-point scale with exclusive heterosexuality at zero and exclusive homosexuality at six.[13] Among twenty-five–year-old males in the United States, he claimed that 79% were at zero (exclusively heterosexual) and 2.9% were at six (exclusively homosexual).[14] He claimed the following about white American males between the ages of sixteen and fifty-five:[15]

♦ 10% were "more or less exclusively homosexual (i.e., rate 5 or 6) for at least three years."
♦ 8% were "exclusively homosexual (i.e., rate 6) for at least three years."
♦ 4% were "exclusively homosexual throughout their lives, after the onset of adolescence."

His findings showed that 10% of the males had seven or more homosexual experiences. Further, he claimed that as many as 37% had some kind of homosexual experience after adolescence.

Kinsey's research methodologies have been questioned. Although he used a large number of subjects—they took sex histories on more than 18,000 people and used data from 5,000 men and 6,000 women—he did not use methods of random sampling that scientists commonly use today. His subjects came from boarding houses, college fraternities, prisons, mental wards, and wherever else he could get them. As many as 20–25% had prison experience and 5% may have been male prostitutes. Since one would expect that this group would have higher than average homosexual experiences, the findings of Kinsey's studies may not be representative of the population as a whole.[16]

Current research

There has been significant research since the 1950s to indicate that the occurrence of homosexuality in America and in other countries is much lower than the Kinsey statistics would indicate.[17] Milton Diamond of the John A. Burns School of Medicine at the University of Hawaii analyzed studies of populations in the United States, Scandinavia, Asia, and Europe, and found that including all individuals who have *ever* engaged in *any kind* of same-sex behavior, the numbers would be "5–6 percent for males and 2–3 percent for females."[18]

A large study by the Alan Guttmacher Institute reported in 1993 that of sexually-active men aged 20–39, only 2.3% had any same-gender sexual activity and only 1.1% reported exclusive homosexual contact during the last ten years.[19]

Perhaps the largest and most scientifically-based modern survey was concluded in 1994 by academics at the University of Chicago's National Opinion Research Center.[20] They asked 210 pages of questions of 3,432 Americans, ages eighteen to fifty-nine, and published their findings in *The Social Organization of Sexuality*.[21] On the subject of homosexuality, this survey found the following:

Have you had sex with someone of your gender?

2.7% of men (and 1.3% of women) had sex in the past year

7.1% of men (and 3.8% of women) had sex since puberty

Are you sexually attracted to people of the same gender?

6.2% of men (and 4.4% of women) said yes

The survey also showed larger percentages in urban areas. The twelve largest cities in the United States showed more than 9% of men identifying themselves as homosexual, as opposed to only 1% in rural areas. Since homosexual people tend to migrate from the rural areas and suburbs to larger cities, these larger urban groups feed the perception that a larger percentage of the total population is homosexual.

Conclusions on existing research

Different studies show different findings. Kinsey claimed that 4–10% of the male population was more or less exclusively homosexual for at least three years. Other research since that time shows the figure to be a more conservative 1–3%. However, if you consider everyone who has had homosexual contact since puberty, the numbers are more in the neighborhood of 5–10%.

Whatever the numbers, homosexual problems are significant and touch the lives of many people. If we use the conservative figure of 5%, of the ten million members of the Church there are 500,000 who have some degree of homosexual problems. And if you count their parents, spouses, brothers and sisters, it could add up to ***nearly three million members of the Church directly affected.***[22] Add to that grandparents, uncles, aunts, and concerned Church leaders, and you can see that many more people are affected.

The truth about your homosexual feelings

You did not choose to have homosexual feelings. These attractions usually develop because social and emotional needs were not met in the developmental years.

You did not develop homosexual problems because you are afraid of women. In reality, relationships with women generally have little to do with homosexual problems; instead, they have to do with relationships with men.

For further reading

"Same-Gender Attraction," Dallin H. Oaks, *Ensign*, Oct. 1995, pp. 7–14.

Setting the Record Straight: What Research Really Says About the Social Consequences of Homosexuality, Larry Burtoft, Ph.D., Focus on the Family, Colorado Springs, Colorado, 1995, pp. 24–26.

Homosexuality in America: Exposing the Myths, American Family Association, Tupelo, MS, 1994.

Kinsey, Sex and Fraud: The Indoctrination of a People by Judith A. Reisman and Edward W. Eichel, Huntington House, LaFayette, LA, 1990.

Chapter Two

Why Am I Attracted to Men?

Many factors contribute to the development of homosexual attractions. Dr. Elizabeth Moberly, author of *Homosexuality: A New Christian Ethic*, explained, "[M]any things are capable of causing the disruption in attachment that underlies the homosexual condition. It is not a question of one particular cause leading of necessity to one particular effect."[23] It is difficult to develop theories about the origins of homosexual attractions because no single theory fits every situation. Although there are some commonalities among people, there are no constants. Factors are different from person to person, or at least individual reactions to the same factors vary. Humans are complex beings and our behaviors are the result of many complex interactions.[24] This chapter discusses how personality, biological inheritance, and developmental experiences influence you. As you read, keep an open mind and consider how each concept may apply to you.

Personality

Before you were born, you existed as a spirit, and before that as a unique intelligence (see Abraham 3:21–23). Your personality was not created at physical birth, but has been developing long before that. It is no wonder that every person has different likes, desires, dreams, and moods. We see ourselves and the world in different ways and each of us hopes for something a little different from life. One child may be content with the affection he receives from his parents, while his sibling who receives the same attention feels a deficit and requires more. Some children seem content to play by themselves, while others who have many friends seem to need even more.

Many men with homosexual attractions have a heightened sense of emotional sensitivity which can make them vulnerable to emotional hurt when their high expectations are not met. Since we all have different needs and perspectives on life, it is easy to see why two people in the same situation will react differently. For one person, a negative situation may be manageable, while for another it is a devastating crisis.

Biology

Science has not shown that homosexuality is an inborn or biologically-determined characteristic. Biology may play some small role in influencing behavior or feelings. Some people seem susceptible to particular actions and may be drawn toward them or become addicted to them more easily than other people.[25] One person may be able to dabble with gambling, while another becomes a compulsive gambler. Some may drink only socially, while others have an unusual attraction to alcohol. Studies indicate that genetics may be a factor in susceptibilities to some behavior-related disorders, such as aggression, obesity, or alcoholism. Likewise, there are theories that claim biological predispositions influence the development of homosexual attractions when other life experiences are also present.[26]

Beyond such predispositions, some scientists search for more direct genetic causes—a gene or chromosome that actually determines sexual orientation.[27] News reports on these studies have misrepresented the facts. If you read the reports published by the researchers, you find that they admit their current findings are not conclusive. Most scientists today give genetic theories little credibility.[28] The more significant research in these biological areas is described below.

Twin studies

Drs. Michael Bailey and Richard Pillard studied identical and fraternal twins.[29] They identified homosexual males who had identical twin brothers and found that 52% of the brothers were also homosexual. Among fraternal twins, they found the ratio to be 22%. They concluded that since identical twins had a higher incidence of mutual homosexuality than fraternal twins, there must be a genetic component in the development of homosexuality.

However, if genetics caused the homosexuality, the correlation between the identical twins (who have exactly the same genes) should have been much higher—even 100%. Since all the twins in this study were raised together, it is impossible to determine whether genetics or the same family environment contributed to the brothers' homosexuality. If the genes are identical and the brothers are raised in the same family environment, a correlation of only 52% in identical twins shows that other factors are involved.

Many question the validity of the twins study. The researchers commented that since their subjects were not selected by random sampling, they may have collected a biased sample with skewed results.[30] Another twin study was conducted a year later, which showed a correlation of only 25%.[31]

Brain studies

In 1991, Dr. Simon LeVay, a neurobiologist at the Salk Institute in La Jolla, California, reported his findings from studying the brain structures of forty-one cadavers.[32] He concluded that an area of the hypothalamus (the INAH3) was smaller in homosexual men than in heterosexual men. (It was also found to be smaller in women than in heterosexual men.) However, these findings do not show any direct link between the hypothalamus and sexual orientation and, furthermore, are dubious at best because of the following reasons:

♦ It has not been determined that the INAH3 is involved in the development of sexual orientation.[33]

♦ The sample size of this study was small (only forty-one). Furthermore, Dr. LeVay did not know the sexual histories of the cadavers he studied. Nineteen men apparently were homosexual and he assumed that the other sixteen men and six women were heterosexual.[34]

♦ Since most of the subjects had died of AIDS, the HIV virus may have affected the brains in various ways, especially the hypothalamus, which is a major player in the immune system. LeVay himself admitted this was a serious flaw in the study.[35]

♦ There were many inconsistencies in the findings. Three of the allegedly heterosexual men had a smaller INAH3 than the mean size for the "homosexual" men and three of the "homosexual" men had a larger INAH3 than the mean size for "heterosexual" men.[36]

♦ Many neuroscientists charge that LeVay deviated from protocol when he measured volume rather than the number of neurons in the INAH3. This is critical, since the area LeVay measured is very small (about the size of a snowflake).

♦ Dr. LeVay himself cautions that the results of his study "do not allow one to decide if the size of INAH3 in an individual is the cause or consequence of that individual's sexual orientation."[37]

Anne Fausto-Sterling, a professor of medical science at Brown University, said, "My freshman biology students know enough to sink this study."[38]

Chromosome studies

In 1993, Dr. Dean Hamer announced that he had found a correlation between DNA markers on the X chromosome (region Xq28) and sexual orientation in a selected group of homosexual men and their relatives over age eighteen. In other words, "it appears that Xq28 contains a gene that contributes to homosexual orientation in males."[39] In his book, Dr. Hamer stated, "We can make only educated guesses about the importance of Xq28 in the population at large." He concludes that "Xq28 plays some role in about 5 to 30 percent of gay men. The broad range of these estimates is proof that much more work remains to be done."[40] Scientists have since questioned the validity of these findings and what they purport to show.[41] Dr. Hammer has been charged with research improprieties and is under investigation by the federal government for improperly excluding from his study men whose genetic makeup contradicted his findings.[42] A later study by the University of Western Ontario "found no consistent pattern of DNA similarity on the X chromosome."[43]

Hormone studies

Studies have shown that in some cases the mothers of homosexual males suffered a high degree of stress during their pregnancy. Since stress affects hormonal levels, some researchers suggest that decreased levels of testosterone could lead to a demasculinization of the developing brain. However, multiple studies over the years have not been able to substantiate the theory, and the available evidence is to the contrary. Ehrhardt and Meyer-Bahlburg wrote, "In the majority of intersex patients with known hormone abnormalities, the sexual orientation follows the sex of rearing. Consequently, we have to assume that prenatal hormone conditions by themselves do not rigidly determine sexual orientation."[44] Dr. John Money also states there is no evidence that prenatal hormonalization alone determines sexual orientation.[45]

Experiments have been conducted wherein testosterone was given to homosexual males, both those who were effeminate and those who were not. "When there were any behavioral changes at all, the subjects became more like themselves than ever. Their sex drives were usually increased and sometimes their effeminate mannerisms as well (when they had any), but there were never any directional changes in their sexual interests. From these experiments . . . it has become abundantly clear that the sex hormones play a considerable role in powering human sexuality, but they do not control the direction of it."[46]

Biological conclusions

Drs. Byne and Parsons of the Department of Psychiatry at Columbia University reviewed the biologic theories of human sexual orientation in 1993 and concluded, "[T]here is no evidence at present to substantiate a biologic theory."[47] No study suggests that a simple cause effect relationship exists.[48] And Dr. Earl Wilson wrote, "the disputed evidence for physical causes of male homosexuality is even weaker when it comes to lesbianism."[49]

Regardless of the role that genetics play in the development of sexual attractions, such attractions are changeable and treatable. In analogy, although the City of Hope National Medical Center researchers found a certain gene present in 77% of the alcoholic patients they studied, we have not abandoned treatment for alcoholism.[50] Many former alcoholics have changed their behavior and lead productive lives. You have control over your destiny. As a child of God, you have moral agency and can determine the course of your life. Regardless of any biological thread, thousands of men who struggle with homosexual attractions have made changes in their lives for the better.

Developmental experiences

Professionals agree that environment influences a child in significant ways. Your family, friends, society, and experiences influence how you feel, how you view life, and how you act. Dr. William Consiglio refers to this myriad of social and psychological factors as a "conspiracy of factors," meaning that many factors "conspired" or came together in the right amounts at the right time to divert sexual desires in you as a developing boy toward other boys.[51] Some of these factors include your relationship with your family and peers, your ability to identify with masculinity, the degree to which your emotional needs are fulfilled, your feelings of self-worth, and early sexual experiences.

Relationship with father

When I first tried to understand how my homosexual attractions had developed, I didn't think my family was dysfunctional. We loved each other and my father did not beat us. We lived in peace and love and were active in the Church. However, I later came to realize that these good things did not guarantee that all my emotional needs would be met.

It is important that a boy have a healthy emotional relationship with his father or with another significant male. (This is much more than Sigmund Freud's theory that a homosexual male child is the product of a strong mother and a passive, indifferent, or hostile father.) The boy needs to feel love from his father and needs to identify with him. It is through this male bonding that a child develops a sense of himself as an individual and as a male. If this relationship was not functional for you, the needs that would normally be met through it may remain unmet.

This bonding may not have occurred if your father was physically or emotionally uninvolved in your life as a child, or the bond may have been broken if he was punishing or authoritarian. Since this can be very painful, you may not have wanted to reestablish the connection. Even if he tried to build a good relationship, you may have prevented it out of fear of further hurt. Dr. Elizabeth Moberly of Cambridge University refers to this as *defensive detachment.*[52] As a child, you may have defended against further trauma by blocking yourself from relating normally with your father, and in so doing, unknowingly insured that your needs for attachment with him would not be met. It may have become an approach-avoidance conflict. The drive for a renewed attachment showed your need for love from him, but the defensive detachment prevented the attachment and so the needs continued unmet.

As a child, your interpretation of this relationship was critical. Even if your father was available and loved you, if you did not perceive that love or could not connect with him, there could have been a deficit. There is a difference between *being* loved and *feeling* loved. The more sensitive and the less able to relate to your father, the greater the chance of a relationship problem. To children, parents are their source of being, and if the attachment to them is disrupted, their very being feels endangered. If you became hurt as a child, you may have become unwilling to trust and may have learned to repress the need for attachment. You may have then distanced yourself from your father and later carried it over to men in general by avoiding closeness with male peers. If this is true in your case, you became emotionally needful as a result of not having the supportive, affectionate relationships required to develop a good sense of identity. When these psychological needs remain unfulfilled, although the boy has grown to be a man, you are still essentially a child trying to fill basic emotional needs. In many respects, you may still be a dependent child who needs to be loved by his father and not yet an adult with adult emotional needs.

To learn more about the father-son relationship and defensive detachment, read *Homosexuality: A New Christian Ethic* by Elizabeth R. Moberly.

Relationship with mother

The relationship with your mother is also important. A mother can either reinforce and strengthen a boy's relationship with his father or she can dominate and minimize the father's role. A strong relationship with your mother is not a problem unless it gets in the way of a strong relationship with your father. In the triangle of relationships between the boy, mother, and father, the three sometimes become imbalanced. If the father-mother relationship was not healthy, you may have missed out on learning what a husband-wife relationship should be. Further, you may have tried to take care of the emotional needs of your mother and become a surrogate male companion to her. If this disordered mother-son relationship occurred, you would not have been able to develop a normal male image as a boy, nor would the emotional needs have been met as a son from your mother. Needless to say, you also would not have gotten your emotional needs met from the father-son relationship. If this happened, you may have become enmeshed with your mother, in part to compensate for not having the emotional support from your father.[53]

Gender identity

As you develop, it is important to gain a healthy sense of self as a man. In normal development, the concept of masculinity (what it means to be a man) is internalized before puberty by interaction with, and validation from, other boys and men. If you were confused about what it means to be a man or did not feel affirmed in your masculinity, you may have internalized the concept of masculinity in unhealthy ways with frustrating results. If this happened, you likely did not realize that anything abnormal was happening. As you entered puberty and sexual feelings emerged, they may have become confused with your masculine longings.

Having diminished feelings of masculinity does not mean you feel you are feminine—that is the case for only a small percentage of men. There is a considerable difference between feeling inadequate as a male and feeling feminine. Many men who have homosexual feelings are masculine in appearance and action. They simply have not affirmed within themselves their validity as a man.

Boys who exhibit less masculine behaviors and prefer feminine things have a higher chance of developing same-gender attractions during the socialization process.[54] Dr. Richard Green reports that although more than half of the boys who show pronounced effeminate behavior develop homosexual problems, a substantial minority of them does not. He suggests that the boy's behavior, along with contributing life experiences, can predispose them toward developing attractions toward the same gender. Dr. Judd Marmor wrote, "Thus, a little boy whose behavior is effeminate, who does not like competitive athletics, and who prefers music and art, may be disappointing to a macho father, who tends to reject the boy and distance himself from him. The mother may respond by overprotecting her son. Such reactions disturb the boy's capacity to identify positively with his father and cause him to over-identify with his mother. He may ultimately then develop homosexual erotic responses which are reinforced by later experiences."[55]

Defensive detachment may also express itself in the development of gender identity. The effeminacy of some men with homosexual attractions and the quasi-masculinity of some women with homosexual attractions are examples of defensive detachment from the person's gender. They feel the need to identify with their own gender, but they reject it because they perceive it to be harsh or hurtful, and they prevent its normal development in a defensive way. In these cases, the development of their identity as male and female was likely stopped at an early stage of development.

Male emotional needs

As a boy, your need for the love and identification with other males was a normal, legitimate requirement every boy has; your needs may have been greater than average. These needs would usually be met by your father or another significant male during early childhood and later reinforced by peers, teachers, and society as a whole. If your perfectly natural needs for love, acceptance, and identification with other males were not fulfilled, you may have developed insecurities that now hold you back from legitimately fulfilling them. You may long for the companionship, love, and acceptance of male peers, but when it is offered you resist because of fear of hurt or rejection. You may then feel hurt that the opportunity for companionship and attention has passed you by. You may secretly fear that you are not worthy of companionship or attention and therefore stay where it is safe but lonely rather than venture out to interact with other men.

Many report that during childhood they felt different from their peers. You may have been a loner and didn't play the rough games that boys commonly play. You may have had some friends, but wished for more and felt unable or unworthy of more substantial relationships that were important to you. If this describes you, your attraction to other males may be rooted in the need to identify with and be accepted by other males and feel part of a group of buddies. At a time critical for making friends, your life may have been disrupted by a medical problem or a move to a new neighborhood, or overprotective parents may have interfered with peer relationships. If you had limited contact with other boys, you may not have identified with them sufficiently in healthy ways, but anticipated rejection and expected you would not fit in. You desperately wanted acceptance and comfort from these ideal friends, but instead developed feelings of loneliness and longing.

If you felt alienated from other boys, you may have become attracted to them as an opposite. Watching from the sidelines, you admired the boys and wished you could be like them. Even as an adult, you may be attracted to men who look or dress the way you wish you did. If you are young and carefree, you may envy a professional man who is responsible and mature. And if you are the mature professional, you may wish you could be young and carefree.

This longing for a friend can be intense and may easily turn to adoration and idolization. One day in high school, I remember walking by the gym just as the track team was returning from a meet. I remember noticing one particular boy who was shirtless and sweaty, and in that brief moment, I saw my ideal of perfect masculinity. I wondered what made the difference between him and me. Although he was my age and in some of my classes, I wondered how he could be on the track team and be so manly, and I was not. I admired him for being an athlete. He was everything I wished I was. Those were the beginnings of my feelings of envy toward other men. Although it happened twenty-five years ago, I remember the incident as vividly as if it happened yesterday. Those kinds of feelings and longings can have significant impact in our lives.

"Mysterious [males] are those who possess enigmatic masculine qualities that both perplex and allure," writes Joseph Nicolosi. "Such [males] are overvalued and even idealized, for they are the embodiment of qualities that the [individual] wishes he had attained for himself."[56] As you entered puberty and sexual feelings emerged, this intense envy could have turned to sexual lust, and if you were not able to fill your need for love and acceptance through brotherly relating, you may have begun to seek it through sexual relating.[57] Homosexual behavior may be an attempt to complete your masculine identity as you try to possess valued masculine attributes through sexual intimacy with other males. It may be an effort to solve the mystery of masculinity that arises from the perception of being unlike other men. And it may also be a simple escape from your inadequacies and pain. In the heat of passion, you can momentarily believe any fantasy—that you are beautiful, masculine, loved, and accepted.[58]

These underlying emotional needs are the same for all men whether they have homosexual problems or not. The homosexual drive is actually a drive to fulfill the emotional need to relate to and be accepted by other men. "Love among those of the same sex is right and good," explain Drs. Thomas and Ann Pritt. "Only the sexualization of the attraction is inappropriate."[59] This attraction to other men is a reparative drive and is actually an attempt to resolve the problem, and not the problem itself. The core problem is not homo*sexual*, but homo*social*. It is a continual attempt to remedy earlier deficits and fulfill the social and emotional needs that still exist. The fulfillment of these unmet needs for love and identification can only be solved through nonsexual relationships with other men. The attractions will persist until you are able to develop a healthy identity and relate appropriately with other men in a nonsexual way.[60]

Self-Worth

Low feelings of self-worth and inferiority are common breeding grounds for homosexual problems. Traumatic experiences in your life as a child could have lead to feelings of inferiority. Negative interactions with other boys could have easily damaged a vulnerable self-image and increased your sense of feeling different from other children. Feeling different creates a mind set that can have a tremendous impact on your development and on the way you see the world. These feelings may have separated you from your peers and you may have felt you were living your life from the outside looking in. Knowing that your attractions were not normal, you kept them secret and this secret not only increased your sense of aloneness, but made you feel you were of less value than other boys. Unfortunately, the feelings of isolation, inferiority, and fear of exposure are the very forces that keep the underlying issues from being resolved. Other children may have picked up on your sense of inadequacy and attacked it, causing you to withdraw further, defensively detach, and even develop a fantasy life.

You likely felt a sense of shame because your attractions were wrong, and this made you feel even more different and inferior in relation to your friends. The feelings of being different, inferior, and guilty often lead to self-belittling and self-degrading thoughts. You may have thought that you were inherently defective, not knowing that your homosexual attractions were the result of a *deficit* and not a *defect*.

Early Sexual Experiences

If you had unresolved needs for affection or experienced social or emotional trauma, you would have been particularly vulnerable to negative experiences. Early masturbation, exposure to pornography, or childhood sexual experimentation often introduce sexual thoughts before young men are able to understand them, and they can reinforce homosexual interests. Children who have been victimized by sexual abuse or youth who have early sexual contacts can become confused and develop a gender misidentity and unusual sexual interests and values. Inappropriate sexual activity blurs the distinction between intimacy and sex. Studies show that boys who are sexually abused are four to seven times more likely to have homosexual problems and 65% of the victims say the abuse affected their sexual identity.[61]

Developmental conclusions

Many boys become aware of their same-sex attractions at an early age (sometimes before age five). The most important formative years for the development of sexual feelings and attitudes are during late infancy and before the onset of puberty, and not during puberty and adolescence. Dr. John Money explained, "The hormones of puberty activate what has already formed and is awaiting activation."[62] Your development of heterosexual interests would have proceeded instinctively if emotional maturity has not been obstructed by issues such as those just discussed. Dr. William Consiglio describes homosexuality as a *disorientation* from the mainstream of heterosexual development. "It is not something a person is born with; rather, it is sexual disorientation when the God-designed stream of heterosexuality is blocked. Homosexuality is not an alternative sexuality or sexual orientation, but an emotional disorientation caused by arrested or blocked emotional development in the stream of heterosexuality."[63] But the good news is that the condition is correctable. When these blockages are "successfully reduced, diminished, or removed, human sexuality can resume its natural heterosexual flow toward its proper, God-designed outlet; i.e., wholesome, mature, sexual, and emotional expression in marriage with a person of the opposite sex."[64]

Your homosexual urge is not unrealistic or rebellious. It is not a fear of, or a flight from, heterosexuality. It is actually an unconscious attempt to fill your normal emotional needs and when these needs begin to be filled, you can begin again progressing toward full heterosexual maturation.[65]

Summary

Personality, genetics, and developmental experiences all have a place in influencing the development of homosexual attractions. Drs. Byne and Parsons at Columbia University believe it is important to "appreciate the complexities of sexual orientation and resist the urge to search for simplistic explanations, either psychosocial or biologic."[66] They emphasize that in addition to the influences of genetics or the environment, the individual plays an important role in determining his or her identity.

Dr. John Money stated, "Many wrongly assume that whatever is biological cannot be changed, and whatever mental can be. Both propositions are in error. Homosexuality is always biological and always mental, both together. It is mental because it exists in the mind. It is biological because the mind exists in the brain. The sexual brain through its extended nervous system communicates back and forth with the sex organs."[67]

Our character is the net result of our choices and life experience. An article in *Harvest News* stated, "Some of us are shy, some anxious, some have problems with anger or chemical dependence, some of us fear commitment. Did we 'choose' any of these things? Actually, *all* of our adult personality is the result of a complex interplay of heredity and family environment with thousands of small personal decisions dating back as far as we can remember. The results are deeply entrenched ways of feeling, thinking, acting."[68] Although you may have had no control over the emergence of homosexual attractions, you can choose how to respond to them.

Elder Dallin H. Oaks has said that "some kinds of feelings seem to be inborn. Others are traceable to mortal experiences. Still other feelings seem to be acquired from a complex interaction of 'nature and nurture.' All of us have some feelings we did not choose, but the gospel of Jesus Christ teaches us that we still have the power to resist and reform our feelings (as needed) and to assure that they do not lead us to entertain inappropriate thoughts or to engage in sinful behavior."[69]

For further reading

Responding to Abuse: Helps for Ecclesiastical Leaders, Church of Jesus Christ of Latter-day Saints (item number 32248).

Preventing and Responding to Child Abuse, Church of Jesus Christ of Latter-day Saints (item number 33196).

Stolen Childhood: What You Need to Know About Sexual Abuse by Alice Huskey.

The Wounded Heart: Hope for Adult Victims of Childhood Sexual Abuse by Dr. Dan B. Allender.

Chapter Three

Can I Resolve My Homosexual Problems?

You may be struggling to make sense of homosexual attractions in light of the gospel. Although you have a testimony of the gospel, you also know these feelings are very real and strong and in spite of your efforts to live the gospel, the feelings don't go away. You are caught between the gospel which is right and the attractions toward men that are contrary to the gospel. The response of most men is to (1) try to suppress the feelings and live the gospel or (2) decide that the gospel doesn't fit in their life and pursue the attractions, thereby losing out on the blessings of the gospel. Rejecting the gospel was not an answer for me, but suppressing the feelings didn't make them go away either. Suppression means a continual struggle where, at best, you are celibate but miserable, and at worst, lead a double life by pretending to be a good member of the Church but secretly engaging in homosexual behavior. The only way to resolve the problem is to identify the needs that cause the attractions and fill them in legitimate ways

This chapter addresses the reality of resolving homosexual problems. It gives a definition of what it means to resolve these problems, statistics on the numbers of people who have resolved them, and information about the time the process takes. Finally, it discusses how complete the change can be and the ultimate goal of doing all this work.

Is it possible to resolve these problems?

The world has defined concepts such as *homosexual* and *sexual orientation* and tells us that they are inborn and cannot be changed. Many people have bought into this theory and believe that a homosexual orientation is as genetic as race or left-handedness. They say that those who have changed are simply engrossed in a fantasy and some day will come back to reality and realize they are still homosexual.

Although these "pro-gay" arguments are complex and can appear logical, they have little credibility when viewed in the broader perspective of the eternal plan of salvation. To believe that God would give us problems that we could not overcome is to deny the power of the atonement and the omnipotence of God.

Dr. Charles Socarides stated, "The major challenge in treating homosexuality, from the point of view of the patient's resistance, has, of course, been the misconception that the disorder is innate or inborn."[70] But you are not a "homosexual" and do not have an inalterable "sexual orientation."

President Spencer W. Kimball taught, "After consideration of the evil aspects, the ugliness and prevalence of the evil of homosexuality, the glorious thing to remember is that it is curable and forgivable. The Lord has promised that all sins can be forgiven except certain ones enumerated, and this evil was not among those named. Thus it is forgivable if totally abandoned and if the repentance is sincere and absolute. Certainly it can be overcome, for there are numerous happy people who were once involved in its clutches and who have since completely transformed their lives."[71]

I personally attest that it is possible to diminish homosexual attractions, eliminate homosexual behavior, and lead a happy life in full alignment with the gospel. I know this because I have done it. I used to be conflicted by my feelings and tormented by my desires to act out. Now that I have resolved these issues, I feel peace and comfort as a whole person. And mine is not the only case. I personally know many other people and have read about hundreds more who have resolved significant problems and are now much happier and at greater peace with themselves and with God.

What does it mean to resolve these problems?

The process described in this book is *not* one of learning to suppress the feelings and control the behavior through willpower. The goal is to *resolve* the issues that created the homosexual attractions in the first place and now continue to sustain them. A transition out of homosexuality might include the following:
♦ reducing or eliminating homosexual desires.
♦ eliminating homosexual behavior.
♦ developing a secure sense of self and male identity.

Desires

As men begin to resolve their homosexual issues, they note that their sexual attractions toward men significantly decrease. They may reach the point where they are no longer sexually attracted to men at all. Others may continue to be attracted to men as strongly as before, but they can learn to cope with the attractions without being overwhelmed by them.

Many men still experience some feelings or attractions from time to time, but they are able to deal with them with a minimum of anxiety and they do not dominate their lives or behavior. Over time, the feelings diminish both in number and intensity until it becomes easy to dismiss these fleeting thoughts, much like they do any other unwanted thought that enters their minds. As Joe Dallas describes, for most men these desires are "reduced from a major issue into a minor one, a problem that does not dominate their lives or keep them from experiencing healthy friendships, healthy marriage, and peace of mind. If it is still a problem to them, it's only one of many, they don't struggle with it daily and they seldom give it serious thought. For them, the battle is not even considered a battle anymore."[72]

Most find that heterosexual feelings awaken or increase within them.

Behavior

With a greater understanding of their issues, men with homosexual struggles recognize they can choose to avoid sexual activity with other men and are able to control their actions. The comforting news is that as you resolve deeper issues, you will find that your compulsions to act out diminish and in many cases disappear. As time passes, homosexual behavior becomes less and less appealing, and in some cases even repulsive.

If you have been heavily involved in sexual behavior for a number of years, you will have a greater struggle overcoming habits and sexual addictions. But if you are sincerely motivated and make a significant effort, you can overcome these addictions.

Identity

You may be attracted to other men because of a distorted view of yourself and others. If you have accepted a "gay" identity, you can change that perception and accept yourself as a son of God with eternal potential. With increased levels of self-acceptance, your feelings of self-worth and masculinity will increase, you will begin to see your value in relation to other men, and stop comparing yourself with other men. As you become more pro-active rather than reactive, you will be able to develop increasingly healthy relationships with men and sexual attractions will decrease.

How many people change?

Since homosexuality is the outward manifestation of unresolved issues that are central to your personality, deciding to work on these issues involves reevaluating your core person and working to change it. This may be a long and painful process, and not everyone who begins it sees it through.

Personal observations

For the past seven years, I have been involved with LDS support groups for men with homosexual problems. I participated for half that time to work on my own problems and during the remainder of the time have served in leadership capacities. During those seven years, I estimate there have been more than a thousand men attend at least one meeting and I have personally met about 350 of them. Their success has varied because of several factors, chief among which I believe is their level of commitment.

♦ Many attend only a few meetings, then drop out. They learn a little about the philosophy of change, but do not pursue it because they don't believe that change is possible for them, they decide they don't want to change, they are not ready for change, or they did not find the support group helpful to them.

♦ Others go to support groups because they enjoy the friendships they build with others who are likewise struggling with homosexuality. It is a great relief for them to find other LDS men who understand their value system and empathize with their situation. But for them, it is a social meeting and they lack the commitment to do much beyond showing up at meetings.

♦ Still others attend because of feelings of guilt. They know they should change but they are not willing to put forth the effort to change. Without much commitment, they participate on a superficial level to pacify their conscience and appease their family.

Unfortunately, the majority of the thousand people who have attended support groups for one of these reasons have found only limited success. Their token efforts may bring about some changes, but few make significant, lasting progress.

However, there is hope if you are committed to the process and put forth a significant effort. Although it was the hardest thing I have ever done, it was worth the effort. I no longer struggle with homosexuality. It no longer controls my life or dominates my thoughts. For me to get to that point, it required the following:

♦ personal study, prayer, pondering, and journaling over a period of four years.
♦ reaching out and building important male relationships.
♦ individual therapy for five months.
♦ group therapy (two six-week groups).
♦ support group meetings for three and a half years.

Of those who make this kind of commitment, most are able to resolve their problems and make significant, long-lasting changes in their lives.

Observations of others

Fortunately, you don't have to rely solely on my word. Read the following opinions and studies by professionals in the field.

Dr. William Consiglio is an associate professor of clinical social work at Southern Connecticut State University who for more than seventeen years has worked with men and women who seek freedom from homosexuality. He finds that 40% of his clients find personal resolution and enjoy a full heterosexual life, with many entering marriage and parenthood. Another 40% achieve a functional resolution in that they are able to control their homosexual thoughts, attractions, and behaviors, and thus maintain consistent celibacy. The remaining 20% drop out of the process and eventually return to active homosexuality.[73] He reports that even for those people who do not make a complete heterosexual recovery there is great hope. They can "achieve a significant degree of emotional healing, growth in self-esteem, and spiritual well being and are able to move on in life freed of the homosexual obsession and preoccupation. It allows them to form rewarding and fulfilling relationships and live more integrated and satisfying lives which are compatible with their spiritual values and convictions. And that's powerfully good news in itself."[74]

Dr. Reuben Fine, Director of the New York Center for Psychoanalytic Training, stated, "I have recently had occasion to review the results of psychotherapy with homosexuals, and been surprised by the findings. It is paradoxical that even though the politically active homosexual group denies the possibility of change, all studies from Schrenck-Notzing on have found positive effects, virtually regardless of the kind of treatment used. . . ."[75] He further stated, "Whether with hypnosis . . . , psychoanalysis of any variety, educative psychotherapy, behavior therapy, and/or simple educational procedures, a considerable percentage of overt homosexuals became heterosexual. . . . If the patients were motivated, whatever procedure is adopted, a large percentage will give up their homosexuality. In this connection, public information is of the greatest importance. The misinformation spread by certain circles that 'homosexuality is untreatable by psychotherapy' does incalculable harm to thousands of men and women."[76]

In 1994, Dr. Houston MacIntosh reported in the *Journal of the American Psychoanalytic Association* a survey of 285 psychoanalysts who treated 1,215 homosexual patients. The psychoanalysts reported that 23% of the patients changed to heterosexuality and 84% received significant therapeutic benefit.[77]

Dr. Charles Socarides, who teaches and serves as attending psychiatrist at the Albert Einstein College of Medicine in New York, reports that in treating forty-five "overt homosexuals," 44% developed full heterosexual functioning.[78] These success rates are as good as, or better than, those for treating other conditions. Let us compare the success rate of overcoming homosexual problems with that of overcoming problems from depression, one of the most commonly treated behavioral issues. Of those treated for depression, about one third get better, one third stay the same, and a third actually get worse. This division of thirds holds true for the treatment of many conditions. If homosexuality is indeed a treatable, changeable condition, we would expect about the same success rates. In fact, we find much better. Clinical evidence shows that the recovery rate for homosexual problems is even greater than for drug addiction and alcoholism. The professional community generally considers treatment a success if more than half the patients show improvement; the recovery rate for drug and alcohol addiction is about 50%. A Masters & Johnson study showed the recovery rate from homosexuality at 71.6% when there was motivation and support.[79]

Dr. Irving Bieber, former president of the New York Medical College, lead a nine-year study of male homosexuality. His research team concluded that "many homosexuals became exclusively heterosexual in psychoanalytic treatment. Although this change may be more easily accomplished by some than others, in our judgment, a heterosexual shift is a possibility for all homosexuals who are strongly motivated to change."[80] After following some of his patients for as long as ten years, he claimed success rates from 30–50%.[81]

Dr. Gerard van den Aardweg made an extensive analysis of 101 people he had in treatment and found that 60% of those who continued treatment reached "at least a satisfactory state of affairs for a long period of time. By this is meant that the homosexual feelings had been reduced to occasional impulses at most while the sexual orientation had turned predominantly heterosexual, or that the homosexual feelings were completely absent, with or without predominance of heterosexual interests. Of this group, however, about one-third could be regarded as having been changed 'radically.' By this is meant that they did not have any more homosexual interests but had normal heterosexual feelings, and in addition that they showed a fundamental change in overall emotionality from negative to positive—from instability to reasonable, normal stability. . . ."[82]

For her doctoral dissertation at Brigham Young University in 1978, Elizabeth James conducted perhaps the most comprehensive review of the literature on the treatment of homosexuality that had been conducted to date. In her analysis of 101 studies that had been published from 1930 to 1976, she found that approximately 35% of the clients recovered and 27% improved. She concluded that "significant improvement and even complete recovery are entirely possible."[83] She noted an 81% recovery and improvement rate for bisexuals, 69% for long-term therapy clients, 53% for short-term therapy clients, and 42% for exclusively homosexual clients. She noted that "there is certainly room for the development of new treatments and combinations of techniques that will enhance the effectiveness of those procedures already in use."[84] Since 1978, a great deal has been done to increase the effectiveness of treatment techniques. New theories and methodologies have been developed and many therapists are receiving specialized training. Numerous books have been written to help both therapists and individuals seeking greater insights to their feelings. Today, the outlook for successful change is even more encouraging.

Drs. Thomas and Ann Pritt state that "freedom from homosexuality is truly available to men and women as they come to recognize the underlying causes of their attractions, and as they are able to realize legitimate, healthful, identity-securing affections with valued heterosexuals of their own sex."[85]

These are just a few of the many studies and experiences that show that many people are resolving their homosexual problems. If you don't personally know someone who has made these changes in his or her life, you might assume that no one has, because you don't often hear accounts of people making such changes. People seldom appear on television or stand up in church meetings and admit that they used to be sexually attracted to the same gender but now are not. They typically keep these issues to themselves and when they make these great internal changes, people around them are often not even aware that anything has happened. Content with having put together the pieces of this internal jigsaw puzzle, they move on quietly with their lives. Psychologist Gerard van den Aardweg said, "I think these cases are perhaps more numerous than we would presume, because many of them prefer to stay anonymous and not be public examples of 'the converted-and-cured-homosexual.'"[86]

Hopefully, the questions in your mind about changing homosexuality are no longer questions of *if*, but *when* and *how*.

How long does it take?

The length of the transition varies depending on many factors, such as the following:
- ◆ your motivation and commitment to the process.
- ◆ your willingness to take responsibility for your life.
- ◆ your efforts in personal study, prayer, pondering, and journaling.

♦ the closeness of your relationship with your Heavenly Father and Jesus Christ.

♦ the amount and quality of individual and group therapy you receive.

♦ the level of support you receive from those who are close to you and from support groups.

♦ your efforts to reach out and build new relationships.

♦ the degree to which you have accepted a homosexual identity.

♦ the amount of abuse in your past and the severity of problems it has caused.

♦ your willingness to leave your homosexual past behind.

♦ the length and degree to which you have been involved in homosexual behaviors.

♦ the degree to which you have addictions and compulsions.

Those who are able to define their problems and begin working on them early, before compulsive behaviors turn into addictions and before attitudes turn into identity, may be able to make the transition in a matter of months. Those who begin the process later in life after years of sexual habits and mental conditioning find it takes much work and substantially more time. Most men I have spoken with report it takes somewhere from three to ten years. However, don't set time frames for yourself and expect that changes will happen within a certain period of time. Your problems didn't develop overnight and they likely won't be resolved in a short time.

Gradual progress

In today's society, we often expect instant results. Satellites, computers, and microwave ovens allow us to accomplish things in a matter of seconds. When things don't happen instantly, or when solutions are not forthcoming at computer-like speed, we tend to panic. We forget that some of the more important things in life take more time—usually in terms of months and years.

Don't set time limits on change. Some people begin to see progress in the first few weeks, while others don't see substantial progress for months. While God does work miracles, few people are freed from homosexual feelings in a blinding moment. Rather than a quick 180–degree reversal of their sexual attractions, most men experience gradual changes in their spiritual, physical, sexual, and emotional understanding of themselves. After some work, you will notice that your sexual attractions toward other men begin to diminish and have less control over you than they once had. They will be less frequent and intense and you will feel less compelled to seek homosexual connections. This kind of gradual progress requires patience and endurance and is the true test of your commitment to God. The key is in recognizing you are improving and in keeping the momentum going. My friend Garrick said, "I am content to change little by little and learn what Christ would have me learn from all this same-sex attraction stuff. I am content to struggle with everyone else on the planet to be happy regardless of life's circumstances. I am thankful for the ride."[87]

Some people maintain that since the person often struggles for many years—and sometimes for his entire life—this is proof that change is not possible. However, the gospel teaches that one of the purposes of this life is to have experiences that test our faith. The scriptures exhort us to put off the natural man and become a new person in Christ (see Mosiah 3:19). It is expected that throughout this life we will struggle between our old nature and our new nature and the scriptures are filled with advice on how to win this struggle.

In the Lord's due time

Don't become frustrated if your progress is slower than you originally expected. Remember that this is a complex process that will not be resolved overnight. If you have righteous desires and are doing all you can, be patient. Answers will come and change will happen, but on the Lord's timetable and not necessarily your own.

In the allegory of the olive trees in Jacob, we read, "And it came to pass that the servant said unto his master: How comest thou hither to plant this tree, or this branch of the tree? For behold, it was the poorest spot in all the land of thy vineyard. And the Lord of the vineyard said unto him: Counsel me not; I knew that it was a poor spot of ground; wherefore, I said unto thee, I have nourished it this long time, and thou beholdest that it hath brought forth much fruit" (Jacob 5:21-22). We must be careful not to counsel the Lord, but to take counsel from Him (see Jacob 4:10). We are given the challenges in life that we need. "Trust in the Lord with all thine heart; and lean not unto thine own understanding. In all thy ways acknowledge him, and he shall direct thy paths" (Proverbs 3:5-6). Don't ask God to do it your way. Rather pray "Thy will be done."

Eternal progress

Homosexuality seems to be an overwhelming problem to many people because they include in it a whole life of problems. But remember that *everyone* deals with issues of self-worth, relationships, intimacy, lust, comparing themselves with others, and a whole host of problems that are part of a lifelong process of growing, overcoming, and improving. These issues of personal growth and development are part of the larger plan of eternal progression. Changes we begin to make in this life will continue into the next. Therefore, whatever progress we can make in the short term or long term, we should begin it now.

My friend Brad has worked hard to resolve many difficult issues in his life. He has significantly increased his feelings of masculinity and sees himself in a new light. Heterosexual feelings have awakened in him, he is beginning to date, and is looking forward to marriage. However, he also has an advanced case of AIDS that he contracted during his earlier promiscuous days. I admire that he hasn't let the progression of AIDS diminish his desire to work out his problems. It would be easy for him to stop working toward marriage, knowing that he most likely doesn't have time to get married in this life. But he has an eternal view of his growth and development and realizes that whatever progress he makes in this life will be to his benefit in the next. (See Brad's story in the Testimonials section of this book.) The goal of becoming a whole man of God is certainly attainable and is worth whatever work it takes. Begin now.

How complete will the change be?

For most people, going through this transition process does not guarantee that they will never again have a homosexual thought. Joe Dallas explained, "If a man has been a drunkard for 20 years, then joins Alcoholics Anonymous and stays sober, he has definitely changed. His sobriety will have an impact on all parts of his life, improving his attitude, relationships, and job performance. Will an occasional desire for a drink nullify his claim to have changed? Hardly."[88] Dr. Dean Byrd said, "It's not so unlike treatment outcomes for other emotional struggles. Do we expect the individual to never struggle again? No, we simply expect that they will have the resources to respond to their struggles appropriately."[89]

Don't measure your progress simply by the types of temptation you still experience. Remember that temptation is not sin. Satan will likely try to remind you of your past and try to get you to doubt whether you have really changed. But remember that everyone is tempted. Christ was tempted His entire life but did not succumb to temptation. Life is a continual process of putting off the natural man and moving toward God. Temptations do not define us; we are defined by how we respond to the temptations. Therefore, if you dismiss the homosexual temptations and act responsibly, you can be confident that the changes you have experienced are real.

As Joe Dallas explained, "*All* Christians deal with sin, *all* Christians have stubborn areas of weakness, and *all* Christians at times feel overwhelmed by their personal issues. . . . Yet all Christians don't feel as though they must either completely overcome their weaknesses or else abandon the faith."[90] In the book *A Place in the Kingdom*, Leo Hall explains that his homosexual attractions have not disappeared. "I choose not to worry about *when* or *if* my SSA [same-sex attraction] feelings will go away. My immediate hope is that, day by day, I can control or master any sexualized thoughts or behaviors that come. I am learning to replace unwanted feelings with concern, love, and empathy toward all men. . . . In fact, I do not wish my SSA feelings to simply disappear. Rather, I hope that they will be replaced by or enhanced into a more celestial love."[91]

What is a miracle?

"And now, O all ye that have imagined up unto yourselves a god who can do no miracles, I would ask of you, have all these things passed, of which I have spoken? Has the end come yet? Behold I say unto you, Nay; and God has not ceased to be a God of miracles" (Mormon 9:15).

My friend Alan wrote the following: "A woman in our ward was in a terrible automobile accident last summer. Her neck and back were broken and they expected she would be paralyzed for life. But she was given a blessing that she would recover in some important ways. She went through spinal surgery and for a long time had to wear a halo cast. She has slowly regained functioning, and now is able to come to church with two canes; she doesn't even need to use a wheelchair or walker. She can go up stairs and actually has quite good use of her hands, although not complete. I looked at her Sunday, and felt I should go up to her and tell her how much joy it gave me to see her at church because it is a witness to me of a modern-day miracle.

"It is interesting to me, because her miracle is different from the way miracles are portrayed in the Bible. It wasn't sudden. It wasn't complete. She is still a lot more hampered than she was before the accident. Yet in my own heart, the Spirit witnessed to me on that day—and has on other occasions when I have looked at her—that, in fact, she was incredibly blessed in her recovery. It is a miracle, regardless of the time span involved, regardless of the fact that it wasn't all at once or that it still isn't complete or even that it may never be complete.

"I am just now making the connection with my own situation. The miracle of my recovery may take a long time. It may be gradual. It may not ever take me to the point I think I really want to be, in terms of no homosexual desires at all and no remnants of homosexual thoughts ever. (Even straight people have inappropriate thoughts, don't they?) But that doesn't mean the miracle won't happen in other ways that can be just as wonderful. And whatever faith and effort it takes to bring about the miracle—whatever that miracle may mean in my life—will be worth it."

In the Doctrine and Covenants we read, "And again, to some it is given to have faith to be healed" (D&C 46:21). Can God change you? Is there anything too hard for God? "For with God nothing shall be impossible" (Luke 1:37). No matter how monumental this struggle may seem to you, it is not too hard with God's help. "For I am God, and mine arm is not shortened; and I will show miracles, signs, and wonders, unto all those who believe on my name" (D&C 35:8). Miracles do happen. They don't necessarily happen overnight, and they don't always happen in the way we expect. But miracles certainly happen. I have seen them in my life and in the lives of many of my friends.

How should I describe the process of change?

The phrases "*resolving* homosexual issues," "*overcoming* the effects of homosexuality," "*changing* homosexuality in your life," and "*transitioning* out of homosexuality" are good descriptions of the process. It is a process of fulfilling legitimate emotional needs. Dr. Elizabeth Moberly explained, "One should not try to cure, or ask God to cure, something for which cure is not necessary. God does not 'cure' people of legitimate needs. . . . It is not merely ironic, but tragic, that people have attempted to 'cure' what should rightly be fulfilled."[92]

It would be easier to coin a term to describe the process if homosexuality were a condition that was the same for everyone and if it had a definable beginning and end. If we could measure it, we could determine how and when we moved out of it. But the individual elements that make up the homosexual condition are simply life's challenges that everyone faces to one degree or another and may have to work on for a good part of our lives. For example, there may not be a definable time when we can say we have overcome issues such as envy, lust, or denial. We may gain considerable progress toward overcoming them, but still struggle with some aspects for the rest of our lives. I'm not sure that in a lifetime anyone should stop working on improving their feelings of self-worth, and we can always work toward a more correct self-perception, constantly reminding ourselves who we really are and striving to return to our loving Heavenly Father.

We are part of a human family that has challenges in life to overcome. We all work on a unique set of problems and try to become better today than we were yesterday. Our divine nature tells us that we will continue to learn and grow and improve through eternity.

The ultimate goal

The ultimate goal of this transition process is to achieve the following:

♦ a sense of belonging to the male gender.
♦ a comfortableness with heterosexual men.
♦ male relationships that are emotionally healthy.
♦ the ability to relate to women emotionally, spiritually, and physically.
♦ the ability to function effectively as a husband and father.

◆ the personal satisfaction of understanding, controlling, and feeling good about yourself.

For further reading

Homosexuality: Opposing Viewpoints (William Dudley, book editor, Greenhaven Press, San Diego, CA, 1993). This book objectively analyzes the two sides of the question whether change is possible.

Chapter Four

Agency, Freedom, and Responsibility

In one of my support groups I developed a close friendship with a man who had a beautiful family and a testimony of the gospel. Although he tried hard and made some progress, he eventually gave up the Church and his family for a single, carefree life. I think part of the reason he made that choice was because he felt he had no choice. This chapter tells you that you *do* have a choice. Many men are making correct choices in difficult situations and as a result are making significant changes in their lives.

Our lives are made up of small choices. Seldom do we make a large, consequential decision. The little decisions shape our character and make us who we are. Our character is the composite—the net result—of all those small choices. This chapter explores our power to choose and how those choices influence our eternal lives.

In the Doctrine and Covenants we read: "I prepared all things and have given unto the children of men to be agents unto themselves" (D&C 104:17). What does it mean to be agents unto ourselves? Let's look at the concepts of agency and freedom.

Agency, *free agency*, and *moral agency* all refer to our internal power to exercise our will and make choices. *Freedom* refers to the external power and opportunity to carry out those choices.[93]

Agency

Before we came to earth, God gave each of us our agency—the power to choose (see Alma 13:3). In fact, one of the principal reasons we came to this earth was to be proven, to see if we would do everything we are commanded to do (see Abraham 3:25). In the council in heaven, Satan presented an alternative plan that denied agency. When it was rejected, he rebelled, "and sought to destroy the agency of man, which I, the Lord God, had given him" (Moses 4:3–4).

Knowing that Satan is anxious to have us misuse the power of agency, we need to be careful in the choices we make. "Wherefore, the Lord God gave unto man that he should act for himself" (2 Nephi 2:16).

"Therefore, cheer up your hearts, and remember that ye are free to act for yourselves—to choose the way of everlasting death or the way of eternal life" (2 Nephi 10:23). God has given us our agency—the power to choose—and no person or organization can take it away.

Freedom

What can be taken away or reduced in this life is our *freedom*, which is the power to act on our choices. Elder Dallin H. Oaks explained that "free agency is absolute, but in the circumstances of mortality freedom is always qualified."[94] He explains that freedom may be qualified or taken away in three ways:

1. *By physical laws.* For example, we are bound by the physical law of gravity and cannot choose to disobey it. There may also be some physical limitations with which we are born.
2. *By the actions of others.* We choose to live under governments that impose laws and restrictions for the common good of society.
3. *By our own actions.* We may choose of ourselves to impose restrictions on our individual freedom, such as when we buckle our seat belt or sign a contract. In these instances, we use our free agency to choose to temporarily limit certain individual freedoms to help us achieve more important eternal freedoms. You may choose to set personal boundaries. For example, if you know you are susceptible to certain addictive behaviors, you can decide to limit your access to places or conditions that might make it easy for you to fall into temptation.

A restriction of freedom in these ways "reduces the extent to which we can act upon our choices, but it does not deprive us of our God-given free agency."[95]

Consequences

We tend to think of agency as a personal matter. Often overlooked, however, is the fact that choices have consequences. We are free to consider our options, to make choices, and to act, but once an action has been taken we are not free from its consequences. An astronaut, for example, makes the choice to enter the rocket. He can withdraw any time before the rocket fuel is ignited, but once it is, he is bound by the consequences of his choice. In the eternal principle of the Law of the

Harvest (see Galatians 6:7–9), we reap what we sew. Actions have consequences.

President Gordon B. Hinckley said, "Each of us has a choice between right and wrong. But with that choice there inevitably will follow consequences. Those who choose to violate the commandments of God put themselves at great spiritual and physical jeopardy. The Apostle Paul said, 'The wages of sin is death' (Romans 6:23)."[96]

Responsibility, accountability, and authority

In my profession, I consult with company executives to teach them management and leadership skills. A problem I see time and time again is a breakdown in the balance of responsibility, accountability, and authority. Not only can it be a source of failure in companies, but also in individuals.

Responsibility is an agreement between two or more people for the purpose of achieving a desired result. The expected results should be mutually understood and accepted by all parties.

Accountability is a consequence of assigned responsibility. When a person has the responsibility over a given task, he must answer for achieving the desired result.

Authority is the ability given to a person to complete the assigned responsibility. It includes access to the appropriate resources (personnel, money, equipment, etc.) to complete the job.

It is important that these three elements be in balance. A manager must assign responsibility, hold the person accountable, and delegate the proper authority. How does this relate to you if you wish to take control of your life and make significant changes? You need to

♦ take personal responsibility for your actions and the direction of your life.
♦ be accountable to someone.
♦ exercise the proper authority (1) by giving yourself permission to take action and (2) by giving permission to someone else to check up on you.

Responsibility

Satan would have you believe you are not responsible for your agency in this life because you were "born this way" and have no control over your homosexual actions. However, the gospel of Jesus Christ teaches that individual responsibility is an eternal law. We *are* responsible for controlling our impulses so we can keep the commandments and realize our eternal destiny.

The first step is to take full, personal responsibility for what you have been, what you are, and what you will become. Even though you didn't ask for homosexual desires, take responsibility for your life today. Don't feed your self-pity by acting like a victim of life and external situations. Don't blame your environment or your genes for your problems. You are not a helpless victim of circumstance. You are a son of God with divine rights and abilities. You did not choose to have homosexual feelings and attractions but you *do* choose how to respond to them and your ability to change will be determined by the control you decide to take over your life.

In the short term, it may be easier to avoid problems than to face them. I have a friend who is an expert at denial. Denial is his best friend. But hiding from things that are troublesome only makes them worse in the long run. Problems are best solved by facing them head-on.

Accountability

Accountability is an eternal principle. We read in the Doctrine and Covenants, "It is wisdom in me; therefore, a commandment I give unto you, that ye shall organize yourselves and appoint every man his stewardship; That every man may give an account unto me of the stewardship which is appointed unto him. For it is expedient that I, the Lord, should make every man accountable, as a steward over earthly blessings, which I have made and prepared for my creatures" (D&C 104:11–13).

In life, we are accountable to God for everything He gives us. In the parable of the talents, the servants were held accountable for the talents they received and they were expected to increase them (see Matthew 25:14–30). In Church callings, we are held accountable to our priesthood leaders who hold regular interviews with us. Those who have received their temple endowments will remember the instruction they received about reporting progress and being accountable. Accountability helps us keep our integrity and helps us grow.

In your struggle with homosexuality, identify those to whom you will be accountable:

♦ *To yourself,* honestly admitting your problems and weaknesses.
♦ *To God* in daily prayer, confessing your weaknesses and asking for His strength to make it through the day.
♦ *To your bishop* or branch president for sins that should be confessed
♦ *To your therapist* for how well you are following through on the things you need to do.
♦ *To a confidant.* We often need a friend in whom we can confide. This may be someone who also has a personal struggle with homosexuality or simply a close friend who cares about you.

In the book of James, we read, "Confess your faults one to another, and pray one for another, that ye may be healed. The effectual fervent prayer of a righteous man availeth much" (James 5:16).

Once you identify those who will help you be accountable, talk with them about the specific things you want them to hold you accountable for. For example, you may wish to commit to call someone whenever you feel tempted to act out. Or if you have a problem with cruising on the way home from work, commit to call a person each evening to account for what you did on the way home. Give them specific questions you want them to ask you. It is very important to be completely honest with them. If you slip, you may be tempted not to tell them the whole truth. But remember, you have made an agreement with them for the purpose of helping *you* and it will do no good to hide the truth from them even a little.

Authority

The next step is to give them the authority or permission to check up on you. Since you asked them to follow up on you, don't get upset when they ask difficult questions. If you feel frustrated or controlled, remember that *you asked them* to check up on you.

With this accountability agreement, be careful that you don't try to shift to them part of the responsibility for your actions. You cannot blame them if they do not call you or if you could not reach them in an emergency. You are fully responsible for your own actions. Their job is to remind you of that. As you learn to be accountable, you will feel self-empowered.

Another aspect of accountability is to recognize you have authority over your own life if you will give yourself permission to take action. Because of past failures, you may feel powerless to take action. But as you exercise authority over your own life, you will soon find that you can make significant changes in your life. You can take action and it will make a difference.

Chapter Five

Life Choices

Each person has to find his own way of dealing with homosexuality. Some choose to espouse a homosexual identity, "come out," and live openly in that identity. Others choose to find resolution of the homosexual problems so they can live the gospel fully. The choice to resolve the homosexual problems is a choice for growth and self expansion. Deciding to resolve homosexuality is a major life choice. Since homosexuality is the outward manifestation of unresolved issues that are central to your personality, deciding to work on these issues will involve reevaluating your core person and working to change it. This chapter outlines the steps to go through and some issues to consider as you make these important life decisions.

Step One: Define your personal values

The first step in this process is to determine your personal beliefs and core values. Spend a considerable amount of time thinking about your inner values and writing them down. As I went through this process myself, I realized that I could not just accept the beliefs of my family or society, but had to identify what mattered most to me so I could make decisions based on that. In a sense, it meant getting in touch with my inner self and clarifying for me what I believe to be true. It meant identifying my own beliefs as separate from those of others. I had to question my testimony. Did I believe things because others around me believed them or did I believe them of myself? Once I discovered for myself what is eternally true and internalized those values, I could make choices and not waste time trying to change what is everlastingly true or arguing that it had no right to be true.

Now, I must warn you of a liability in this process. Once you determine what is personally valuable, you cannot blame anyone else or hold a grudge because someone forced you to do something. Obtaining self-clarity empowers you to do things because *you* want to do them. You no longer perform out of duty, or respect, or fear. Discipline comes from within and you have the will and integrity to subordinate desires and impulses to the values you determine are important. It is a process of creating a deeper conscience and awareness of the values that govern your behavior. Look to yourself and no one else, and you can become the master of yourself.

Some men blame their failures on a lack of discipline. While discipline is important, it is not enough. If you struggle day-by-day and decision-by-decision trying to change behavior by self-discipline alone, you will likely fail. If each time you are faced with a temptation you have to make a choice, you will finally tire and make wrong choices. The problem is not a weak will, but that values and priorities have not become deeply planted in your mind and heart. You need a firm foundation rooted in the principles and core values that are personally important. How much better it is to decide once and for all what you will be and do! Each time you are faced with an alternative, you already have the decision made and merely need to yield to it. How much better to give in to the right choice than the wrong one! When you act in accordance with your core values, you will feel personal satisfaction and increased feelings of self-worth. (For a more in-depth discussion on this topic, read *The 10 Natural Laws of Successful Time and Life Management*, by Hyrum Smith.)

Step Two: Consider your options

There are really only three options.[97] First, you could straddle the fence. Some men try to have their cake and eat it, too. They want the comfort, security, and acceptance of their family and they want to remain active in the Church. But at the same time, they seek sexual gratification on the outside. But if you understand the scriptures and the plan of salvation, you know this is not a sensible option (see Revelation 3:16). Living a double life—living a lie—is a life of desperation and unfulfilling relationships both at home and on the outside.

A second option is to come down off the fence on the side of homosexuality. This includes the fantasy of finding Mr. Right and living happily ever after. Sadly, many people seek this idyllic condition but never find it. If you understand the scriptures and the plan of salvation, you will realize this is not a reasonable option.

The third option is to accept the eternal plan of salvation. This means devoting yourself to God, your family, and eternal truths. Why spend your energies fighting what you know to be true? Decide to live the gospel plan your loving Father in Heaven designed for your total happiness. President Howard W. Hunter taught, "Christ's way is not only the right way, but ultimately the only way to hope and joy."[98] The sooner you align your life with eternal truth, the sooner you can find true happiness. Surrender your homosexual activities and fantasies, give up your refuge in pornography (if that is a problem for you), and give up all else to follow Christ.

When I finally faced my homosexual problems and used the "h" word for the first time, I was happily married and had children. I loved them very much and felt secure in my marriage. Nevertheless, the pull of the homosexual desires was so strong that my life was turned upside down. People in the gay world told me I should be true to myself and act on my feelings. They said that if I suppressed this newfound sexuality, I would some day regret all the life experiences I would have missed. I soon realized, however, that I could not experiment with these sexual desires on the side and at the same time pretend to be a faithful Mormon husband and father. If I did not want to live a double standard, I had to make a decision. Should I leave my wife and family and dive head first into the gay world? My Mormon life seemed quite dull compared to the excitement and mystique of the gay life! I saw a gay lifestyle as powerfully alluring. It appeared romantic and sensual, and at the same time outrageous and enticing. I found it hard to be objective because rational thinking would quickly get swept away by the emotional fascination. I finally had to sit down and write down all the pros and cons I could think of. The following is the list I wrote in my journal.

Should I move out and accept a gay lifestyle?	
Pro	**Con**
Stop being a hypocrite; no hiding; no lying.	
Could accept myself as I am and wouldn't have to try to change.	

Should I move out and accept a gay lifestyle?	
Pro	**Con**
Freedom with my time to pursue hobbies, travel, exercise.	Increased financial obligations (two households, two cars, etc.).
Could live with Daniel, whom I feel deeply for. ♦ I've known him six weeks. ♦ I can't be sealed to him. ♦ Romantic relationship with him can't last forever.	Would lose my wife, whom I feel deeply for. ♦ I've known her eight years. ♦ I'm already sealed to her. ♦ Romantic relationship with my wife can last forever.
	Limited access to children; could not be the father to them that I want to be.
	I would be excommunicated from the Church.
	Eternal joy and progression would be limited until I began living as I should.

I then wrote in my journal about the risks, my needs, and my fears.

"Risks: After a few years, I'll probably decide I really want what I had. Even after I made the long trek back and was rebaptized, my wife and children would likely be gone forever and I'd have to start over again at nearly age forty.

"Needs: I need the love of a man. Even with the love of a wife and family, I feel a big emotional deficit. I hurt inside and am left wanting.

"Fears: If I were to try to change, I am afraid I may not be able to, and I would continue trying to live the lie for many years while I see my relationship with my wife deteriorate."

Once I had all this on paper, I could objectively see the options open to me.

Step Three: Discern truth from error

Consider eternal truths

Eternal truth stands on its own and is not subject to our opinions. There are not several versions of truth that we may choose to fit our personal situations. God has a plan for the salvation of all His children. As you evaluate your options, consider the following three questions to help clarify your thinking: "Who am I?" "Why am I here on earth?" "Where am I going after this life?" Truthful answers to these three questions will remind you of eternal principles to consider as you make your decisions. (You may also wish to read "Choices," by Russell M. Nelson, *Ensign*, Nov. 1990, pp. 73–74.)

Elder M. Russell Ballard reminded us, "If we are anchored to the correct understanding of who we are, why we are here on this earth, and where we can go after this mortal life, Satan cannot threaten our happiness through any form of temptation. If we are determined to live by Heavenly Father's plan, we will use our God-given moral agency to make decisions based on revealed truth, not on the opinions of others or on the current thinking of the world. Those who understand our Heavenly Father's eternal plan for the joy and happiness of his children will be better prepared to make good choices. If we truly believe that we are his children and are here on earth to learn to live, by faith, the teachings and the commandments of God, we will make the choices that will qualify us to one day return to live in His presence."[99]

Use all the resources available

Your Heavenly Father has given divine gifts to help you in this journey and you must use them to receive the promised blessings. Get a patriarchal blessing or read it if you already have one to be reminded of the blessings you have been promised. It should give insights into your potential and remind you that decisions have eternal consequences and will also affect the lives of other people. Ask your father or bishop for a priesthood blessing to get additional insight as you make these important life decisions. If you have received your endowments, reflect on the covenants made in the temple and remember the promises that were made to you. You are part of a chosen generation reserved to live on the earth in these last days. You have an important mission to fulfill, which for some reason includes homosexual challenges. Since the decisions you make will determine the course your life will take, be sure to make choices that will give eternal joy rather than temporary happiness.

Follow the Holy Ghost

Be careful how far you trust your feelings. Emotional feelings can be fleeting and can change from time to time. If you pursue your current whim, you will be tossed to and fro by every emotion. But since the Holy Ghost works through feelings and impressions, be sure to follow those from the Holy Ghost—they will always be in line with revealed truth. The Spirit will never prompt you in a way that is contrary to the teachings of the prophets. The promptings from the Holy Ghost come from deep within and can be distinguished from the surface emotions that may change from time to time.

President James E. Faust taught that "by the power and gift of the Holy Ghost, we can know what to do and what not to do to bring happiness and peace to our lives."[100] Mormon wrote, "For behold, the Spirit of Christ is given to every man, that he may know good from evil; wherefore, I show unto you the way to judge; for every thing which inviteth to do good, and to persuade to believe in Christ, is sent forth by the power and gift of Christ; wherefore ye may know with a perfect knowledge it is of God" (Moroni 7:16).

Don't be deceived by worldly teachings

Hosts of lies today say that homosexuality is a healthy, alternative lifestyle. Even people in the Church are sometimes beguiled by Satan's clever twists of the truth and they begin to think that they know more than the leaders of the Church about the needs of people who struggle with homosexual desires. With a sincere desire to help, these people write letters to Church leaders and pray that God will inspire the Brethren to understand homosexuality and change Church policies to be more favorable toward those who have homosexual desires. The leaders of the Church seriously consider homosexual issues and have a clear understanding of what God would have them do. There will likely never be a revelation on homosexuality that will become a section in the Doctrine and Covenants to answer all our questions. I likewise don't see a section about overcoming alcoholism or other mortal conditions. Revelation on these matters comes individually. The gospel already has the answers we need, and we can receive individual revelation as we need it to understand how to apply gospel principles to our specific problems.

See your situation for what it is

Several years after beginning to work on my homosexual problems, I reflected back on where I was and recorded the following in my journal, entitled, "What I wanted from a gay lifestyle":

"Relationships: I searched for love in all the wrong places. Now I am learning how to build healthy relationships. I am meeting new people at my support group meetings, at my therapy group, and at the sports program. I am also learning how to reach out and build relationships with other men at work and at church.

"Romance: I wanted men to love me and care about me, and I tried to feel it through a romantic involvement with them. I now realize that the physical involvement destroys any hope of real love and caring. I can develop caring relationships with men, but I can only have a romantic relationship with my wife. I need to date my wife more and spend weekends away occasionally to awaken the romantic feelings we have. We need to go out dancing.

"Excitement: In the gay lifestyle, I found new friends and new activities that added excitement to my life. However, I can feel the thrill of exciting activities with male friends (waterskiing, SCUBA diving, river running, or wind surfing).

"Individuality: Involvement in the gay lifestyle was a way to prove that I wasn't a dull, stereotypical Mormon. I need to find healthy, constructive ways to show my individuality.

"Intrigue: The gay lifestyle was exciting because it is a mystery to most of the world. Most people don't know about it and don't want to know about it. I enjoyed its mystique. However, there are other ways I can feel that same excitement. I am now working with Evergreen International in a pioneering effort to apply new theories to counseling and support groups to help myself and others resolve homosexuality in our lives. I can write materials to help others understand homosexual issues.

"Freedom: I want to feel I have freedom to do what I want. As I come to trust myself more, and earn my wife's trust, I'll feel less confined and more free. As I bring my actions more in line with my value system, I'll realize that when I am doing what I want to do I am free."

Step Four: Decide and commit

After prayerfully evaluating your options, make a decision. "[Y]ou must study it out in your mind; then you must ask me if it be right, and if it is right I will cause that your bosom shall burn within you; therefore, you shall feel that it is right. But if it be not right you shall have no such feelings, but you shall have a stupor of thought that shall cause you to forget the thing which is wrong. . . ." (D&C 9:8–9).

A decision alone is not enough. You need to make a firm commitment to follow through, no matter how hard the way. If you believe you can be free of unwanted homosexual desires and behaviors and your life can be happier because of it, you must make a solemn commitment to do whatever to achieve it. The worst thing you can do is make a half-hearted effort, fail, then become convinced that you cannot overcome homosexuality.

"And Elijah came unto all the people, and said, How long halt ye between two opinions? if the Lord be God, follow him: but if Baal, then follow him. . . ." (1 Kings 18:21).

Speaking on how to get control of our lives, Stephen Covey said, "As we make and keep commitments, even small commitments, we begin to establish an inner integrity that gives us the awareness of self-control and the courage and strength to accept more of the responsibility for our own lives. By making and keeping promises to ourselves and others, little by little, our honor becomes greater than our moods."[101] As a member of Christ's Church, you have made sacred covenants with Him. You have taken upon yourself the name of Christ (see D&C 18:28; 20:29, 37). You have promised to always remember Him and keep His commandments and in return He has agreed to grant you His Spirit to be with you (see Moroni 4:3; 5:2; D&C 20:77). (See also "Choices," Russell M. Nelson, *Ensign*, Nov. 1990, pp. 73–74.) Covenants should not be taken lightly. We draw strength from making and keeping covenants. You may wish to read President Boyd K.

Packer's address from a general conference about the choice to live a gay lifestyle and how it relates to covenants (see "Covenants," Boyd K. Packer, *Ensign*, Nov. 1990, pp. 84–86). You may also wish to contemplate the words to the hymn "Lord, I Would Follow Thee" (*Hymns*, number 220).

Step Five: Make a clean break

In the New Testament, Paul says we must make a sincere decision to follow the Lord. To show our decision to leave our homosexual past behind, we need to make a clean break from all items and relationships that remind us of it. Although you want to make changes, a part of you may cling to the past that is familiar and holds fond memories. It is important to break from these things because they can keep the old feelings alive in your emotions and undo many of your efforts to make changes.

Make a careful inventory of your life to determine what you need to break from. Are there people you associate with that remind you of past events that will hold you back? Are all your friends uplifting and supportive of your efforts to change your ways? If you are serious about leaving homosexual things behind, you need to leave behind those people that encourage you to associate with homosexual things and develop friendships with men who have the light of Christ in their eyes and they will encourage you in righteousness.

Take inventory of your possessions to see if any have a strong association with a person or event you need to leave behind. These might include mementos, gifts, photos, jewelry, or clothing. As hard as it may be to get rid of these, holding on to them will only hold you back. Avoid all activities or places that are homosexual in nature or that trigger temptations. You may even need to look at the area you live in and the route you travel to work. Does any of this remind you of the past you are trying to leave behind? You must be willing to burn the bridges to the past with no thought of returning.

As you identify all these things you plan to eliminate from your life, it will likely seem quite bleak if you don't replace them with new, wholesome activities that will allow you to associate with men you would like to be friends with. Learn to play tennis or racquetball or engage in some other physical activity that will not only help you feel better about yourself, but also give you the chance to associate with new people. When you are ready, you may consider playing sports with men in your ward. Many worthwhile community service agencies will not only help you grow by serving others, but also give opportunities to meet and associate with other men.

Once you make important life decisions that are in harmony with your inner values and make commitments to follow through with them, it doesn't necessarily mean that the way will be easy. Over the years, you have likely developed sophisticated methods of denying or avoiding pain and difficult situations. By now, you probably have realized that these ways of getting short-term relief have turned into your long-term enslavers. It will take some work now to change these methods of denial and avoidance into more healthy ways of facing problems honestly. It may be painful at times, but it can also be richly rewarding. And if you have friends, family, your bishop, a support group, and God on your side, you shouldn't feel alone in the process.

For further reading

"Making the Right Decisions," Richard G. Scott, *Ensign*, May 1991, p. 36.

Chapter Six

Personal Plan of Action

Homosexual problems wouldn't be so difficult to resolve if there were a step-by-step plan that everyone could follow. However, because the factors that *cause* homosexual problems differ from person to person, there is no magical formula that will *resolve* them for everyone. The concepts discussed in this book can teach basic principles of healing, but you will have to develop a personal action plan considering the specific things you need. It won't be as simple as sitting down in an hour with your day planner because the issues are complex, but your success is too important to leave to chance. This chapter outlines steps in developing a personal plan of action as well as some concepts to consider as you develop your plan.

Determine readiness

Before you begin this journey to resolve homosexual problems, it is important to determine if your personal desire is strong enough to carry you through because success will depend on your level of desire and commitment. Do you believe you can change? In quiet moments when you get in touch with your spirit deep inside, the part that really knows who you are in an eternal sense, do you believe you can overcome this temporary condition called homosexuality? Have you really decided that you *want* to overcome its power over your life?

Make a self-inventory

Before beginning, it is important to do a careful self-examination to determine where you are. Plan to spend several hours defining your current feelings and actions in some detail. Don't get impatient with the time it will take; the reward will be well worth the investment. Evaluating where you are now is an important beginning in developing a strategic plan. It can also be a helpful comparison later to measure the progress you make. Your therapist and bishop can help give some objectivity as you ask questions such as the following:
♦ What are my current feelings and desires?

- How strong are they?
- How are they directed?

♦ What are my current habits, compulsions, and addictions?
  - Specifically identify the behaviors, their frequency, and intensity. (Be sure to include fantasies, pornography, masturbation, and other sexual behavior.)

♦ What problems do I have with envy, lust, and pride?

♦ How well do I understand myself?
  - What do I understand my divine nature to be?
  - How do I describe my current feelings of self-worth?

♦ Am I honest with myself and with others?
  - Do I see things as they really are or do I pretend some problems don't exist? (List them.)
  - Do I make excuses or lie to cover my actions? (What actions and in what situations?)
  - Do I make excuses or lie to hide my feelings? (What feelings and in what situations?)
  - Do I make excuses or lie to avoid confrontations or situations that make me feel uncomfortable? (What situations?)

♦ In what things do I trust myself and in what things do I not trust myself?

♦ How do I feel about myself?
  - Do I like myself? (How much and why?)
  - Do I love myself? (How much and why?)
  - Do I enjoy spending time alone with myself? (Why or why not?)

♦ How would I describe my relationships with other men?
  - What close friendships do I have?
  - What do I long for in relationships with men?
  - To what degree are those needs currently being fulfilled?
  - Do I develop unhealthy dependencies? (Give examples.)

♦ How do I describe my relationship with my father?
  - Do I enjoy spending time with him?
  - How well do we communicate emotionally?
  - In what ways are we honest and not honest with each other?
  - Do I hold grudges? (List them.)
  - Do I *believe* that he loves me? (Why or why not?)
  - Do I *feel* his love? (Why or why not?)

- Do I feel he is proud of me? (Why or why not?)
♦ How do I describe my relationship with God?
  - Do I believe that He knows me personally?
  - Do I believe that He loves me? (Why or why not?)
  - Do I *feel* His love? (Why or why not?)
  - Do I feel He is proud of me? (Why or why not?)
  - How often do I pray? (Is it quality time talking with Him?)
♦ How well do I understand gospel principles?
  - Do I understand faith, repentance, and forgiveness and do I do anything about it?
  - What do I understand the atonement to mean to me personally?
  - How much or how little do I let Christ into my life?
  - How often do I think of Christ when faced with temptations?

Not only should you take the time necessary to carefully consider questions such as these, but it is important to *write down your answers*. Although this may seem like busy work, it will be valuable both now and later. It will help you and your therapist now as you put together a strategic plan of action because the answers can help you consider areas that need improvement. The information will also be helpful to you later. Sometimes we make progress in such small increments that we don't even notice the progress. Being able to look back later and read the answers you gave will help you see the progress you have made. It will give you a basis on which you can make periodic evaluations of how far you have progressed toward your goals and determine how much further you have to go. When you get discouraged, you can read where you were and gain encouragement by seeing the progress you have made.

Develop an action plan

With your initial self-inventory in hand, you can sit down with your therapist and identify the areas where you need to concentrate. Be sure to include specific things do to repair, build, and grow. Pick a few areas and write down specific things you can do to improve. A goal without a written plan of action is just a wish. As you read the remaining chapters of this book, consider how each issue relates to you personally and write them down in a special section of your journal entitled "Action Plan" where you can frequently refer to them, reevaluate them, and add to them. When you have completed an action, you can remove it from your plan.

The chapters in this book cover basic issues that most men need to address, and you can begin to concentrate on them. However, you may have issues beyond these that you will need to address in your particular situation. As you put together your plan, be sure to consider both emotional and spiritual aspects.

Emotional and spiritual aspects

The *emotional repairing and maturing* may include such things as coming to grips with past emotional trauma, resolving current emotional conflicts, overcoming emotional detachments and dependencies, learning to love appropriately, building healthy relationships, correcting self-perceptions, and building feelings of masculinity and self-worth.

The *spiritual development* may include growing in ways such as surrendering to God, having a mighty change of heart, overcoming envy and lust, giving Christian service, and developing spiritual wholeness. Personal growth and healing come as you put total faith in your Savior who has the power to change your life. There is no condition you could be born into that He cannot repair. There is no condition that could obstruct your temporal and eternal happiness and potential that He cannot correct. And when you have done all you can, He will take it from there and do the rest.

Both the emotional and spiritual aspects need to be addressed during the process, or it won't be complete. I talk with men who say "I've tried fasting and prayer and scripture reading. I've tried to be good. But it just doesn't work!" I also talk with men who say "I've been in therapy for years and the feelings just don't go away." Some men develop healthy relationships to meet their emotional needs, but neglect the spiritual needs. If you grow emotionally, but not spiritually, you won't have the spiritual help necessary to make it through this difficult transition. If you move along the spiritual track, but not the emotional one, the temptations won't go away and the intensity of the urges and desires may be so great that you will find it difficult to resist the temptation. The process of transition is one of both grace and truth. There is truth in the therapeutic process, but it is also a healing process of grace.

Ask your therapist to help you gauge how you are growing both spiritually and emotionally. Follow his advice if you need to increase work in one area or the other to keep them in balance. When the effort is not in balance, people appear to make good progress, but the progress is temporary and they eventually relapse. While they take care of some of the deficits in their lives, their progress is not permanent because it is not whole.

Repair, then build

It may be helpful to think of your efforts in terms of a two-step process:

1. *Reparative:* fixing the mess (such as correcting your self image, bringing completion to past trauma, resolving masculine identity conflicts, and controlling compulsive behavior).
2. *Developmental:* building a better future (such as making life choices, growing emotionally, developing healthy relationships, and following Christ).

Keep a long-term perspective

We make poor choices in life when we change our focus from eternal, long-term goals to the short term and choose the easy way rather than the more difficult but more important. As Stephen Covey explained, "We are more in need of a vision (or destination) and a compass (a set of principles or directions), and less in need of a road map. We often don't know what the terrain ahead will be like or what we will need to go through it; much will depend on our judgment at the time. But an inner compass will always give us direction."[102]

Multiple factors

Homosexual problems are caused by many factors coming together at critical times in your life. It therefore stands to reason that to resolve it you need to bring together several specific factors at the same time. Those who are successful in resolving homosexual issues have found that attending meetings and therapy groups is not enough. They discover that numerous things have to be in place at the same time for such a change to take place. Almost invariably, it requires sincere spiritual growth, individual therapy, and sticking with a program for several years. Those who commit to this level are able to resolve their homosexual issues in significant ways.

Remember that homosexuality is not the real problem. It is a symptom of deeper struggles such as rejection, envy, abuse, identity, distrust, or fear. However, men who have homosexual problems seldom recognize this because (1) the specific issues vary from person to person and (2) the men are often masters at hiding the real issues in their lives. To resolve the homosexual problems, you need to determine what the underlying problems are, and once you resolve them you resolve the homosexual problems. Once you discover what you have been looking for by relating homosexually, you can find nonsexual ways to fill those needs. Although you can stop homosexual behavior in the short term by exercising willpower, the emotional deficits and unmet social needs will not go away until you legitimately fulfill them.

The remaining chapters in this book discuss topics that most men need to consider. As you read each chapter, consider how it relates to you and set specific goals in each area. Remember that since many of these components are interdependent, neglecting one area can make progress in another area ineffectual.

Keep balance

In my own life, I have come to recognize the need for balance. I believe that a lot of the difficulty I have had is the result of an imbalance. I had too few close friendships during certain childhood and adolescent years. I had too much preoccupation with sex during some adolescent years (but who doesn't?). I had too little access to a father model during early childhood. I had too little acceptance by my older brother when I looked up to him. For several years, I felt too comfortable spending time with my mother and therefore did not go outside and play with friends.

Not only can the imbalance contribute to the *development* of homosexual problems in the first place, but a continued imbalance can contribute to *failure* as you try to resolve them. For example, you may spend so much time reading and studying about homosexual issues that you do not take time to build relationships. Or you may rely on support groups and not get individual therapy. Or you may get therapy and build relationships, but ignore the spiritual aspects.

In The Book of Mormon, we read, "And see that all these things are done in wisdom and order; for it is not requisite that a man should run faster than he has strength. And again, it is expedient that he should be diligent, that thereby he might win the prize; therefore, all things must be done in order" (Mosiah 4:27). Your life is like a quilt. The colors and textures of the individual pieces and threads all combine to make a work of art. Remember that homosexuality is the symptom of deeper problems. As you work on things that may seem unrelated, your homosexual problems disappear.

Luke's description of how Jesus grew provides a good formula for the areas we need to work on. "And Jesus increased in wisdom and stature, and in favour with God and man" (Luke 2:52). Be sure you work on intellectual, physical, spiritual, and social-emotional goals.

Set boundaries

Another reason people fail in their attempts to make changes in their lives is because they fail to set boundaries for themselves. A recovering alcoholic, for example, may need to draw the line at entering a bar. If he rationalizes he can enter the bar and socialize with his drinking buddies but not be tempted to drink, he is fooling himself. Likewise you cannot be involved in gay organizations and not be tempted to flirt and be attracted to other men. You need to establish boundary lines that you commit not to cross.

Physical boundaries may be easy to define but there are also other boundaries to consider that may be more difficult to define, such as emotional boundaries.[103] If you find it easy to fall into emotional dependency, you may need to establish emotional rules and hold to them. Although you may not always be able to control how you feel, you can choose how to respond to those feelings. Your emotions give you clues to understanding yourself. To help you understand emotional boundaries, you may read *Human Boundaries and Personal Abuse* by Melanie Geyer.

Abuse can also affect the concept of boundaries. All forms of abuse (sexual, physical, emotional, intellectual, and spiritual) involve a violation of boundaries. Abuse may cause confusion as to what boundaries are and where they can or should exist. To avoid being abused, define your own boundaries. To avoid being abusive of others, respect their boundaries.

You are the steward of your body and have the right to determine who can touch your body. If you have been the victim of abuse, you may have come to feel that others have a right to touch and use your body. This false perception can be changed by discovering your self-worth and working through the effects of abuse with a therapist. If you have become enslaved in sexual addictions, you may feel you are helpless in controlling physical intimacy. But with professional counseling and God's help, you can overcome addictions and gain control and self-respect.

Take the time now to evaluate current boundaries because they may be nebulous. Setting and obeying personal boundaries is a way to show self-integrity and self-respect. Setting boundaries is not just a one-time event; it is a constant process of defining, redefining, evaluating, and maintaining boundaries.

Monitor progress

It is common to have recurring doubts as you work on your action plan. Gerard van den Aardweg, a psychologist with many years of successful clinical experience treating homosexuality, observes that "the homosexually inclined, even if they are in principle willing to change, initially have serious doubts whether there are realistic chances of a profound improvement. These are periodically returning doubts, notwithstanding clearly observable progress, and they only die away when the change in feelings has become much more obvious."[104] To overcome these doubts, look back at your previous self-assessments from time to time and compare your current conditions with them. This will not only give you encouragement, but can help you make adjustments to your plan as needed.

Being accountable and journaling

We can receive support by being accountable to others—to God, to your bishop, to your therapist, and to a close friend. It is important to be accountable to yourself through introspection and journaling. Spend time thinking and writing in your journal about the events and feelings you experience each day. Stephen Covey reminds us that "keeping a journal of our thoughts, experiences, insights, and learning promotes mental clarity, exactness, and context."[105] Don't just record events superficially. Think and write about deeper levels including your thoughts, feelings, dreams, and ideas. Record anything that moves you, whether the event is happy or upsetting. Describe your feelings and try to determine why you feel the way you do. Studies show that people who write regularly in journals feel less stressed about their lives and more in control.

Journal writing is a way to monitor and direct your life. With the fast pace of life, it can be helpful to pause for a few minutes each day to reflect on what happened and why. The act of writing in a journal gets your thoughts outside your head and slows down your thinking process so you can make connected, complete thoughts. When Jacob, the brother of Nephi, was writing on the plates, he commented that "our lives passed away like as it were unto us a dream" (Jacob 7:26). Life is not a dream and journaling is a way to help you recognize what is happening in your life and keep it directed. As time passes, your interpretations of the past will change. So don't just write down facts and events, but also describe how you felt at the time. When you clearly know your thoughts you will be less afraid of them and will see them for what they are. You may also compare current entries with previous ones to evaluate the progress you are making. Journaling can be especially helpful if you do not have someone available to talk things through.

Journaling is also a process by which you can work out grief and healing. If you have unresolved issues with your father, writing him a letter in your journal can be a way of working things out and bringing closure to painful situations. When I do not write in my journal regularly, I find myself wandering and regressing. Journaling helps to analyze my feelings, assess my actions, and stay in control.

Requirements for change

The following are important elements for successfully resolving your homosexual problems:

♦ *You are personally dissatisfied with your current condition.* You are aware of the negative consequences of your current situation and want to change it. The stronger your dissatisfaction, the stronger your motivation to change.

♦ *You believe it is possible to change.* You have heard that change is possible and have seen changes in others. You believe you can change because: (a) you believe you are capable of something better, (b) you believe in God's promises, and (c) you believe that through God's power you can change.

♦ *You develop and follow through on a plan of action that addresses your specific needs.* This process differs for each individual and includes specific things that need to be done to repair, build, and grow.

♦ *You have adequate support during the process* from peers, family, Church leaders, and professional counselors who provide information about the change process, encouragement to continue when it is difficult, feedback, insight, validation, love, and friendship.

Use a multifaceted approach

You will be more successful if you use all the relationships and resources available, such as family, friends, counselors, Church leaders, faith, prayer, group and individual therapy, books, and support groups. You will have to grow in other areas like coming to understand your true self, confirming your masculine identity, healing old wounds, forgiving, reconciling your relationship with your father or others, and learning to control your behavior. And most important, spirituality will need to play a major role. Commitment to and faith in Jesus Christ is the key to applying the healing power of the atonement in your life. If you are ready to do these kinds of things, there is hope. You can find your way out of homosexuality just as I and many of my friends have done.

Who should you tell?

When and who you should tell are matters that each individual must determine through prayer and inspiration. What is best for one may not be for another. Besides your bishop or stake president, I don't feel it is necessary or prudent to tell many people beyond your family or closest friends. You may feel those who are closest to you should know about this part of your life so they can be an integral part of your life. It will help them understand you better and they will be in a better position to provide support.

Wife

If you are married, your wife deserves to know about your struggles. You cannot be of one flesh (see Matthew 19:5) if you hide such important parts of your life from her. Wives are often in tune with their husband's feelings before the husband ever understands them. I was married and had children before I realized I had homosexual problems. After I saw a therapist a few times, I knew I had to tell my wife. I spent quite a bit of time preparing just how I would tell her. I picked Labor Day weekend so we would have several days to thoroughly talk things out. I explained to her that I had emotional problems I was trying to work out and that I was seeing a therapist to try to understand them. I explained my feelings of loneliness and we talked about gender identity and the need for male companionship. We talked about my difficulty in developing satisfying relationships with men. It was several hours before I ever used the "h" word and I tried to help her see it as an emotional problem and not just a sexual one. I told her I could not make it on my own. I needed to share these experiences with her. There was a lot of talking and crying, then more talking and more crying. Although it was difficult, she was supportive and committed to help me through it. I am grateful that my wife knows about these challenges in my life and that she is there to support me. After a particularly good therapy session or support group meeting, I needed to be able to share my positive feelings and successes with her. This experience has helped us grow together in ways we never did before.

The following is the experience of one wife: "My husband . . . told me about his struggles with same-sex attraction (SSA) after we had been married for one year. As he talked to me that day, I remember feeling a deep outpouring of love for him, and a profound sense of sadness that he had struggled all alone for so many years. I was impressed that he would share something so intimate and painful with me. [He], in turn, was amazed that I didn't kick him out of my life. He told me it was his first experience with unconditional love. The thought of leaving my husband never occurred to me. He was still the same man I loved, and I felt even closer to him that day because of the way he opened up his heart to me. That day was a turning point in both our lives."[106]

Parents and siblings

I have disclosed my struggles to my older brother since I suspected he also had homosexual problems. Although in his case he has chosen to pursue homosexuality at the expense of the gospel, the fact that we have shared this part of our lives with each other has brought us closer together.

I have chosen not to tell my parents or other family members because I feel it would not be helpful or necessary to do so. Steve Andersen wrote the following about telling his parents: "On Sunday, I told my parents and what a relief it was! I never could have expected their response. Had I known they were going to be as supportive as they were, I would have told them years ago. I guess I underestimated them. They were totally shocked, which actually surprised me, because I thought they suspected it when I was growing up. I shared with them all the things I thought about myself growing up and was surprised to find out that they were just my perceptions and not necessarily how other people viewed me, particularly my parents. My dad said that he knew he was nonemotional and that he often has considered trying to change. He said if it would help me and boost my self-esteem, then he would like to try. He then came over and gave me a big hug—the first I can remember in thirty-six years—and I'm thirty-six! He even called me at work the next day, which he never does, just to tell me how sad he was and that he felt like crying, not because he was sad that I was dealing with this, but sad that I had been unhappy for so long and he never knew. What a positive experience!"

Children

Scott wrote the following about his experience telling his son: "The moment we knew would come had arrived. My oldest son (almost fourteen) finally asked the question! I was working on the computer writing about my life experiences when my son came home. He wanted to use the computer and I wouldn't give it to him, so he kept coming in and out of the room and walking over to see what I was working on, and I kept trying nonchalantly to keep him from seeing what I was typing. I was nearly finished when my hovering son finally came out and asked, 'Dad, are you gay?' I dodged the question, and he said, 'You didn't answer me.' So I said something dumb like, 'Why? Are you?' He answered that he wasn't. Then I answered, 'Yes. I have been.' Then I looked at him and asked, 'Does that bother you?' Having the basic question answered seemed to satisfy him and he just went back to asking when he could use the computer. Later that evening he was very loving. He came by several times and hugged me and told me that he loved me. I read to him for a while at bedtime and when we finished I said to him, 'Son, it's important for you to know that I love Mom, and that I always have.' He just gave me a hug and went to bed. It wasn't nearly as painful as I'd imagined or feared it would be. In fact, it wasn't painful at all."

Children who are loved and respected by their parents tend to love and respect their parents. However, beware that many adolescents are not mature enough to be as accepting or understanding as Scott's son. You and your wife should prayerfully decide when—or whether—to tell your children. If you tell them, explain that you are not perfect (if you have made behavioral mistakes), but don't discredit yourself or demean men in general. If the children don't respect the role of men and fathers, they may develop gender identity problems themselves.

Friends

Some men have also found a very positive experience in telling a close friend who does not share homosexual struggles. They have generally been very surprised to learn that others will still accept and love them even when they know their "deep, dark secret." This has helped them feel loved for who they really are, rather than for the facade they tried to present. This realization often improves their self-perception.

My friend Todd described his experience sharing personal struggles with friends. He wrote, "True friends will always accept us, even though they cannot completely relate. Having said that, it is amazing to find how many people can relate to homosexual issues even though they may not have personally experienced such issues. For example, I know a lot of men I can talk to about their struggles with relating to their father, even though their difficulties may not have contributed to sexual issues. Similarly, female victims of sexual abuse have been able to relate to my difficulties, and vice versa. In the end, I have found that everyone I have shared my 'terrible secret' with has accepted me and become a closer friend because of the sharing. Indeed, the process was a necessary part of my healing."

Use caution

Although the above stories are positive experiences, don't expect that everyone's reaction will be positive. Some men have been ostracized from their families or have lost close friends when they told them of their attractions. The people you tell are human and come from varied backgrounds. They have their own limitations and hangups, and each will react differently. Some are able to display Christlike love; others may lash out at you. Some may blame themselves while others may blame your friends or other situations in life. Be patient and give them time to come to understand, just as you expect them to be patient with you. If they hesitate initially, don't interpret it to mean that you are unacceptable or unlovable. Recognize that now having shared with them, your relationship can grow to increased levels. Deeper relationships are worth the initial pain they may cause.

To help as you explain your struggles to a loved one, about your struggles, I have written a booklet, *Understanding Male Homosexual Problems: An Introduction for Latter-day Saints*, that explains in a condensed form the concepts discussed in this book.

Make it work!

Amulek taught, "And now my beloved brethren, I would exhort you to have patience, and that ye bear with all manner of afflictions. . . . But that ye have patience, and bear with those afflictions, with a firm hope that ye shall one day rest from all your afflictions" (Alma 34:40-41).

In closing the general conference in April 1995, President Gordon B. Hinckley admonished us to "put behind us our weaknesses of the past and go forth with new energy and increased resolution. . . . We have work to do, you and I, so very much of it. Let us roll up our sleeves and get at it, with a new commitment, putting our trust in the Lord." Such an accomplishment is possible, he said, if "we will be prayerful and faithful. We can do better than we have ever done before." A few moments later, he added "May we go with determination to try a little harder to be a little better. Please know that we are not without understanding of some of your problems. We are aware that many of you carry very heavy burdens. We plead with the Lord in your behalf. We add our prayers to your prayers that you may find solutions to your problems. We leave a blessing upon you, even an apostolic blessing. We bless you that the Lord may smile with favor upon you, that there may be happiness and peace in your homes and in your lives, that an atmosphere of love and respect and appreciation may be felt among husbands and wives, children and parents. May you 'look to God and live' with happiness, with security, with peace, with faith."[107]

Chapter Seven

Personal Study

The Lord tells us, "And as all have not faith, seek ye diligently and teach one another words of wisdom; yea, seek ye out of the best books words of wisdom; seek learning, even by study and also by faith" (D&C 88:118). One of your biggest challenges in resolving homosexual problems is to overcome your confusion by getting good, true information. Many men report that this helps them make sense of their feelings and see things in a more enlightened perspective.

As one man commented, "I received the [Elizabeth] Moberly and [Jeff] Konrad books from a gentleman in Evergreen. For two or three days I read them continually until I got through them. And I had an experience reading those books like some people have when they read The Book of Mormon, where they just become totally absorbed in it and it rings true and they say, 'This is the true religion!'"[108] Another man said, "[I]t was a tremendous experience to read these books and agree with them and say 'Aha! This is what's been going on!'"[109]

A number of good books can help you understand your situation. I found it helpful to read books about different psychological theories of homosexuality, as well as those that gave practical suggestions of things I could do. They didn't all fit my personal situation, but in every one I found some elements that gave me a perspective that helped me understand and come to terms with my feelings. It is critical to increase your understanding of basic Gospel principles. Although you may think you already know the gospel, gaining a more in-depth understanding of the atonement, faith, repentance, and forgiveness will be at least as beneficial to you as gaining an understanding of the emotional aspects of your homosexual attractions.

It seems that those who have the most success in understanding their feelings and controlling their behavior are those who read the most. The more you study, the more you are exposed to ideas that may help. Good information from books, manuals, audio cassettes, videos, newsletters, and other educational resources can help offset the demoralizing confusion you hear in the media at large. In the section

Selected Readings, I list publications that were helpful to me. The description that follows each book can help you decide if it is a book that may be helpful to you.

Beware of books—some even written by LDS authors—that do not adhere carefully to gospel fundamentals. In a review of one such book, Scott Peterson explains that "rather than adjusting their behavior to accommodate the values of their religion, they adjust their own religious values to accommodate their behavior. What they seek is not explanation, but rationalization."[110]

I recommend that you subscribe to newsletters. You can get from Exodus International a list of the ministries that publish newsletters and for a small donation of $5 or $10 a year, you can receive regular newsletters that have valuable insights. I found the following newsletters to be particularly helpful:

Harvest News, P.O. Box 11469, Philadelphia, PA 19111, phone 215/342–7114, e-mail: HarvestUSA@aol.com.

Regeneration News, Regeneration, Inc., P.O. Box 9830, Baltimore, MD 21284–9830, phone 410/661–0284.

Nexus, Metanoia Ministries, P.O. Box 33039, Seattle, WA 98133–0039, phone 206/783–3500.

The Journey, Evergreen International, P.O. Box 3, Salt Lake City, UT 84110, phone 800/391–1000, e-mail: evergrn999@aol.com.

Chapter Eight

Support Groups

Most men find support groups to be very helpful. A support group should be a safe and confidential place where you can come to know that you are not the only one with homosexual problems. No one will say, "You're dealing with *what*?" It is a place to find encouragement from other men who are working to resolve the same problems you are, and that helps reduce your feelings of being alone, different, and isolated. This chapter discusses the purpose of support groups and tells you what to look for in choosing one. It then discusses how to support each other in a group and the need for spirituality and safety. Finally, it explains how specialized support groups, such as sports programs, can be helpful.

Joe Dallas writes that the function of a support group is to "provide a safe, godly environment where people can openly discuss their homosexual struggles; learn from the experiences of others who've gone through similar struggles; be accountable to a group of Christians who are genuinely concerned; and know they have friends who are regularly praying for them, available to them, and rooting for them."[111]

A support group is about helping others. In the beginning, you attend to help yourself, but you soon discover that you find the help you need when you extend help to others. When you begin to care more about their needs than your own, you find yourself healed in the process.

Support groups emphasize dialogue as a way of learning to openly and clearly deal with issues that are at the root of feelings of homosexual attractions. As you listen to each other, perhaps for the first time you will listen to yourself. The typical newcomer sits and listens, and about half way through the discussion realizes he has finally found people who think and feel like he does. When he recognizes that he is safe and can trust the group, he begins to open up and the healing process of sharing begins. He discovers that even when others know all about him, they still accept him. Once the fear of rejection is gone, he finds that he has the courage to relate to men in the group and eventually to men outside the group. Support groups can help you by providing:

- ◆ a safe environment where you can face your problems.
- ◆ feedback, insight, and practical ideas from men who have experienced the same things you experience.
- ◆ a place to begin to build healthy relationships with other men.
- ◆ interpersonal experiences in validation, love, and friendship.
- ◆ direction, vision, goals, and encouragement to continue when it is difficult.
- ◆ accountability for your actions.
- ◆ positive experiences to offset the effects of negative peer pressure.
- ◆ reduction of your sense of isolation.
- ◆ understanding, empathy, and acceptance from other men.
- ◆ encouragement to continue through the lengthy process.

A support group alone is not enough

A support group will not solve all your problems; it has no magical "cure" for homosexual problems. Participating in a support group is one of the many things you may need to do. Some men get a false sense of security by participating in a support group and when it doesn't solve all their problems they may feel frustrated and lose hope that change is possible.

A support group in moderation can be valuable for support and understanding, but in excess, it can prolong and heighten your old identity. The support group should never take the place of the Church, your priesthood quorum, or a normal social life; it is only a short-term supplement.

While your relationships with men in the group will be very fulfilling, they will not be all you need. The support group can be unhealthy if its members only interact with the other members of the group. In a sense, it can become a nonsexual "gay" community. If you live from meeting to meeting because it is your only social interaction, you need to actively pursue relationships with men outside the group at work, in your quorum, and in other male groups. It is when you experience the love and acceptance of men who do not have homosexual problems that you really start to recognize your true worth. Those friendships will be the most rewarding and healing.

In addition to a support group, many men need individual and group therapy. Sometimes support groups can actually do more harm than good if the person is not also seeing a therapist individually to help him correctly process the things he experiences and feels so they can contribute to his growth. If you have addictions, you may also need the help of a twelve-step program like Homosexuals Anonymous or Sexaholics Anonymous (see the Organizations section in this book).

Choosing a support group

President Boyd K. Packer gives the following counsel and warning: "There are groups of many kinds which seek to fortify those struggling to withdraw from drug addiction or to master other temptations. On the other hand, there are organizations which do just the opposite. They justify immoral conduct and bind the chains of addiction or perversion ever tighter. Do not affiliate with such an organization. If you have already, withdraw from it."[112] Some organizations exist to give support and love, but do not seek to help the person find ways to overcome homosexual behavior. These organizations do more harm than good because they help the person justify his behavior and, as President Packer stated, "bind the chains of addiction or perversion ever tighter." Some organizations believe they know more about the homosexual condition than the Church leaders and they plead with them to change Church policies to be more sympathetic to those who have homosexual feelings. They use the scriptures in an attempt to justify the expression of homosexual feelings. The Apostle Paul condemned those who seek to justify homosexual behavior saying that they "changed the truth of God into a lie, and worshiped and served the creature more than the Creator" (see Romans 1:25–32). Beware of the subtle craftiness of such groups.

Before you choose a support group, get a copy of their written literature and read the group's mission statement. (If they don't have one, they likely have not defined their purpose well enough for it to be a healthy environment.) Does the group support the doctrines of the gospel, the scriptures, and the practices of the Church without reservation or exception? If the group has any reservation or finds any exception, it is on shaky ground. Do they teach that change is possible? Does the group inspire respect for the individual and promote personal growth? Does the group have written policies to protect participants in their vulnerabilities and provide a safe environment? Does the program support total abstinence of sexual behavior outside of marriage? This kind of sobriety can be attained through sharing experience, strength, and hope at group meetings. The group is on dangerous ground if it seeks to justify any homosexual behavior. Does the group function according to the written statements?

LDS support groups

Evergreen International is an umbrella organization that can help you find support groups that follow the criteria discussed above. Evergreen can refer you to a local support group or therapist. In addition to support groups for men and women who struggle with homosexual attraction, there are groups for their spouses, family, and friends. The organization also publishes manuals and newsletters, sells books by mail, and sponsors conferences. It provides education and resources to family and friends, professional counselors, religious leaders, and all others who wish to help individuals who desire to change. You may call or write for a list of publications or information on a support group near you. If there is no support group in your area, Evergreen can tell you how to start one. (See the Organizations section of this book for information on how to contact Evergreen.)

Evergreen began in the summer of 1989 in Salt Lake City, Utah, when a group of eleven men met to organize a support group. Believing that homosexual practices are not in keeping with the gospel of Christ, these men were frustrated with their experience with other organizations. They concluded there must be a solution other than destroying spiritual beliefs or denying sexual longings. They drew on information from Christian ministries in other parts of the country that had been helping men and women resolve their homosexual problems for more than thirty years.[113] From these small beginnings, Evergreen International has grown into a network of referral and educational services for men and women throughout the world.

Joining a support group

The first step in joining a support group is to make the phone call to the group leader. He will generally want to talk with you before you attend a group meeting to determine your sincerity and readiness to participate with the group. He will explain to you the format and rules of safety and confidentiality that are critical to the success of the group. When you first attend a support group, you will likely go through the following stages:

Fear and anticipation. You may have a number of fears and concerns as you attend your first meeting. Will the other men accept me? Will I be able to open up to them? Will I be attracted to someone there? These are legitimate fears that are common to nearly everyone.

Sense of relief. Although your first meeting can be frightening, you will soon find that it is easy to make friends because people are there to lend support. Most men report an enormous sense of relief to have found a group of LDS men who also struggle with attractions and are trying to find righteous solutions to their situations.

Curiosity and sharing. The next phase is one of learning all the new information that is available. You will become aware of many books with good ideas about the causes of your problems and their potential solutions. You will also have the chance to exchange ideas with others in the group and hear what has helped them to be successful.

Boundary testing. As you mature emotionally through your experience in the group, you will find yourself testing the boundaries to determine what is appropriate.

Disillusionment. After the initial excitement wears off, you may become disillusioned as you realize that the support group in itself will not solve all your problems and there is a lot of hard work ahead of you. This is the phase where some men drop out of the group in search of an easier answer.

Hard work. This is the phase where you settle in and do all the work.

Termination. Some men make the mistake of leaving a support group before they are ready and others remain much longer than is healthy. You may need the help of your therapist to determine when the time is right for you. If you are able to see your issues objectively, you will know when it is time to move out of the group. Be aware that sometimes group members panic when someone else is "graduating" and they may try to hold the person back for their needs and not for his. If you know it is time for you to move on, do it.

Open and closed group formats

An *open group* is one where you can attend the group meetings whenever you like, as long as you agree to abide by the group's rules. A *closed group* is one where the participants are identified and each makes a commitment to attend all meetings. Closed groups are more stable because people are not always entering and leaving. Because of this continuity, the participants are more dedicated and accountable to each other and they can make more progress.

How to support each other in a group

The Bible exhorts us to bear one another's burdens (see Galatians 6:1–2). We also read, "Two are better than one; because they have a good reward for their labour. For if they fall, the one will lift up his fellow: but woe to him that is alone when he falleth; for he hath not another to help him up" (Ecclesiastes 4:9–10).

The men in my support group were able to give me a lot of support and help. They understood my feelings and helped me find solutions to my problems. When I felt vulnerable, I called them and they talked me out of desires to act sexually. They were genuinely concerned about me and I was genuinely concerned about them. I relied on them many times. I never would have made it without the love and support I got from my friends who were always there when I needed them.

The following suggestions can help you have effective relationships in your group.

Be a consistent support to others in the group. Make attendance at the group meetings a matter of high priority. Consistency is very important both for your own progress and that of other participants.

Be honest with yourself. The controversial nature of homosexual problems encourages people to keep it hidden and festering. Many of us have felt that we were the only ones to have these feelings. Admitting a problem to yourself is the first step to recovery. The next step is to decide what you intend to do about it. What is your purpose in joining a support group? Do you really want to overcome evil thoughts and behaviors or are you just looking for justification of your incorrect ways?

Be honest with others in your group. Admitting your problems to others in the group can help relieve feelings of isolation. As you openly explore your feelings in regular meetings, you can get much needed support from those who have experienced or who still experience struggles, and you can acquire a sense of accountability to each other. The group will teach you how to disclose and be honest with others in the group. It is not easy to disclose things that are deeply disturbing and personal, but it is the first step in healing. You will discover that there is no need to lie to others in the group or cover up the way you feel about things. They will understand your troubles and be willing to share with you the solutions they have found. By asking a lot of questions, or even just by listening quietly to what others say, you will begin to understand how this process works.

Confront and challenge other group members. Sexual activity thrives in secret and the group can be a place to bring it into the light. Group members can confront each other kindly and respectfully when they see rationalization or denial. In the beginning, this kind of total honesty can be difficult, but if you are sincere in your desire to make changes in your life, you will welcome it.

Respect the rights of others. Respect the right of others to have opinions different from yours. No one should ridicule or belittle another participant, even jokingly, nor should they be judgmental or critical of others or their situation. Like you, they are struggling through difficult circumstances.

Recognize that group members are on different levels. One night in the group meeting, Bill talked about the group and the way we did and did not support each other. He had felt at times that the group brought him down. For example, when he slipped up once he almost felt a cheer from us. He felt us say 'Hurray! Bill is human.' Although we didn't want him to fail, that was the message he felt. At times, I felt like I want to be on the same level as the other guys. As strange as this sounds, there were times I felt I wanted to be as messed up as Alan so I could feel I fit in completely. It is important to recognize that each member of the group is on a different level and that is okay as long as each works and progresses from where he is.

Give equal time. Don't dominate the discussion time, but allow others the chance to express themselves as well. Allow equal time even to those who appear not to want to talk. You have a responsibility to help them feel comfortable and bring them out of their silence.

Invite the spirit to every meeting. Although the meetings don't need to be somber, they should have a tone of respect for each other, for the difficulty of the process of change, and for the power of the Spirit that is essential to guide you through the process. Every meeting should begin and end with prayer. Watch your conversations so they don't drive the spirit away.

Avoid inappropriate conversations. Share your feelings and experiences with others, but don't give graphic details of sexual activities or divulge locations where sex or pornography is available. Don't assume that everyone knows what you know, but spare them from temptations by not divulging such information. Profanity has no place in the meetings. It is also important to keep conversations about other men positive and not let the discussions become a pity party where you devalue other men, but instead encourage each other to get out and build relationships with other men.

Help others recognize and develop feelings of self-worth. Group members should be positive and build each other up and encourage each other in righteousness. Help others see their value as individuals. Always be watching out for others and when it appears they need extra help, do all you can to include them and help them feel a part of the group. In addition to *acts* of kindness, *tell* them you love them and appreciate their friendship. Help them see their friendship is of great value to you.

Move to deeper levels of conversation. It is usually easy to talk about surface-level things like the weather, school, work, politics, and other knowledge-based things. Although a certain amount of this kind of conversation is necessary to build a relationship, be sure that you soon move from the knowledge area to feelings. It is when you begin talking about your feelings and emotional reactions to things that you move into the areas that will be the most beneficial.

Be accountable to each other. Group members should hold each other accountable by asking each member to report on their progress each week. During the week, you may want to organize a buddy system so that when you are tempted to do something inappropriate, you have a buddy you can call to help.

Be wise in your activities with other participants. Don't participate in activities that cause you to be vulnerable, which may arouse homosexual feelings, or include any degree of physical intimacy with other men. Avoid campiness (acting "gay") and inappropriate jokes or innuendo. Behave with them the way you would with men who do not experience homosexual attractions. Don't spend excessive time with any one participant to protect yourself from emotional dependency or from the possibility of physical intimacy. Limit the time you spend with group members. Spending excessive time with them limits your time to associate with men from outside the group, and you should give top priority to those relationships.

Relationships with men in the group. You will develop strong relationships with other men in the group and although you will have a lot of clean, wholesome fun, remember that the support group is not a social club. Your purpose in the group is to learn how to relate in wholesome ways so you will have the confidence to relate with other men at work and at church. While the group is a safe place to learn to relate to each other, it should not be the ultimate goal. You should work on making your primary relationships with men outside the group.

Relationships with men outside the group. When you disclose your "dark secrets" to other men in the group, you find that they still love and accept you. And although this love and acceptance will be meaningful, the voice of the Adversary will whisper, "Of course *they* love you, because they are attracted to men themselves." Your next step will be to reach out into the mainstream world and discover that love and acceptance is available there as well. Someone else needs to be allowed into the deepest levels of your life. That doesn't necessarily mean that they need to know all about your attractions, but you need to open up and let them in.

For additional guidelines on creating an environment of support, you may read the book *Group Techniques* by Gerald Corey.

Confidentiality and anonymity

Many men who have homosexual attractions have chosen not to disclose such to others outside the group and could be deeply hurt by the release of information about their situation. In some cases, even spouses may not be aware of their husband's participation in the group. Rules of confidentiality ensure privacy for individuals in the group. It is a safeguard of special significance to men who may hesitate to participate in an organization if they have any reason to believe that their homosexual problems could be revealed to others.

In addition to protecting the identities of fellow participants, it is vital to keep confidential what is said in the group. A helpful phrase to remember is: "What we say here stays here." Outside the meetings, don't mention the people you saw or repeat the things you heard. One careless slip of the tongue overheard by someone else could have a devastating effect on a fellow participant. While this principle may be clear in theory, putting it into practice may not always be easy. The following general guidelines may be helpful:

Keep identities anonymous. Most groups have guidelines about using only first names and last initials.

Membership lists. Lists of names, telephone numbers, and addresses should be kept only when absolutely necessary. If you keep lists of members, guard them with strict care.

Return addresses on mailings. Most organizations associated with homosexuality do not include the name of the organization in the return address of mailings.

Telephone messages. When leaving messages, be careful not to identify the individual with any group or meeting or to inadvertently divulge information that may be revealing. Assume that the person who receives the message knows nothing about the individual's involvement with any group. Be aware that some people pretend to know more than they actually do to get information from you, sometimes unintentionally (out of curiosity) and sometimes willfully (out of spite). Either case can be damaging. Since others may have access to the individual's voice mail or e-mail, leave only the information you would give to a stranger.

The place of spirituality in group meetings

Because Christ's atonement and the plan of salvation play an important role in the process of recovery, it is critical that you draw on gospel principles, refer to the scriptures and the words of Church leaders, and incorporate all these into every aspect of your support group program. However, when engaging in gospel discussions, be sure to stay away from the myths and on solid doctrinal ground. It is entirely appropriate in an LDS group to support each other by sharing testimonies, praying for each other, encouraging each other in righteousness, and attending the temple together. "Therefore, strengthen your brethren in all your conversation, in all your prayers, in all your exhortations, and in all your doings" (D&C 108:7). I have heard encouraging stories from groups about spiritual experiences that have had a profound influence on their growth and recovery. If your group is not having similar experiences, evaluate your activities and plan for ways to invite the Spirit into all you do.

Be careful that you do not confuse priesthood responsibility. When a person needs particular strength or comfort or enters a leadership position in the organization, he may go to his father or priesthood leader and ask for a priesthood blessing. If a participant cannot turn to his father or a priesthood leader, friends can help. However, be careful about the exercise of priesthood ordinances within the group. The group is not the Church and should never become a substitute for the priesthood quorum. You can benefit greatly from relationships you develop within your priesthood quorum, so rely more on quorum members, priesthood leaders, home teachers, and your father. The support group's programs should be temporary and point you back to your priesthood quorum and leaders for support and fellowship.

One evening at our support group meeting, two women came by invitation. One was previously married to a man with homosexual problems and wanted to understand him better and know what to do to support him. The other had a brother who died the previous week of AIDS and wanted to find a measure of peace about his death. They were both anxious to learn and understand, and part way through the meeting one of them began to cry because the Spirit was so strong. She said she was overwhelmed by being in a group of LDS men who believed they could overcome their problems and were trying desperately to do so.

The need for safety in the group

Support groups for individuals with homosexual attraction have an inherent risk—the ever-present danger that participants could become involved with each other sexually. This is why it is of primary importance to have controls in place to make the environment safe. Getting the men together in a support group provides opportunities for growth and the development of relationships which is the key to resolving the attractions, but at the same time, the risks need to be carefully monitored and controlled. It is critical to the success of the group to establish and enforce policies of safety and confidentiality. There should be strict rules of no sexual or seductive conduct with other members of the group. Absolutely none. Never.

Safety boundaries

In addition to the safety rules of the group, it is important to establish personal boundaries. While the group process is helpful, it can also open you to dangers you need to manage. In the group setting, you experience emotional intimacy with other men on levels that perhaps you have not experienced before. Although you do not talk about sexual details, the fact that you discuss sexual problems may put you in a vulnerable state. If your discussions open up old wounds, you may experience anxiety or hurt and be tempted to revert to old patterns of behavior to relieve the pain. Since each person in the group discusses his area of vulnerability, others can wittingly or unwittingly take advantage. Therefore, boundaries must be established for the protection of everyone in the group. These external controls are safeguards during your period of growth to prevent you from responding to situations in unhealthy ways.

You will likely need to set personal boundaries on what you will and will not do after the meeting. When my friend Randy first joined his support group, he was so relieved to find other men with similar goals, that he didn't want to go home after the meetings ended. He would stay in the parking lot talking with his newfound friends for hours. He also discovered he was vulnerable during these late-night chats alone with other men, and sometimes found himself getting intimate with one man. He quickly had to set boundaries to stay out of trouble and committed never to be alone with another man because he knew there was safety in numbers. He also set for himself a limit of thirty minutes after the meeting, at which time he would get in his car and go home. He found that from 9:00 to 11:00 P.M. after the meeting he could undo all the good he did from 7:00 to 9:00 P.M. in the meeting. Go home while you are still on a high so you can continue to think through new ideas and keep positive thoughts on your mind. Keep the momentum going and don't lessen the experience with something less uplifting.

If two members of the group car pool to the meetings, it may be a good idea to hold them accountable each week for the time they were alone together. When they arrive at the meeting, ask them how the drive went, and before they leave after the meeting, ask them if they feel they are vulnerable and what they intend to do about it.

For many people entering a support group, boundaries are nebulous, and while there is room for growth, there is also the potential for sexual problems if it is not managed properly. Watch for people who cross boundaries or don't set boundaries. Challenge people to look at how they respect themselves, how they set boundaries, and how they maintain integrity for themselves.

Sexual problems in a group

An incident of sexual activity among group members brings serious personal consequences and weakens the group as a whole. Are you a highly committed person with a deep addiction, or a person who keeps acting out because you are ambivalent about the healing process? The group can tolerate a motivated participant who is sincerely trying to overcome an addiction, but not one who is just playing games.

Warning signs

The following are warning signs of sexual activity: seductive behavior, needing undue attention, not willing to work on their own issues, challenging authority, playing the role of the helpless victim, inside jokes, rebellion, resistance, not willing to follow rules regardless of their prior agreement to them, paranoia about being watched, and avoiding another participant (may indicate shame because of sexual involvement). Those who are isolated and not involved with others may be especially vulnerable.

Interventions

When group leaders suspect problems, they should confront those involved to determine if there are problems. Such confrontation should not be accusatory, but in a spirit of concern for their welfare and a desire to help them grow beyond any problems. This can be a good learning opportunity for those who may not know how to interact with each other socially in appropriate ways.

If sexual activities occur, group leaders should intervene immediately since sexual activity can quickly destroy the unity of the group. The leaders should confront those involved and discuss the occurrence to help them understand what led to the behavior and to set in place precautions to avoid a recurrence. The leaders should help them understand the consequence and responsibility of what they have done. If sexual activity continues, those involved should be asked not to participate in the group. When a participant is removed from the group, the ultimate goal is restoration. He should not be told that he isn't wanted in the group, but that he needs more individual counseling before he is ready for the group setting.

"Brethren, if a man be overtaken in a fault, ye which are spiritual, restore such an one in the spirit of meekness; considering thyself, lest thou also be tempted" (Galatians 6:1).

If a leader falls, he should step down from his leadership position immediately so he does not bring the rest of the group down, and also to relieve him of the burden of leadership so he can concentrate on his own problems.

Sports programs

In addition to the conventional support groups, you may find an experiential group helpful. Experiential groups exist to provide you a specific experience. Men's groups of various kinds hold retreats and provide opportunities for men to experience rites of passage that may have been missed. A common type of experiential group is a sports program that teaches basic skills in basketball, softball, or another sport, and provides opportunities to play the sport. Participants learn how to function on a team and have the chance to work through defensive detachment and face and resolve their fear of the sport. For many men in the group, sports may have been one of the things that separated them from other boys. Participation in a sports program can help you:

♦ learn the rules of the sport and through practice gain a certain level of skill. These skills can improve his ability to relate to and father his own children.

♦ learn teamwork by playing with other men.

♦ experience friendly competition in a team sport.

♦ develop a healthier body image and increase feelings of self-worth.

◆ face and resolve old fears and feelings of rejection and feel accepted as a member of a team of men.

Basketball

I enjoy individual sports such as weight lifting and running, and have even played competitive, nonteam sports like racquetball. But I always feared team sports. The first time I showed up at an experiential group basketball practice, I froze in the hallway when I heard the balls bouncing inside the gym. However, when I finally got the courage to go in, I found the other guys were just as uncoordinated and fearful as I was. I found it was a nonjudgmental environment where I could learn the rules of basketball and enjoy playing the game with other guys. Participating in the sports program really built my feelings of self-worth. My lack of skill in sports had been a reason for me to distance myself from other men, but with a little practice I found I was actually a good basketball player, and then had the confidence to play on the ward basketball team.

Softball

The next season was softball, and I had greater fears. Even though I actually enjoyed basketball, I *dreaded* the thoughts of softball because it brought back old feelings of ridicule that I experienced on the ball field in elementary school. I wrote the following essay after my first softball practice in the sports program.

Take Me Out of the Ball Game

"The last time I was on a softball field was in the third grade, when we occasionally played softball for physical exercise. When they chose up teams, I was always the last to be chosen (even after the girls!). I always played outfield, because out there no one expected you to actually catch the ball or to be able to throw it all the way to the infield. In the batting lineup, I would say that I had already batted and continually slip to the end of the line.

"Now I am thirty-five years old and I can do anything I want—except play softball. And it still separates me from other men. I don't care to become very good at softball; I just want to feel comfortable enough to join in an occasional game. So I determined that I would be at the first Saturday practice. After all, with basketball I found that I actually knew most of the rules of the game, and with some practice I wasn't a bad shot. By the end of the season, I could mix it up with the best of them. Now, why couldn't I do the same with softball? Besides, most of the guys learning softball were the same klutzes I had played basketball with.

"I showed up in the parking lot with my brand new Dale Murphy Rawlings mitt. How was I to know that you're supposed to oil down a new mitt before you use it? I didn't even bring a baseball cap. How can I act like I know what I'm doing without a baseball cap? And besides, where's Buzz? He played little league, so he'll know what to do. I need him! I got nervous and turned back to get something I suddenly 'remembered I had left in the car.' I met Buzz halfway back, and my confidence waxed strong again.

"Buzz and I picked up a softball and threw it back and forth. He showed me how to hold the ball and how to throw. Now that wasn't so hard. I even caught almost every throw. The group then gathered for introductions and a little stretching, then the inevitable decree, 'All those who want to play a game go over there. And everyone else comes over here.' Of twenty-five guys, I was the only one to 'come over here.' I didn't intend to play a game that day. I just wanted to practice throwing and batting, and learn some of the rules of the game. The coach gave me a few more pointers and we threw for a minute until he had to coach the game. I found a spot on the bleachers and watched my friends bat and run the bases. And everyone cheered. My mind went back to grade school, and suddenly I was a fat, uncoordinated little boy again. I was up to bat and the pressure was on to perform. Everyone was counting on me. And everyone knew I would fail. Why does it matter if you hit a ball with a stick or if you miss? With a few swings of the bat I would be a hero or a felon. Self-images are created and destroyed so easily. For some reason, softball represented all the negative experiences I had as a child. It reminded me how I felt as a fat, clumsy boy trying to fit in with the crowd. It represented peer pressure and inadequacy. And the tears came freely. Thank heavens for sunglasses. But soon the sunglasses couldn't hide the tears that were streaming down my face and I had to leave. I found a shady spot under a tree about a hundred yards away where I could still see and hear the game. It was safer there. I could see them but they couldn't see me. And no one could see me cry.

"Before long, Buzz found me and I cried on his shoulder. He reminded me how I started basketball without any experience and ended up doing well and how softball could be the same. He reminded me that courage is not the absence of fear, but acting in spite of fear. As I left the field that day, the immature side of me said, 'Never set foot on this field again. You don't have to go through this humiliation.' But the side of me that wants to grow assured me that I had to face my fears head-on. I have something at stake. My four-year-old son plays t-ball on a community team and I am scared to play catch with him. (As I write this, I am overcome with emotion that a thirty-five-year-old father would be scared to play catch with his four-year-old son.) It won't be easy to show up for practice next Saturday. The fears won't be gone, and the tears will probably be near the surface again. But it's something I have to do. And if it does not kill me, it will make me stronger.

"The next Friday, my friend Buzz took me to the batting cages to learn how to bat. He showed me how to hold the bat, how to stand, and how to swing. We were both surprised at how well I did. I missed only a half dozen out of fifty pitches! All it took was a little time and encouragement to give me the confidence I needed to go to the next practice.

"The next Saturday practice was a good experience. Since Buzz had helped me the day before, I went up to bat with confidence. The coach helped me in a kind way without being condescending. In the practice, I hit my five balls with only seven pitches. We then played a short game, and I hit both times I was at bat! After the practice, Andy talked with me about my fears of softball. He had only seen the confident side of me and was glad to see that I had fears and doubts and hesitations like everyone else. He admitted that although he feels comfortable about softball, he is scared to think about playing basketball. Since I feel comfortable with basketball, I promised to help him when basketball season comes. As I think back on what Buzz did to help me with softball, it is surprising what little it took to get me through what I viewed as an unsurmountable fear. All it took from Buzz was a little time and concern for me to feel comfortable to show up at practices and now I can do the same to help Andy."

Chapter Nine

Therapy

As helpful as support groups can be, they are not a substitute for individual and group therapy because there are issues that can only be dealt with effectively in sessions with a trained therapist. Therapy can help you clarify your identity and make life choices that are consistent with your personal values. It is a process of self-understanding, self-acceptance, and growth. For most people, that means difficult, painful compromises. Although your life becomes more clear, it may not become easier; there are no shortcuts to personal growth. Human emotions are complex and difficult situations are not easily unraveled. This chapter explains different therapeutic approaches and gives information on choosing the right therapist. It then discusses individual and group therapy and explains how each can be beneficial.

Modern therapy for those who struggle with homosexual problems bears little resemblance to the sordid history of treatment for emotional problems. In the late nineteenth and early twentieth centuries, the medical profession regarded homosexuality as a mental illness and attempted to cure it by drastic measures such as electroshock therapy, hormone injections, castration, hysterectomy, and even lobotomy.[114] Today, professionals use more humanistic approaches to help people understand and deal with their feelings. There is no need to fear therapy and certainly no reason to feel inadequate because you see a therapist. In today's complex world, most people can benefit from therapy for some reason at some time in their life. If you consider the suggestions in this chapter and choose your therapist wisely, it can be a richly rewarding experience.

Therapeutic methods

Within psychotherapy, there is a broad range of treatment approaches, some of which are helpful and others damaging.

Approaches to avoid

Many mental health professionals practice "gay-affirmative" therapy, which encourages individuals to "come out of the closet" and accept their homosexual orientation, which they say is a natural and healthy sexual variation. This kind of therapy proposes that the reason the person is unhappy with his homosexuality is because of his own self-hate and because of society's anti-gay prejudices. This approach is not in harmony with gospel principles and should be avoided.

Approaches that are beneficial

Other forms of psychotherapy allow individuals to determine for themselves if homosexual attraction fits within their personal values. If it doesn't, the therapy helps them learn to love themselves and grow in self-worth through becoming congruent with their personal value system. Dr. Joseph Nicolosi proposes reparative psychotherapy, which can help people "explore the source of their problem, develop nonerotic same-sex relationships that diminish the sexual attraction they feel toward men, become more secure in their gender-identity, and enjoy heterosexual relationships."[115]

Reparative therapy is based on the view that homosexual attractions develop because of incomplete gender-identity development and defensive detachment from other males. "Reparative therapy is not a cure in the sense of erasing all homosexual feelings. It is, however, a successful treatment strengthening masculine identification."[116] By growing beyond their homosexual problems, individuals can find inner happiness and peace of mind. For a more in-depth understanding of reparative therapy, you may read *Reparative Therapy of Male Homosexuality: A New Clinical Approach* by Joseph Nicolosi.

There are other helpful approaches similar to reparative therapy. Dr. William Consiglio's reorientation therapy is explained in his book *Homosexual No More: Practical Strategies for Christians Overcoming Homosexuality* and Elizabeth Moberly's re-education therapy is described in her book *Homosexuality: A New Christian Ethic*.

Choosing a therapist

Choosing the right therapist is critical because the wrong therapist can do you more harm than good. Since reparative, reorientation, and reeducation therapies are not as widely practiced as gay-affirmative therapy, you may have to search to find the right therapist for you.

Choose a therapist that can understand and support you in your personal values. In this respect, the ideal counselor would be LDS or at least a man who upholds Christian values. He needs to understand and support your religious motivations to change in the context of the eternal plan of salvation. He needs to understand and be able to teach you the divinely-appointed roles of men and women and he needs to be a good role model of a Christlike man because in many ways he will be your friend and mentor. Dr. Elizabeth Moberly advises that the therapist is emotionally involved in the process, within therapeutic guidelines. Depending on your particular needs, you may wish to look for a psychoanalyst, a psychiatrist, a psychologist, or a licensed clinical social worker (LCSW).

It is advisable that men choose a male therapist for several reasons. Since part of the problem is due to defensive detachment from men, a male therapist is in a better position than a woman to help you work through some of the developmental blocks you had with your father or with other men. A male therapist is also in a better position to help you understand other men and guide you into relationships with them. If your therapy experience is successful, the intimate relationship you develop with your therapist will be healing in itself and will encourage you to develop relationships with other men.

You may contact Evergreen International to get a recommendation on a therapist who fits the descriptions above. (Information on contacting Evergreen International is found in the Organizations section of this book.)

Since therapy is a major investment of time and money, be sure that your therapist will be able to provide you the help you need. Discuss with him how he will approach therapy with you. Talk about your value system and what you expect from therapy. Don't hesitate to talk with him about the finances involved and be sure they fit within your budget. Your medical insurance may cover some of the visits.

The therapeutic process

Part of the therapeutic process will be to explore the past. Joe Dallas writes that "we can learn from the past and thus improve the present." Further, "the past helps us to understand the present. And what we understand, we can deal with."[117] This process was helpful to me and I recommend it. However, I suggest four cautions:

Don't blame the past for your situation and assume the role of a victim who has no control over the present. No matter how painful the past has been, you cannot avoid responsibility for what you do in the present. Your goal now is to try to understand the causes of your struggle to learn what you can do to resolve them.

Watch out for invented memories. There is a tendency to invent past experiences to explain the present. If you read that certain childhood experiences can cause certain reactions, you may come to believe that those things happened to you in your childhood. You may reinterpret or skew the past or even invent in your mind events that never happened, all in an effort to make sense of the present.

Not finding all the answers in the past does not mean you can't resolve the present. At one point during my therapy I was trying to understand why I developed certain feelings during grade school. My therapist gave me an assignment to go back to my elementary school and spend an hour walking around the playground and try to recreate the feelings I had during a certain event. I did as he suggested, but never found any clues. To this day, I don't understand why I reacted to the event the way I did. Although I didn't find any clues to the present, I don't let that bother me. The past doesn't need to be completely explainable.

Don't concentrate on the past to the exclusion of the present. Although the past may hold keys to help you understand the present, concentrate the majority of your time on your current feelings, actions, plans, failures, and successes. The past is only valuable inasmuch as it helps deal with the present. The extent to which the past is important depends on the level of trauma in the past. If you have not suffered abuse, you may not need to spend much time dealing with the past. If you have been abused, you may need to grieve and resolve past trauma.

If therapy is not available to you

If you cannot afford therapy or if there is not a good therapist available, you can still benefit by reading carefully-selected self-help books, journaling, and trying to analyze your life. Set up a plan of action and follow through on that plan. Look at your life as though you are watching a video tape and identify the things you want to change, then make specific assignments to yourself to develop relationships and do things to build your self-image. You can be accountable to God through prayer, to yourself by using your journal, and to a friend in person or by telephone, letters, or e-mail. However, be careful not to let e-mail, letters, or even the telephone replace face-to-face contact with other men because this personal interaction is critical.

Individual therapy

A trained therapist can guide you through your personal growth process. He is your personal counselor to help you put all the pieces of the puzzle together. He can help you see how to integrate your personal study, spiritual growth, support groups, personal relationships, and behavior modification. He can help you see in an objective way how to keep your life in balance. He can be your mentor and your confidant.

Individual therapy is an essential part of the process for most men who resolve their homosexual problems. Although it will not take care of all your needs, it can give direction to all your activities. For example, if you also participate in a sports program, group therapy, support group, or a community men's group, your therapist can help you see how all these pieces fit together and help you keep them in balance.

As you talk with your therapist, you will discover things about yourself. Often, because of shame or guilt we have buried some things so deep within us that we don't even realize them ourselves. The therapist is trained to ask the right questions to help you see things in perspective and guide you through the process. Use him as a sounding board. Be honest with him about your problems, concerns, and fears. Don't keep any secrets from him. Therapy will be most effective when you have a completely open and honest relationship. The therapist is bound by ethical standards to keep everything you say completely confidential. He can't even tell someone else that you are seeing him. Together you can develop action plans to take you through each step of the process and you can report back to him on both your successes and failures. The journey won't seem so lonely or so hard if you have a therapist by your side the whole way. Individual counseling can help you to:

♦ identify and resolve personal issues and underlying factors.

♦ identify and clearly define your personal goals.
♦ develop a personal action plan then help you keep working on the plan.
♦ identify and work around the roadblocks.
♦ receive encouragement when you get discouraged.
♦ increase your awareness of things you need to work on.
♦ give insight into your feelings and actions.
♦ give an outside perspective (help you see black and white when all you see is gray).
♦ identify your personal strengths and weaknesses.
♦ give a forum to talk things out and get feedback.
♦ give someone to be accountable to for your behavior, growth, and personal plan of action.
♦ learn to generalize lessons learned to other situations.
♦ learn to internalize new information (make your heart believe).
♦ learn how to live congruently with your personal values and belief system.
♦ learn to control compulsive behaviors and overcome addictions.

Make your sessions count. Not only are these therapy sessions expensive, but if change is important to you, do all you can to make them as helpful as possible. I found it helpful to make written notes about my sessions and refer to them often. I wrote in my journal as much detail about each session as I could. It was helpful to review the things we discussed and it gave me something to refer back to later and monitor my progress. I especially made notes about things I wanted to think about further or pursue in a future session. I did not want to let fleeting ideas escape me; they were often inspiration that turned out to be helpful. Be sure to write down the assignments you receive from your therapist and be sure you follow through with them.

Group therapy

Group therapy can also be helpful, but is of secondary importance to individual therapy. Group therapy has some of the same advantages as a support group. The difference is that group therapy is always run by a trained therapist who is there to facilitate the discussion in meaningful ways. Since support groups are not guided, it is easy for members of the group to hide or even deny their feelings. But in a therapy group, the therapist can help members confront issues head-on and then be sure the issues are brought to healthy conclusions.

If you are involved in group therapy, it is important that you also receive individual therapy so you can work out issues that come up in the group setting. Group therapy can help you to:

♦ get the mutual support of others who share your struggle.
♦ hold each other accountable.
♦ learn to accept others and feel accepted by them.
♦ learn to disclose.
♦ discuss issues of importance and get the feedback of others.
♦ learn to generalize to other situations the lessons you learn.
♦ learn to internalize new information (make your heart believe).
♦ learn relationship and communication skills.
♦ learn to be assertive.
♦ reinforce newly learned traits.
♦ experience relationships and activities in a safe environment, as a bridge to the real world.
♦ learn compassion for others as you begin to see their challenges from their perspective.

My friend Todd had been so closed up that no one in his life really knew much about him. Then he went to group therapy where he had the chance to explain his troubles to others and he began to open up. He wrote, "Each time, it became a little easier. I noticed that rather than being dangerous, opening up and sharing feelings and being really close to people on an emotional level was kind of nice. For the first time in my life, I no longer felt like I was unacceptable because I started to find out that people could know everything about me and still want to be my friend. In fact, through the sharing of deep emotions, I gained some of my closest friends."

Chapter Ten

Behavior

I often see men try one of two approaches to solve their homosexual problems. Some try to stop the behavior and suppress the desires but don't work on identity issues or other deeper problems. Unfortunately, they find that sooner or later both the desires and the behavior return. My friend Alan tried numerous times to control his behavior by exercising willpower alone. Although he put up a good fight, he always found that the urges were stronger and more persistent than his willpower and he eventually gave in. Other people work on self-identity issues but don't stop the behavior. They find that the continuing behaviors reinforce the feelings and obstruct their efforts to improve how they feel about themselves. The answer to both these situations lies in a balanced approach. A major focus of this book is on discovering the underlying causes and working on resolving those inner conflicts that generate the desires for homosexual actions. But at the same time, you must get your behavior in control so it does not reinforce the feelings you are trying to understand and redirect in appropriate ways. Although controlling your behavior is of utmost importance, it alone will not solve your problems. Long-term change depends on your perception of yourself and on your devotion to God. Behavior management is a prerequisite to behavior change.

This chapter explains that you can choose your behavior, how habits and addictions can compromise your power to choose, and how you can be safe by carefully setting personal boundaries on your actions. It warns against justifying homosexual behavior and discusses the concepts of temptation and sin. The chapter then gives suggestions for changing your behavior patterns and warns of the dangers of homosexual behavior. Finally, it gives specific counsel about controlling fantasy, pornography, masturbation, cruising, and homosexual behavior

Changing your behavior

President Boyd K. Packer said, "Many of you are burdened with unhappiness and worry and with guilt. Many of you struggle under the bondage of degrading habits or wrestle with loneliness or dis-appointment and failure. . . . We are not offended at all of these things. All of these things may be set aside—overcome. Whoever you are and whatever you are, we reach out to extend to you the hand of fellowship so that we can lift one another and lift others."[118]

One of your priority tasks is to make constructive, positive changes in your habitual ways of behaving and relating to your environment. At first, you may have to take drastic measures to get your behavior under control. If you have not been deeply involved in sexual behaviors, your job will be less difficult. However, if you have been heavily involved in sexual activities you may have a more demanding struggle to overcome habits and sexual addictions. But if you are sincerely motivated and make a significant effort, you can overcome them and control your behavior. The comforting news is that as you resolve deeper issues, the compulsions and desires to act out will diminish or disappear and the struggle to control your behavior will be less demanding. As time passes, homosexual behavior will become less and less appealing, and even repulsive.

Understanding your behavior

Behaviors are purposeful, and are governed by valid, ordered sequences of experience. While homosexual behavior may appear strange and without logic to many people, it served what you viewed as a useful purpose and was rational from your point of view. Barney Swihart wrote, "Sexual bondage is never about simple lust or external behavior. It is in response to the deep wounds of life that sexual strugglers develop self-protective relational walls to insulate themselves from further hurt. However, the sad irony is that the very walls they have cultivated to 'protect' themselves now have become the 'prison' that keeps them in bondage.[119]

Why change your behaviors?

Do your current behaviors build you up or tear you down? Look back at the values and goals you set for yourself in the chapter Making Life Choices. Do your current behaviors take you toward or away from your ultimate goals? When you behave contrary to your personal values, your internal feelings of self-worth decrease, but when you behave consistent with your personal values, those feelings of self-worth increase. Integrity is to have the moral courage to make your actions consistent with your knowledge of right and wrong. As you look at your behaviors, if you find any that are incongruent with the things you really value in life, change them to actions that are congruent with your deep values and with eternal gospel principles. President Spencer W. Kimball taught, "All normal people have sex urges and if they control such urges, they grow strong and masterful. If they yield to their carnal desires and urges, they get weaker until their sins get beyond control."[120]

Elder William R. Bradford observed, "We give our lives to that which we give our time."[121] We become "oriented" to that to which we repeatedly give our hearts. Do you spend your time cruising or in righteous pursuits? Everything you do today affects your eternal future. You can destroy your future or build your future by the choices you make today. "Wherefore do ye spend money for that which is not bread? and your labour for that which satisfieth not? hearken diligently unto me, and eat ye that which is good. . . ." (Isaiah 55:2) Behaving in harmony with eternal principles brings positive consequences, while violating them brings negative consequences.

Behavior is a choice

Stephen Covey wrote, "Our behavior is a function of our decisions, not our conditions. We can subordinate feelings to values. We have the initiative and the responsibility to make things happen."[122] You may not have had a choice about the emergence of your homosexual attractions, but you do have a choice in how you respond to them. Although a person may crave food, he can learn to control his appetite and does not have to become obese. You have the choice of engaging in inappropriate activities or avoiding them. Each new choice in your life is an opportunity to move away from unwanted behaviors and toward a more desirable state.

Elder Delbert L. Stapley taught, "No man is free who is not master of himself. True freedom of agency exists with the observance of God's laws."[123] In an address in a general conference, President Boyd K. Packer spoke about homosexual attractions and gave the following counsel: "You may not be able, simply by choice, to free yourself at once from unworthy feelings. You *can* choose to give up the immoral expression of them."[124] Abstinence from homosexual activity is required for healing to take place. Abstinence will help the behavioral patterns wither and die.

President Gordon B. Hinckley declares that "the Lord has made it clear, and the experience of centuries has confirmed it, that happiness lies not in immorality, but rather in abstinence. The voice of the Church to which you belong is a voice pleading for virtue. It is a voice pleading for strength to abstain from that which is evil. It is a voice declaring that sexual transgression is sin. It is contrary to the will of the Lord. It is contrary to the teachings of the Church. It is contrary to the happiness and well-being of those who indulge in it. . . . You should recognize, you must recognize, that both experience and divine wisdom dictate virtue and moral cleanliness as the way that leads to strength of character, peace in the heart, and happiness in life."[125]

Committing to change

If you want to change your behavior, you must be committed to do it. You have to decide to stop and determine to do it. You have to choose which will be "the last time." Will it be this one? Or the next one? Or the next? There will always be a "next" time until you decide that it must stop. If you don't decide ahead of time, the situation will decide for you, and when faced with familiar situations, you will act in old, familiar ways. Perhaps your bad desires are not too strong, but your good desires are too weak. You need to encourage, sustain, and strengthen the good desires, rather than spend so much time trying to eradicate the bad ones.

Bob Ragan explained, "For some, the question of homosexuality as an option has not been resolved. The door is still being left open. Homosexual behavior isn't deemed completely wrong. Mr. or Miss Right might still be out there. The heart decision has not been made to follow Jesus, no matter what. Wide is the path that leads to destruction and as long as we hold that homosexual behavior may be a viable option, we are not truly embracing the process."[126] You have to decide once and for all that you will forsake incorrect ways and devote yourself to what is right before you can arrive at the attitude of having "no more disposition to do evil, but to do good continually" (see Mosiah 5:2).

Avoid homosexual behavior

If you have never acted on your homosexual urges, congratulations! Many men have to spend a great deal of time and energy undoing behavioral habits and addictions. If you are not burdened with overcoming these, your task will be less difficult. You may be tempted to engage in homosexual activity thinking that if you were to experience it, you could "get it out of your system" and your fantasies could be put to rest. But this false illusion ignores the seductive power of sexual sin. Many people know that homosexual behavior doesn't satisfy, but are enslaved by it anyway! It is much harder to close a door that has been opened than it is to not open the door in the first place.[127] Be strong and don't give in to homosexual behavior no matter how long your transition may take. Leo Hall wrote, "I have refrained from ever becoming sexually involved with another man. I choose not to 'act out' and sexualize my SSA feelings, but rather to 'act on' my need to love and be loved in Christlike ways."[128]

Habits, addictions, and compulsions

Sexual behaviors can be extremely addictive, whether they involve fantasies, solitary activities, or actions with others. Habits and addictions are self-defeating behaviors that trade short-term benefits for long-term ones. Such behaviors are emotional, but not necessarily logical. Being in an addictive cycle is like drinking salt water. Although the salt water cannot fill your thirst, you continue drinking it because after all, it is water and you are thirsty. But the more you drink, the thirstier you become.

Elder Russell M. Nelson taught, "From an initial experiment thought to be trivial, a vicious cycle may follow. From trial comes a habit. From habit comes dependence. From dependence comes addiction. Its grasp is so gradual. Enslaving shackles of habit are too small to be sensed until they are too strong to be broken."[129]

Some people are more susceptible than others to addictions. Some people are more easily addicted to smoking than others. Some cannot take an occasional drink without becoming alcoholics. These tendencies may restrict the person's freedom, but not his free agency. He may not be free to drink without addiction, but his free agency allows him to choose not to drink at all. Elder Dallin H. Oaks taught, "We all seem to have susceptibilities to one disorder or another, but whatever our susceptibilities, we have the will and the power to control our thoughts and our actions. This must be so. God has said that he holds us accountable for what we do and what we think, so our thoughts and actions must be controllable by our agency. Once we have reached the age or condition of accountability, the claim 'I was born that way' does not excuse actions or thoughts that fail to conform to the commandments of God. We need to learn how to live so that a weakness that is mortal will not prevent us from achieving the goal that is eternal."[130]

Elder Nelson explained, "While we are free to choose, once we have made those choices, we are tied to the consequences of those choices. We are free to take drugs or not. But once we choose to use a habit-forming drug, we are bound to the consequences of that choice. Addiction surrenders our later freedom to choose. Through chemical means, one can literally become disconnected from his or her own will!"[131]

Since behaviors become increasingly strengthened through repetition, we should avoid any behavior that is habit-forming or addictive. This is particularly important with sexual behaviors, because the intensity of the sensual pleasure adds to the addictive nature of the action. Joe Dallas wrote, "Compulsive sexual behavior . . . includes lust and poor self-control, of course, but it is much more than that. It is a repetitive, constant form of sexual activity that a person feels *compelled*—not just tempted—to indulge in. Usually this behavior is acted out in secretive, anonymous sexual encounters. . . . Seldom does it include one lover; most often it means brief trysts with several partners, most of whom will never be seen again. Or it may be a solitary addiction to pornography. Regardless, it's bondage of the worst kind because there's so much shame and remorse attached to it, making it terribly secretive and usually dangerous."[132]

Joe Dallas continued, "To be sexually addicted is to literally rely on sex to stabilize you. It's a state in which the rush of sexual pleasure, with all its accompanying chemical forces has become to you what a drug has become to an addict. And like a drug, it begins to interfere with all parts of life. Breaking the cycle of sexual addiction is not just a matter of will in this case; it's a matter of *strategy, consistency, and patience*."[133]

If you are engulfed in habits and addictions, they can be overcome by the incredible power of the human will, with the support of friends and loved ones, and through the omnipotent power of our Savior. Elder Russell M. Nelson taught, "Your willpower becomes strong when joined with the will of the Lord."[134] Whether such mastery happens overnight or takes a significant amount of time, it can happen nonetheless. You may need to enlist the help of a twelve-step program, a support group, and a therapist to overcome addictions.

Avoid addictions by keeping the commandments. Addictive behavior compromises our will and serves Satan's purposes. Behaviors that are reinforced continue and even become stronger. Those that are controlled become manageable. President Boyd K. Packer promised, "If you can control your thoughts, you can overcome habits, even degrading, personal habits. If you can learn to master them you will have a happy life."[135]

It is interesting to note the similarity between homosexual addictions and other compulsive behaviors. The things that trigger men to act homosexually tend to be the same things that those immersed in other addictions cite as instigating factors for their addictive behaviors. The instigating factors (stress, insecurity, depression, etc.) are the same; they simply have different methods of expression.

Addictions have physical, emotional, and spiritual components. Physically, you may be hooked on the excitement, the "rush," the adrenaline "buzz" of the sexual experience. You may be emotionally hooked through envy or shame. And spiritually, you may feel rejected by God and tempted to act in rebellion.

Passions

Passions can be powerful. Jack Hickey wrote, "Throughout history men have killed and have been killed for no other reason but to satisfy their passions. To feed their sexual drive some have lied, cheated, stolen, and murdered; have given up family, friends, and jobs. . . . A man who covets his friend's wife will risk destruction of both families in order to satisfy his passion." He explained, "Most of the time, they never even stop to think of the consequences. If they do stop to think, the drive is often so strong that it doesn't matter."[136]

As bad as you may consider your passions to be, they have a useful purpose. Don't ask to be rid of your passions, rather, "see that ye bridle all your passions, that ye may be filled with love. . . ." (Alma 38:12). Wise use of your passions can help you develop true love which comes through controlling and directing your passions, not by allowing them unrestrained expression. In the classic musical production *Camelot*, there is a line with good advice for us all. When the love triangle between King Arthur, Guenevere, and Lancelot began to deepen, King Arthur said, "We must not let our passions destroy our dreams."

Personal boundaries

It is important to set and maintain boundaries for personal growth and development. Most Christian acts require restraint and boundaries. In fact, a critical lesson to learn in this life is to become masters of ourselves. In contrast, people of the world say that to deny yourself of worldly pleasures is to deny your true self. They emphasize *feeling good* rather than *being good*. They describe any form of self-restraint as self-loathing or homophobia. However, a peaceful society requires restraint, boundaries, moderation, and temperance.

Setting safe boundaries

You will likely need to set boundaries to get your behavior under control. By setting personal boundaries, you use your agency to temporarily limit certain individual freedoms to help achieve more important eternal freedoms. If you know you are susceptible to certain addictive behaviors, you can decide to limit your access to places or conditions that might make it easy for you to go astray. Since addictions can limit or compromise more important freedoms, it is important to forgo less important, temporary freedoms for more important eternal ones. If you are tempted to go to an adult bookstore on the way home from work, you may have to take a different route that does not pass by the bookstore. Choose boundaries that keep you well inside a zone of safety. Old habit patterns have to be starved before they shrivel and die.

Personal and interpersonal boundaries

In addition to the outward boundaries discussed above, it may be helpful to define boundaries in personal and interpersonal areas.

Physical boundaries. It is important to show affection, and through the healing process, hugging and physical touch can be important. However, it is also important to recognize that each person comes from a different background and has his own limits of personal space. What may be an appropriate hug for one person may be too intimate for another. When a person is starved for affection and conditioned to respond sexually, an otherwise appropriate hug may arouse or make him think inappropriate thoughts. Therefore, it is important to be aware of what is comfortable and appropriate both for you and for the other person. Once you define your personal boundaries, let others know what they are. And before you hug someone else, be sure you know it is within his personal boundaries.

Sexual boundaries. Your attractions and sexuality are your own and you can set boundaries that define what you will do. As steward of your own sexuality, you are responsible for seeing that others do not use you in sexual ways and that you do not use them. In addition to obvious sexual actions, there are other areas to be avoided. Flirting, "gay talk," innuendo, and suggestive conversation show disrespect for the other person and are a form of manipulation and predatory behavior. Fantasizing sexually about someone else is using them without their permission. Such actions affect your self-concept and your relationship with the other person. This is a particularly difficult area for people who have been abused sexually, because they often have difficulty differentiating between sexuality and true loving feelings.

Emotional boundaries. You often cannot control how you feel. Although you can choose how to respond to your emotions, you may feel happy or sad or angry through no choice of your own. Emotions are not necessarily right or wrong; it is not always good to be happy, and not always bad to feel sad. However, understanding these emotions can give you clues to understanding yourself. Others can violate your emotional boundaries by doing things such as the following: telling you how you should feel, telling you they know how you feel, taking it on themselves to "fix" things for you, dumping their emotions on you, or using you to make them feel better without regard for what it does to you. Of course, you can violate the boundaries of others by doing the same things to them.

Intellectual boundaries. Our thought processes reflect our feelings, opinions, and perspectives, and not necessarily facts. You have a right to sort out what you think, and need to give others the right to think and decide for themselves also. If you disagree with someone, it is not your job to fix their way of thinking.

Spiritual boundaries. Your beliefs belong to you and the beliefs of others belong to them. A violation of spiritual boundaries occurs when you tell someone, "You can't believe that." You cannot force a person to believe something any more than you can force them to think or feel the way you want them to. Likewise, you cannot live on the spiritual beliefs of others; sooner or later you need to determine what you believe for yourself.

Boundary violations

Abuse in any form is a violation of a boundary. If we want to avoid abusing others, we need to respect their boundaries. If we want to avoid being abused by another, we must constantly define, redefine, evaluate, and maintain our boundaries. Respect is a key to avoiding abuse.

Memories

Bob Davies and Lori Rentzel wrote, "Our memory is a marvelous gift, but it can also seem like a curse at times. If we previously indulged in sexual sin, it is hard to forget graphic details."[137] Satan will continually try to bring these memories to the surface to entice us back into old thoughts and behaviors. He will magnify the good times in the past, reminding us how exciting and pleasurable it was, but will leave out the heartache, loneliness, and frustration we felt. In his book *Desires in Conflict*, Joe Dallas explained, "Your memories look good only because you're not seeing them panoramically. Take them to their logical conclusion, considering not only what you did and enjoyed, but where it was leading you, and you get a more accurate picture of your past. That's how you shake off the power of 'good' memories—you view them with an eternal perspective."[138] When you are reminded of the past, pray for an accurate and complete picture of it.

It takes time to get over old habits. Even after I found healthy ways to meet my emotional needs with other men, I was still occasionally drawn toward sexual activity because of previous habit-forming experiences. Our minds and emotions remember those experiences and continue to be drawn toward them long after we have satisfied the needs that originally drove us to them. Memories take a while to forget and we may be vulnerable to those possibilities until we forget the memories of them. But over time, the memories will fade if we don't dwell on them or reinforce them. And the best way to hasten that process is to make new, better memories to replace the old.

Justifying homosexual behavior

Emotional difficulties do not grant any special rights to engage in illicit sexual actions. God's commandments apply universally to everyone and we are on dangerous ground when we seek to justify our behavior, assuming we know more about what is best for us than God does. Some are tempted to believe that they have a unique situation and therefore God's commandments don't apply to them. Some men believe that since they are not attracted to women, and feel they cannot marry and enjoy heterosexual relations, they should be allowed some sexual expression with men. But God has revealed only one law of moral conduct, which is abstinence outside of lawful marriage between a man and a woman, and fidelity within marriage. A 1991 letter from the First Presidency addressed to all members of the Church said, "Sexual relations are proper only between husband and wife appropriately expressed within the bonds of marriage. Any other sexual contact, including fornication, adultery, and homosexual and lesbian behavior, is sinful."[139] Notwithstanding these clear counsels, some still argue it is not fair that they are prohibited from acting on their homosexual feelings. They apparently don't understand that one purpose of this life is to learn self-control and obedience to God's commandments. Life appears not to be fair to teenagers who are restricted from acting on their sexual impulses, nor to a physically disabled person who is not able to function sexually, nor to divorced or widowed people who no longer have a lawful outlet for their sexual desires. Speaking in a general conference on the subject of homosexual attractions, President Boyd K. Packer said, "Now, in a spirit of sympathy and love, I speak to you who may be struggling against temptations for which there is no moral expression. Some have resisted temptation but never seem to be free from it. Do not yield! Cultivate the spiritual strength to resist—all of your life, if need be. . . . The suffering you endure from resisting or from leaving a life-style of addiction or perversion is not a hundredth part of that suffered by your parents, your spouse or your children, if you give up. Theirs is an innocent suffering because they love you. To keep resisting or to withdraw from such a life-style is an act of genuine unselfishness, a sacrifice you place on the altar of obedience. It will bring enormous spiritual rewards."[140]

Some try to justify homosexual behavior by saying that our enlightened modern society now sees it as an acceptable expression between two men who love each other. President Spencer W. Kimball showed the fallacy in this kind of thinking when he explained that "right and wrong, righteousness and sin, are not dependent upon man's interpretations, conventions and attitudes. Social acceptance does not change the status of an act, making wrong into right. If all the people in the world were to accept homosexuality, as it seems to have been accepted in Sodom and Gomorrah, the practice would still be deep, dark sin."[141] You may wish to read President Boyd K. Packer's general conference address in which he spoke about those who try to justify a gay lifestyle (see "Covenants," *Ensign*, Nov. 1990, pp. 84–86).

Another subtle form of justification is to accept a lower standard for ourselves than the one revealed in scripture and through modern prophets. Alan Medinger counsels us to be on guard against "the attitude that says, 'God, I am doing the best I can do; this is just the way I am.' Rather than working towards the gospel standard, we adopt a tolerant, indulgent attitude that declares, 'If I only go off on a sexual binge once a year, I'm better off than I used to be. Besides, God understands my weakness.' I have known people who for years have justified their ongoing sin as being reasonable, given their emotional and psychological makeup."[142] It is subtly arrogant to assume that our understanding of ourselves exceeds what God has revealed in scripture and through his prophets.

Temptation

Temptation is not sin.[143] One of Satan's traps is to convince you that you are sinning when you are merely experiencing temptation. Don't feel guilty or ask forgiveness for temptations or attractions over which you have no control. The temptations themselves are not sinful (see Hebrews 4:15), but your reactions to them may be. When a temptation comes, you can either dismiss it or nurture it. If you dismiss it, it is no sin; but if you nurture it, it will grow into lust and then behavior.

Temptation is not identity. Just because you are tempted by homosexual feelings, it does not mean you are a homosexual. Satan may continue to tempt you with things from your past, although you have left them behind.

Temptation is not a sign of low spirituality. Don't feel that you are falling apart spiritually because you experience temptation. Sometimes Satan tempts us more when we are growing spiritually. The scriptures are full of accounts of strong people who were continually tempted. Remember, Satan even tempted the Savior!

Temptation is not unique to you. Everyone faces temptation. Satan may use slightly different approaches with different people, but the basic temptations, such as envy, lust, and selfishness, are common to everyone.

Sin

Dr. William Consiglio gives a good distinction between temptation and sin: "Feelings, attractions, urges, desires, longings, are all temptations. Acting on any of these mentally or physically is sin."[144] When you are tempted, do you dismiss the temptation or indulge it? Do you starve it or feed it? Elder Orson F. Whitney explained, "Sin is the transgression of divine law, as made known through the conscience or by revelation. A man sins when he violates his conscience, going contrary to light and knowledge—not the light and knowledge that has come to his neighbor, but that which has come to himself. He sins when he does the opposite of what he knows to be right."[145]

Joe Dallas explained, "Christ's prohibition against lust (Matthew 5:28) certainly applies to the entertaining of sexual fantasies and erotic desires outside of marriage, but not to the unaroused condition of homosexuality. (Or the unaroused condition of heterosexuality, for that matter. A heterosexual male is attracted to women, but he is not always lusting after them. A homosexual male is attracted to men, but he's not always lusting after them.)"[146]

It is important to do what is right, but it is also important that you *not* do what is wrong. I used to think that it was okay to do some wrong things as long as I did a lot of good things to make up for them.

I looked at it as a mathematical equation and thought I was okay as long as the sum was positive. I finally came to realize that doing what was right was not good enough if I also had a mindset to do what was wrong. As important as it is to do what is right, it is equally important to not do what is wrong.

Although we should abhor sin, we must be careful not to hate ourselves when we sin. Having just spoken in a general conference about those who are attracted to the same gender, President Gordon B. Hinckley declared, "Having said this, I desire now to say with emphasis that our concern for the bitter fruit of sin is coupled with Christlike sympathy for its victims, innocent or culpable. We advocate the example of the Lord, who condemned the sin, yet loved the sinner. We should reach out with kindness and comfort to the afflicted, ministering to their needs and assisting them with their problems. We repeat, however, that the way of safety and the road to happiness lie in abstinence before marriage and fidelity following marriage."[147]

Suggestions for changing behavior patterns

Be clean

President Ezra Taft Benson counseled, "Stay morally clean. This means that you keep a clean mind. Your thoughts will determine your actions, and so they must be controlled. It's difficult to control those thoughts if you submit yourself to temptation. So you will have to carefully select your reading material, the movies you see, and the other forms of entertainment in order to have good thoughts rather than unwholesome desires."[148] Some men say they want to change their behavior, but then flirt with temptation. If you are serious in your intent, steer clear of situations that might present temptations and do all you can to keep righteous thoughts and the spirit of the Holy Ghost with you. Jacob taught, "Remember, to be carnally-minded is death, and to be spiritually-minded is life eternal" (2 Nephi 9:39).

Put on the armor of God

The scriptures remind us to put on the armor of God (see 2 Nephi 1:23 and D&C 27:15–18). When your spiritual defenses are high, you will be much stronger in the face of temptation. Don't leave off any piece of armor or you may be vulnerable to attack.

Identify the cycle and stop it early

Dr. William Consiglio identifies six steps that happen when you notice an attractive man.[149] At any point, you can choose to stop the cycle, but the further down the path you go, the more willpower it takes to stop.

1. *Visual attraction.* Although you can't help but notice a man who has certain features that you consider attractive, you can choose to turn away or continue on to the other five steps.
2. *Visual attention.* You give him your attention.
3. *Visual pleasure.* You experience pleasure looking at him.
4. *Sexual pleasure.* You begin to experience arousal or excitement.
5. *Desire for encounter.* You want to make contact with him (or you keep the eroticized memory of him in your fantasy bank for later recall).
6. *Act to encounter.* You act to make contact with him.

Try to understand your attractions

Search for insight into your motives and an objective view of your behavior. When you are attracted to a man, ask yourself what attracts you. If it is his masculinity, then recognize it for that and turn your thoughts to what you can do to feel more masculine. When you are in need, it is fruitless to chase after something that cannot fill that need. You can never get enough of what you don't need.

I finally realized that part of the reason for my attractions to college-aged men was envy of the lifestyle they lead. When I was in college, I had practically no free time since I had a full-time job in addition to being a full-time student. I feel I missed the fun and exciting college scene and I still desired that lifestyle. The attractions diminished considerably once I recognized that, and I was able to focus my efforts on making my life more fun and exciting.

A while back, I discovered two important questions to ask myself. The first question: "What are the characteristics of men I find attractive?" To this, I answered: twenty to thirty-five, masculine in appearance and action, muscular build, successful professional, over-achiever, and outgoing personality. The second question was quite revealing: "If I could change anything about myself, what are the characteristics I would like to have?" To my surprise, I discovered that my list of answers for both questions was the same. I found I was attracted to men who have the traits I wished I had. I was attracted to those who looked the way I wished I looked and had the masculine characteristics I wished I had. Once I realized that, I knew I couldn't magically possess these traits by chasing after men who had them. I needed to start working to develop them.

Try to recognize your attractions and learn to deal with them on an emotional level without letting them develop into behavior. As you begin to see things in perspective, the temptations for sexual misbehavior will become less enticing and dwindle in number, and you will achieve greater mastery over your fantasies.

See the person behind the attraction

When attracted to another man, many of us dehumanize him. As we fantasize about him, we say, "*that* is gorgeous," and we treat him as an object and not as a real person. Turning a person into an object makes it easier to act sexually with him. If you catch yourself in this trap, try to make the person real by recognizing that he has a family who loves him and that he has feelings and needs of his own. If possible, try to get to know him. I find that when the mysterious becomes familiar, my attractions diminish. I remember a particular night when a new guy showed up at our group meeting. His appearance was stunning. His dark tan, curly hair, and piercing blue eyes caught my attention immediately and I found myself staring at him during most of the meeting. I finally realized that I had dehumanized him and was treating him as an object. So after the meeting, I introduced myself and talked with him so I could humanize him. I found out that it was the first time Tom had been to a support group meeting. Some devastating things had just happened in his life and he was in a vulnerable condition. My physical attraction for him quickly turned into concern for him as a person. The more I talked with Tom, the more I got to know him and I became concerned that his involvement in the group would give him some answers and help him. Knowing that, how could I even consider being attracted to Tom in any way other than as a pure friend? It is much more fulfilling to support a man as a friend than it ever could be to act out with him sexually.

Visualize the consequences

When you are tempted to act sexually, all you think about is the pleasure of the moment. Break out of the erotic enticement by thinking ahead and visualizing how you would feel afterwards. "It would be a setback for me." "It wouldn't really satisfy me anyway." "It would bring me down and I deserve better than that." Follow the action through to its logical conclusion.

Use humor and exaggeration

Dr. William Consiglio suggests this technique to help snap you back into reality. He gives an example of noticing a handsome man: "You begin to idealize his features and take visual pleasure in him as you begin to watch him. Silently, though you can't actually hear it, you're saying, 'What nice, muscular arms he has; what beautiful blue eyes and dark black hair he has; what gorgeous teeth and a strong masculine face he has.' This secret thinking produces erotic feelings and reinforces homosexuality."[150] To counteract this, he suggests that you exaggerate what you say to yourself. In this example, you might say, "'This man must be a Greek god. I've just got to go up and talk with him. I must get close to him or I'll absolutely die. If I can just get to know him, my whole life will be absolutely wonderful from now on. He is so perfect. If I could just touch him I know that I'll never be unhappy again. If I could just gaze into those liquid eyes of blue radiance, I will be in ecstasy forever.'"[151] Gerard van den Aardweg also suggests using humor in his book *Homosexuality and Hope*.[152] Just as children are able to see the silly side of almost anything, you can use humor to get through the crises in your life. When you begin to feel stress, neutralize it by reading an amusing book, listening to a funny tape, or just looking for the humor in life.

Watch for triggers

Learn what sets you up for inappropriate behavior. You may be vulnerable to a number of people, events, and situations that can trigger homosexual feelings. Once you understand what influences you, then you can avoid those situations or change your perceptions. Triggers may include a wide variety of things such as particular songs that bring back specific memories, certain types of music, TV programs, movies, erotic literature, the use of alcohol or drugs, provocative clothing, cruising areas, or specific locations that bring back memories of homosexual events. When you feel triggered, ask yourself why. Examine the attractions and try to determine why you feel the way you do. If you can recognize the reason for your feelings, you will be in a better position to deal with them.

Spiritual highs or other positive events always used to trigger me. Since inwardly I didn't feel I deserved the good experiences, I subconsciously engaged in self-defeating behaviors to counteract the spiritual high or good feelings. I also think it was Satan's direct attempt to dilute the positive effect of the experiences and drive the Spirit away. I urge you to use caution after a positive experience in a group or church meeting and watch your actions and conversations so you can continue to enjoy the Spirit and think about and process the things you experienced.

We are usually the most vulnerable when we feel bored, stressed, angry, lonely, tired, hungry, depressed, discouraged, in pain, inadequate, or guilty. Some people use the acronyms HALT (hungry, angry, lonely, tired) or BLAHST (bored, lonely, angry, hungry, stressed, tired) to remind them of these conditions that can put them at risk for homosexual behavior. When these conditions arise and you feel like acting out, look at the situation and try to find a legitimate fix. If you are hungry and tired, rather than go cruising, get something to eat and go to bed. When you feel the desire to masturbate, try to discover what your real needs are. It may be that you feel lonely or isolated and the real need is for friendship. Do you need to feel appreciated by someone? Are you lonely and just need someone to talk with? Is sex your way of relieving stress? If you have sex, will these real needs be satisfied or only intensified? You may need extra help when you are under stress, lonely, in an unfamiliar setting, or when you are depressed or bored. Plan ahead an alternative course of action to react to these conditions. Set up a network of friends from your support group that you can call when you need help.

When I don't feel good about myself as a man and have self-doubts, I find I am attracted to other men who appear strong, confident, and sure of themselves. The attractions are not sexual anymore, but feelings of curiosity and a desire to get to know these men who have what I feel I am lacking. When I feel this way, it tells me that I am not taking care of myself. I can then look for the stress or the emotional issue that is not being addressed, and find a way to take care of it.

Avoid situations where you will be vulnerable. Don't kid yourself into thinking that you can flirt with temptation without being affected. Alter the route you take to and from work if that route presents problems for you. Do what you can to control your environment. If you want to overcome homosexual behavior, don't associate with those who are constantly indulging in it and boasting about it.

Control your thoughts

President Gordon B. Hinckley explained, "Mental control must be stronger than physical appetites or desires of the flesh. As thoughts are brought into complete harmony with revealed truth, actions will then become appropriate . . . Each of us, with discipline and effort, has the capacity to control his thoughts and his actions. This is part of the process of developing spiritual, physical, and emotional maturity."[153] Thoughts generate actions which lead to habits which develop character which influences our destiny.

President David O. McKay observed, "One chief purpose of life is to overcome evil tendencies, to govern our appetites, to control our passions—anger, hatred, jealousy, immorality.[154] The methods of controlling homosexual temptations are similar to those for controlling any other temptation and there are many good books written on the subject. The First Presidency reminds us of the value of hymns: "Hymns can lift our spirits, give us courage, and move us to righteous action. They can fill our souls with heavenly thoughts and bring us a spirit of peace. Hymns can also help us withstand the temptations of the adversary. We encourage you to memorize your favorite hymns and study the scriptures that relate to them. Then, if unworthy thoughts enter your mind, sing a hymn to yourself, crowding out the evil with the good."[155]

Be accountable

An important part in changing our behavior is to be accountable to someone. You should make an accounting to God in daily prayer, confessing your weaknesses and asking for His strength to make it through the day. You should also be accountable to your bishop in regular interviews for sins that should be confessed. You can be accountable to your therapist for how well you are following your plan of action. In addition, you may need another person in whom you can confide. This may be someone from your support group who also struggles with homosexuality or it could be a close friend who cares about you. In the Book of James we read, "Confess your faults one to another, and pray one for another, that ye may be healed. The effectual fervent prayer of a righteous man availeth much" (James 5:16).

My friend Todd wrote, "When I got tempted to get in the car and go to a cruising spot, I could instead call a friend who knew of my difficulties and I would ask if we could get together and play racquetball, or go to a show, or simply sit down and talk for a while. Often such activity only served to get me through a single night when I was having problems. *But it got me through one night.* Remember that when we are talking about addictive behaviors, the old twelve–step motto of 'one day at a time' is all we can ask for and probably all we should attempt. Over time, I found that my crises tended to diminish in intensity and frequency, but there were definitely many nights I had to call one of my emergency resources."

Take it one day at a time

You can cope with today. Don't worry yet about the challenges you may have to face tomorrow. When you are preoccupied with tomorrow, you miss out on the meaningful experiences of today. Concentrate on the present and you will see that the future takes care of itself. Can you divert a river all at once? No, but you can place one sandbag at a time that will eventually change its course. Don't expect to be able to change your entire character overnight. Remove one bad habit today and replace it with another good habit. It will be a long climb up the mountain but then you'll stand high atop it as a free man.

Experience healthy excitement

Why do we sexualize the solution to our needs? Alan Medinger wrote, "I believe we do this because sex is one of the most intense experiences most people have, and whatever sex touches becomes more alive. Just as salt enhances the flavor of food, sex intensifies the power of any experience."[156] Sex brings excitement when you are lonely or bored. One of the reasons I was enticed by homosexual activities was that I wanted more excitement in my life. The gay world held a certain mystique for me and homosexual encounters appeared exciting.

Use endorphin as the antidote for adrenalin. Endorphin is the body's natural hormone that produces a natural high and lasts longer than adrenalin. Runners experience an endorphin high when they "break through the wall." Endorphin is experienced through good, natural experiences such as laughter, contentment, or spiritual experiences. President Spencer W. Kimball reminds us that "good times and happy lives and clean fun are not dependent upon the glamorous, the pompous, the extremes."[157]

Replace negatives with positives

As you break from negative influences, be sure to replace them with new, positive activities and relationships. President Boyd K. Packer counseled, "Do not try merely to *discard* a bad habit or a bad thought. *Replace* it. When you try to eliminate a bad habit, if the spot where it used to be is left open it will sneak back and crawl again into that empty space. It grew there; it will struggle to stay there. When you discard it, fill up the spot where it was. Replace it with something good."[158] When you remove the seemingly exciting homosexual behavior, your life will seem quite dull unless you fill the void with new, uplifting, and rewarding things. When you take cruising from your life, you will find many hours you can now devote to your family, your church calling, or service to others. You may want to start a new hobby or spend the time developing new relationships with people. Make time for activities you enjoy. Studies have shown that when people work on projects or activities they enjoy, their blood chemistry is altered almost immediately in a positive way.

If you focus on the negative—all the things you *can't* do—the past you are trying to leave will look even more attractive. Instead, focus on the positive—all the great things you are working toward. The old behaviors brought only temporary pleasure, while the new ones will bring lasting joy. Changing behaviors does not have to be viewed as restrictive. Instead, look at it as opening whole new worlds of opportunity. In reality, the old behavioral patterns were restrictive; they locked you into addictive patterns of responding and they held you back from the things you really wanted. Changing your behavior to be in line with your values will release you to move to higher levels of fulfillment and joy. Don't concentrate on the things you are removing from your life, but focus on things you can add to your life.

The Apostle Paul admonished us to "put off . . . the old man, which is corrupt according to the deceitful lusts; and . . . put on the new man, which after God is created in righteousness and true holiness" (Ephesians 4:22, 24). New spiritual things must replace old carnal habits and thoughts. We must diligently seek a new life to replace the old.

Setbacks

As you begin to face issues head on, you may experience increased stress as old wounds are opened and dealt with. As a result, you may experience a greater pull toward old behaviors as a way to cope with these increased feelings. Therefore, be on guard with increased resistence to avoid setbacks. You can stop homosexual behavior. Recommit yourself to live the standards of the gospel, knowing that as you work to resolve your problems the temptations may be strong, but your determination is even stronger.

If you do backslide, don't think that everything has gone down the drain. Don't minimize the consequences of what happened, but realize it is only a temporary setback and don't let it defeat you. A slip or even a fall does not return you to point zero. Get back on your feet with new resolve and remember that all forward movement is cumulative and makes a difference. The very fact that you feel bad about it shows you are progressing. Don't cover up the pain because pain is a warning. Feel it completely, repent, pick up the pieces, and move ahead. Learn from your mistake, so if you see the pattern developing again, you will have the experience and tools to stop it before it develops into homosexual actions. Focus on the progress you have made. Read your journal to remind yourself how far you have come. If you don't reach your goal the first time, don't consider yourself a failure. Failure is not trying at all.

Consider how you would respond if you were to eat something you shouldn't on a diet. You could either tell yourself you slipped and immediately resume your diet or be so weighed down with guilt that you go on a self-defeating bing. If you continue binging, you regain all the weight you lost, then blame the diet for not working. In fact, the diet was working well; it was the way you responded to your setback that caused your defeat.

Your personal plan of action contains specific things you need to do. If you don't keep on guard and follow your plan, there is a chance you could slip or fall. Just like a car, you need to keep yourself well maintained to function properly. If you let spiritual, emotional, physical, or intellectual things slide, you put yourself in jeopardy. Maintenance will be important throughout the rest of your life. President Spencer W. Kimball taught that overcoming the effects of homosexuality "is as permanent as the individual makes it and, like the cure for alcoholism, is subject to continued vigilance."[159]

If you relapse, does it mean you haven't really changed? No. Continued temptation may actually be proof that you are still in the battle. It is only when you accept sin as good that it ceases to be a problem and begins to feel natural. If sin becomes the acceptable solution to the pain, then you have learned to choose it over God. But the fact that you continue to try means that you have not accepted the easy way out and you know there is something better. The scriptures do not promise that we will reach a place in this life where we are never tempted again. We need to continually watch and pray lest we fall into temptation (see D&C 20:33). But we can be reassured we are no longer the people we used to be as we continue to improve and come closer to our goal of becoming like Christ.

Homosexual behavior is dangerous

Homosexual behavior is dangerous to you spiritually, emotionally, and physically. Cruising late at night in dark places can make you vulnerable to physical attack. Sexual behavior may also put your life and health at risk because of diseases that are transmitted through sexual contact. Addictive sexual behavior can be particularly dangerous because the compulsive actions can prevail over a person's better judgement and he may engage in behaviors that are deadly. Men who engage in homosexual behavior account for 80% of America's most serious sexually-transmitted diseases, although they comprise only 5–10% of the population.[160] Those who contract AIDS die at the median age of thirty-nine. Those who don't get AIDS die at the median age of forty-two.[161]

HIV/AIDS

HIV is the Human Immunodeficiency Virus that attacks the body's immune system and weakens its ability to defend itself against disease. A person infected with the virus is considered HIV-positive. When HIV weakens the immune system to the point that the body is no longer able to defend itself—indicated in part by a T-cell count of less than 200—a person is said to have AIDS (Acquired Immune Deficiency Syndrome). Such a weakened immune system is no longer able to fight off serious infections, diseases, and some types of cancer. About half of the people infected with HIV develop AIDS within 10 years; some stay healthy for fifteen years or longer.[162]

The Centers for Disease Control estimate that up to 900,000 Americans—one in 800 women and one in 100 men—are infected with HIV, and perhaps half are unaware of their infection.[163] The Surgeon General said, "Today, most of the people with AIDS are young adults. Although survival times have improved greatly for people who are diagnosed early and receive medical treatment, the disease is usually fatal."[164]

The spread of HIV and AIDS

Everyone needs to become informed about HIV and AIDS and avoid actions that place themselves or others at risk. HIV is in the blood, semen, or vaginal secretions of an infected person. The two main ways of spreading HIV are having sex and using contaminated needles to inject drugs. In addition, infected women can pass HIV infection to their newborns. HIV can be in semen, including the first drop of fluid, even before ejaculation. HIV can enter the body through the penis, rectum, or mouth. Anal sex is especially dangerous. The Surgeon General has said, "Condoms provide some protection, but anal intercourse is simply too dangerous a practice."[165] Performing oral sex is risky because getting semen or blood from an infected person in your mouth puts you at risk of HIV infection.[166] Sores or cuts in your mouth make it even more risky. According to the Journal of AIDS and the Centers for Disease Control, receiving unprotected oral sex also puts you at risk to be infected with HIV.[167]

A person can become infected with HIV through a single sexual contact. The risk of infection increases exponentially with each additional sexual contact. Doubling the number of contacts does not merely double the risk, because you can be exposed to HIV not only directly from the sex partner but also indirectly from all his former partners. It is estimated that half of those who are infected don't know it. Others may know they are HIV-positive but still engage in risky behaviors because of denial or anger, or because they are past caring. Others lie about their HIV-positive status in order to have sex. A survey of HIV-positive men revealed that 11% had lied and said they were HIV-negative in order to have sex.[168] A person under the influence of compulsive sex doesn't think clearly and may take unusual risks that place his own life and the lives of others in jeopardy.

If one in 100 men in America are HIV-positive, how many men who participate in homosexual behavior are infected? One in ten? One in five? How many men who cruise at a given location are infected? One in two? Don't believe you can't get infected. Some men feel that since they don't live in a large city, the chances of infection are small. But infection happens at alarming rates in Salt Lake City and Spokane and Albuquerque and Memphis and Tampa and Cleveland and every other city. I have several friends who thought they were safe and now are infected with HIV. A survey of gay and bisexual males found that in spite of a very accurate understanding of HIV infection, 63% had participated in behavior that put them at "extreme risk."[169] Another survey showed that of those who received anal intercourse, 58% had a partner ejaculate in them without the protection of a condom[170] and only 8% used condoms consistently with their most recent sex partner.[171] Among HIV-positive men who had insertive anal intercourse, 19% ejaculated without wearing a condom[172] and of those who had oral sex, 26% ejaculated in another man's mouth, most typically with someone they had just met.[173]

Dennis wrote the following warning: "I assumed what I thought to be a low level of risk. I had very little anal sex, and always with a condom. I was very careful with oral sex and never let anyone ejaculate in my mouth. I checked my mouth for sores and never had oral sex within a half hour of eating, brushing, or flossing. Although I thought I was being careful, I now realize that I was playing Russian roulette, and I lost. Last spring I tested positive and my T-cell count is now 196, which means I officially have AIDS."

It is important not to judge people who have become infected. Regardless of the actions that allowed the infection, they deserve suffering or death no more than anyone else. What they need most desperately is our love and concern. When tragedy strikes, we should feel sympathy as fellow sinners and fellow sufferers. And if we start looking for an object lesson in the tragedy, we should apply the lesson to ourselves rather than to them. Let the misfortunes of others alert us to the urgency of our own state of affairs.

HIV testing

If you have been involved in even marginally-risky behavior, including giving or receiving oral sex, you should be tested for HIV and other sexually-transmitted diseases. If you are married, your wife should also be tested. Although it may be a frightening thing to do, it is necessary for your own health and that of your family. Early diagnosis can reduce the chance of spreading the disease further and early treatment can slow down the onset of symptoms and HIV-related illnesses, potentially adding years to your lives. For information about testing, contact your county public health office or local chapter of the Red Cross.

Providing support

LDS men who are infected with HIV or have AIDS often have great needs for emotional, psychological, social, spiritual, and financial support. Since most government and private organizations that offer such help have espoused gay-affirmative values, the LDS man may find himself at odds with their goals and find it difficult to get much positive assistance from them. In these cases, it may be especially important to offer him your encouragement, love, support, and acceptance.

In 1988, the First Presidency issued a statement on AIDS and the following year a special four-page bulletin on AIDS was sent to Church leaders throughout the world giving information and guidelines.[174] In these documents, the First Presidency admonishes Church members to become informed about AIDS and to extend Christlike sympathy and compassion to all who are infected or ill with AIDS. They encouraged leaders and members to "reach out with kindness and comfort to the afflicted, ministering to their needs and helping them with their problems."

For more information

Many of your questions about HIV and AIDS can be answered confidentially over the phone by calling the National AIDS Information Hotline sponsored by the Centers for Disease Control at 800/342–AIDS (Spanish: 800/344–SIDA; hearing impaired: 800/AIDS-TTY).

For advice from a Christian perspective, contact Americans For A Sound AIDS/HIV Policy, P. O. Box 17433, Washington, DC 20041 (telephone: 703/471–7350).

To find a support group for Christians with HIV or AIDS, contact the Christian AIDS Services Alliance, P. O. Box 3612, San Rafael, CA 94912.

The perils of homosexual behavior

Less than 2% of the gay population survives to age sixty-five. Gay people commit suicide at much higher rates than national averages.[175] Gay people generally attribute these problems to the oppression and hate they receive from society. However, the internal struggle with homosexuality creates much emptiness and despair.

My friend Spencer wrote the following experience: "This afternoon, as I walked down Christopher Street in Greenwich Village, I saw in a snapshot view both the allure and tragedy of the gay world. Walking toward me was a man in his late twenties. With his gym bag in hand, shoulders back and chest out, he felt proud of his pumped body. I imagined he was headed home to ready himself for a night of entertainment and fun. He was confident and on top of the world. Just after he passed me, I came upon another man also in his late twenties. I almost stumbled into him because he was inching his way down the sidewalk with the help of a cane. Judging from his bald head and the lesions on his face and arms, I assumed he was in the final stages of AIDS. On this beautiful Saturday, he felt well enough to venture out of the house for a short walk in the fresh air. About thirty feet after I passed him, I had to stop and look back on the scene I had just witnessed. In the distance I could still see the healthy young man walking briskly, ready for good times and adventure. In the foreground was the heart-wrenching sight of the other young man who was barely able to walk, a victim of the adventurous lifestyle that the healthy young man was so eager to pursue. I wished I could get the healthy young man to stop and talk with the other young man to see if any advice he would give could save him from a similar plight."

Fantasy

Mark Laaser writes that the three building blocks of sexual addiction are fantasy, pornography, and masturbation.[176] James Allen wrote that a man's mind is like a garden that may be intelligently cultivated or allowed to run wild, but whether cultivated or neglected, it will produce either useful plants or useless weeds. Whatever we allow to enter our minds will always bear fruit. Fantasy is damaging because it keeps us separated from reality. When you fantasize, you build a self-focused, self-pleasing world of fragments of people and situations which you rearrange to meet your needs. Fantasies are not about real or whole people and complete situations, but about imaginary, faceless people and unrealistic situations.

Jesus explained that sexual fantasy is also a violation of the seventh commandment when he said, "Ye have heard that it was said by them of old time, Thou shalt not commit adultery: But I say unto you, That whosoever looketh on a woman to lust after her hath committed adultery with her already in his heart" (Matthew 5:27–28). The gospel standard of chastity calls for cleanliness of both thought and action. The way to keep your actions appropriate is to keep your thoughts clean.

Pornography

In 1984, Elder David B. Haight warned, "Over the past twenty years a plague of pornography has swept across most countries of the world with increasing momentum and devastating impact. What began a few years ago as a few crude picture magazines that startled sensitive people has grown to hundreds of publications, each seeking to outdo the others with increasingly shocking content. . . . New technologies that can bless our lives in so many positive ways are also being used to spread pornographic corruption. Video recorders now can bring to homes. . . lurid portrayals of debauchery that contaminate those who view them."[177] Since Elder Haight said this in 1984, pornography has grown more widespread and more crude, and newer technologies make it increasingly easier to access.

Pornography is harmful

Some people rationalize that viewing pornography doesn't affect anyone but them. They say it is better to relieve their sexual frustrations looking at pornography and masturbating than finding a sex partner. They feel that being the lesser of two evils, it isn't so bad after all. However, many people can attest to the fact that pornography is addicting. I know of one man who over the course of two years had accumulated eighty-seven videos and more than 700 magazines and spent $27,000 in the process.[178]

Pornography drives away the Spirit

More important than financial or other reasons, we should avoid pornography because it drives away the Spirit, and we desperately need the Spirit to guide us. The Spirit of the Lord cannot dwell in unholy places (see Alma 34:36).

Pornography feeds fantasies

The images portrayed in pornographic literature and movies constitute a fantasy unfounded in reality. It is a vision of exaggerated masculinity and sex without consequence. The object of the fantasy can be controlled, picked up, put down, and used as the person wants. It allows an individual the illusion of a sexual encounter without actually having to confront another human being.

Pornography feeds sexual fantasies which reinforce the homosexual feelings you are trying to unlearn. These reinforced feelings can work against all the other efforts you make to resolve homosexuality in your life. The fantasies in your mind are a product of all the garbage you allow to enter your mind and once you allow these images in, they become embedded in your memory and can be recalled even years later. Research has shown that sensory stimulation such as arousal through pornography releases the hormone epinephrine, which tends to lock the experience of stimulation in the brain, unlike the mental storage of less "charged" stimuli.[179] If viewing pornography is accompanied by masturbation, which it often is, the combined effect heightens the mental images. Such images are very difficult to erase from the memory banks of the brain.

Although you are not responsible for the desires that made you want to fantasize, you are responsible for allowing thoughts, stories, and images into your mind to fuel the fantasies. They make homosexual behavior appear enticing and can lead you into the addictive cycle of visualizing, then rationalizing, then acting.

Pornography influences behavior

The primary male response to viewing pornography is to masturbate. Elder David B. Haight explained, "Pornography is not a victimless crime. . . . Pornography is addictive. (See *Ensign*, March 1984, pp. 32–39.) What may begin as a curious exploration can become a controlling habit. Studies show that those who allow themselves to become drawn to pornography soon begin to crave even coarser content. Continued exposure desensitizes the spirit and can erode the conscience of unwary people. A victim becomes a slave to carnal thoughts and actions. As the thought is father to the deed, exposure can lead to acting out what is nurtured in the mind."[180]

Pornography feeds feelings of inferiority

Bob Davies and Lori Rentzel explain that "men who have viewed gay pornography may unconsciously compare their bodies (including genitals) with the 'perfect' standard of statuesque models. Viewing pornography can reinforce feelings of physical and sexual inferiority."[181] No normal person can measure up to the hyper-masculine images found in male pornography. As an individual indulges in pornography, his feelings of inadequacy and envy merge with lust and eroticism and magnify his feelings of sexual attraction toward men.

Andrew Comiskey wrote, "Pornography can become a vehicle through which an individual, empowered by subconscious yearnings, eroticizes another's manhood in an attempt to take it onto himself. Doing so may be a vicarious attempt to complete a perceived sense of lack in his own masculinity."[182] The aesthetically perfect men featured in pornography set up an unrealistic standard by which we compare ourselves, and when we compare their hyper-masculinity to ours, we will invariably feel a deficit and may find it more difficult to accept our own body and gender, as well as to accept other men who don't measure up to the unrealistic illusion of the porn idols. Thus, "pornography seems to distort how one views himself and others, potentially decreasing his capacity to relate realistically to other men."[183]

What is pornography?

Besides the obvious magazines, videos, and books, pornography includes anything that arouses you, even if it isn't graphically explicit. If muscle magazines or clothing catalogs excite you, you may need to avoid them for now. As you work through your problems and become emotionally healthier, you will see these things in a different light.

Eliminate pornography

Dr. William Consiglio counseled, "Rid yourself of all pornographic materials! All erotic magazines, literature, videos, books, pictures, music, letters, or condoms should no longer be a part of your life. It may cost you something financially and emotionally to part with some of these items. The break with all of these things symbolizes a break with a former lifestyle and past and is an indication of a serious decision to change. Don't hold anything back! Get rid of it all; once and for all!"[184]

My friend James wrote about his "giant leap of faith" in deciding to dispose of his collection of pornography. "It was a difficult decision to make. I thought I would never get rid of it. I felt like the guys in those pictures were my friends; they were guys I had related to for years. I knew them well. I knew their bodies well. But it was time. I knew I couldn't just trash them quickly after having a 'relationship' with some of them for ten years. It had to be done in a way that I would never forget, yet something permanent, something with ceremony to it. When I announced to my support group that I was going up the canyon to have a 'burning,' several others decided to join me.

"We parked the car half way up the canyon. The night was cold but a spirit of warmth and goodness penetrated our souls. In the dark, we carried our last rites in our arms as we searched for a fire pit where the final purge would take place. Once a warm fire was burning, we knew it was time for the ritual to begin. I found that it was more than I could bear to resist looking at my 'friends' just one more time—to say goodbye before the permanent destruction. 'Oh, no! I forgot I had that one! I can't get rid of him. He's too beautiful to destroy.' But my soul kept saying, 'it's time.' The flame consumed all my friends one by one. The pain was great, the anguish pierced my side, but my soul kept saying, 'it's time.'

"My companions also threw their pictures on the fire. Bob held back one magazine as though the pain to let it go was too great. Keeping it tucked under his arm like a mother protecting her child, it was safe for a time. Finally the tightly-clutched magazine was thrown into the fire and the pages were separated with a stick so all would be destroyed. Ideal he-man heros disintegrated into nothingness. Envy and lust went up in smoke. Finally, a membership card to a gay club was thrown on the fire as a climax to this funeral of years of lust and envy. As we sat watching the fire burn, the symbolism really hit home. Now that the pornography, lust, and envy had gone up in smoke, we knew that a new era had begun. This was no longer a part of our lives. We felt that our slate was clean. Our self-confidence had been stirred and it had changed us for the better. Several of us felt the presence of heavenly spirits cheering us on in our demonstration of faith."

If you are not yet at the point where you can burn your collection of pornography, consider agreeing not to look at it for a month (or a week). Give any pornographic literature you have to a trusted friend and ask him to lock it away for that length of time. Also agree that for the month you will not to go to a bookstore to find more. By the end of the month, you will have broken some of the compulsive cycles and you can have your friend throw it away.

My friend Garrick wrote, "Most days I think I've got porn licked for good—then I inevitably get stressed out and have a binge fest. I stupidly use it as a crutch when things get overwhelming. The only motivator that has effectively helped me has been to learn to love myself enough that I now believe I am worth the effort to rise above the trash. Ironically, my wife taught me this lesson. One day she confronted me directly and asked me if I had a problem with pornography. I confessed that I had slowly but surely spiraled out of control into a pornography and masturbation addiction. Then, with great power, she said the magic words: 'Dear, you are worth far more than the person you become as a pornography addict.' I finally believed her I am worth more than the trash. Improving my self-esteem and learning to love and respect myself over the past year has made all the difference."

Masturbation

Almost all males who experience homosexual attraction have a particular problem with masturbation. It is a form of sexual immorality that Satan uses to divert men and women from the proper, sacred use of procreative powers. Ancient and modern prophets have warned of the evils of masturbation.[185] It does not edify and inspire, but drives the Spirit away. It also holds you back in old thought patterns and unhealthy ways of responding by isolating you from your feelings and the real task of learning to deal honestly with yourself and the world. Dr. William Consiglio wrote, "Masturbation is sinful because it often becomes the primary means of sexual gratification and because it is accompanied by erotic fantasies."[186] The practice can become habitual and progressive, leading to other immoral behaviors, and is usually associated with pornography and sexual fantasies. Dr. Consiglio states that it can become an addictive habit "because it combines physical pleasure with homosexual imagery. As a result, it becomes a substitute and symbolic sexual experience. . . ."[187]

Eliminating masturbation

On the subject of masturbation, President Spencer W. Kimball wrote, "While we should not regard this weakness as the heinous sin which some other sexual practices are, it is of itself bad enough to require sincere repentance."[188] The following are some ideas to conquer masturbation:

Identify the triggers and stop the cycle early. It may help to identify the events that lead you to masturbate so you can stop the cycle at the first warning signs. It is much easier to stop at the beginning than it is when you are halfway into the cycle. If you find that masturbation is always preceded by looking at pornography, then find ways to stop the cycle before looking at the pornography. If it occurs at a certain time or place, then take actions to change your routine so you can enjoy more healthy habits.

Identify the real needs behind the desire to masturbate. What are your real feelings and needs for which masturbation has become a symbol? Is it a need for friendship? Do you want to feel appreciated by someone? Are you lonely and just need someone to talk with? Is it your way of dealing with stress, depression, boredom, or anger? If you masturbate, will these real needs be satisfied or only intensified? Understanding these feelings and needs, you can make plans in advance to deal with them in a more healthy way.

Keep a log of temptations and how you dealt with them. Record the following in a confidential place for at least a month:

◆ The triggers that started you into the cycle that ended in masturbation. (Was it loneliness, hunger, fatigue, stress, fantasy, pornography?)
◆ What you could have done to stop the cycle. (What specific actions and at what points?)
◆ The actions you plan to take next time you are in this cycle to stop it. (Be specific.)
◆ What you can do to be spiritually, mentally, or emotionally stronger so this won't happen again.

Review this log periodically to see if you can identify patterns, then talk with your bishop and therapist to get their perspectives and suggestions. If your masturbation is excessive or habitual, it may require intense effort on your part and therapeutic help to overcome it.

Be accountable to God in prayer. Acknowledge your weakness to your Heavenly Father in prayer and ask for His strength. Admitting a problem is the first step in solving it.

Be accountable to your bishop. As embarrassing and personal as it may seem, you should talk with your bishop or branch president about this problem. Believe me, you will not be the first person who has talked with the bishop about masturbation. Accountability to a priesthood leader is not only an important step in the repentance process, but his love and support on such a personal matter can be healing. He can give you ideas and a perspective that can be helpful as you overcome your habits.

Be accountable to a trusted friend. You may wish to define an accountability agreement with a close friend or member of your support group. Agree to talk with him about your temptations (avoiding specific details) and how you plan to stop the cycle next time. His perspective and support can be encouraging. A friend of mine committed to his wife that he would tell her each time he masturbated. Needless to say, this was a major deterrent for him!

For additional ideas on overcoming masturbation, see *Eliminate Your SDBs: Self-Defeating Behaviors* by Johnathan M. Chamberlain and the Church's pamphlet *To Young Men Only* by President Boyd K. Packer.

Cruising

There was a time I couldn't drive by a certain place without turning in to cruise. Now I drive by it every day on my way home and most days don't even notice I've passed it. Occasionally, I'll look over as I drive by and thank God that I don't feel any compulsion to go in.

Several years ago, in the afternoon a few days before Christmas, I had gone out to do some shopping and finished earlier than I had expected and the thought entered my mind to cruise. My almost immediate response was "No. I don't want that" and I went straight home and took the family to a movie. Later that night I sat on the bed with the kids and read *The Littlest Angel*,[189] a beautiful story about the littlest angel's gift to the Christ child. While all the other angels gave bright and glorious gifts, all he had to give was a little wood box that meant a lot to him because it contained mementos from earth. Heavenly Father accepted this gift warmly and turned the box into a star that shined brightly over Bethlehem. The littlest angel's gift was accepted because it was a gift from his heart. I thought then that no matter how strong the desires can be at times to go cruising, I can give it up. I can give it up as a gift to God to show my desire to serve him.

If you have learned to relate in the world of cruising by picking up on eye contact or subtle signals, you can also work your way back out of it by consciously ignoring those signals and by not giving out those signals yourself. Avoid staring at other men and if you notice someone staring at you, don't return the look. The eyes are the windows to the soul and brief eye contact with someone may say more than you intend to say. If you don't show interest, the situation won't escalate.

Eventually, you will find that you no longer notice the signals of others and you will avoid the temptations and encounters.

Homosexual behavior

Casual sex

For many men, the majority of their sexual encounters are with strangers or casual acquaintances. Because of their urgent desire for sexual contact, they find themselves connecting with another man for an evening or even a few minutes of pleasure. Anonymous sex is efficient; it may take only minutes or seconds from first meeting to engaging in intimate sex. But it is sex without feelings.

This paradox of having intimate actions with someone one doesn't even know is the Adversary's false substitute for true, fulfilling relationships. This counterfeit intimacy is one-dimensional, substituting physical and romantic intimacy for the true intimacy your friend can have in a relationship with a wife that includes deep emotional ties, acceptance, and love. In fact, the substitute intimacy decreases the possibility of true intimacy because it introduces guilt, plays on his feelings of inferiority, and creates anxiety.

Although casual sex can bring physical pleasure and temporary satisfaction, afterwards, you are left with even deeper feelings of loneliness, rejection, and frustration. Rather than satisfying your need for the love of a friend, casual sex only intensifies the needs. It leads to an addictive spiral that feeds itself. The sexual experience generates more feelings that evoke even more acting out. After each sexual encounter, you feel used and of less value.

Long-term relationships

Some men find another man with whom they have a long-term relationship and do not engage in casual or anonymous sex. The ideal dream of most men who are attracted to other men is to find "Mr. Right" and settle down with him in a romantic, committed relationship. However, the reality is that such relationships are not common. According to a national survey by the gay magazine *The Advocate*, only 33% of the respondents currently live with a partner,[190] 25% are in a relationship that has lasted a year or longer, and only 9% are in a relationship that has lasted more than ten years.[191] Homosexual relationships tend to be unstable and unfulfilling for all the reasons that led the person to develop homosexual desires in the first place, such as psychological deficits, defensive detachment, dependency needs, and the inability to see the real emotional needs. When they realize their partner cannot fill their emotional needs, they continue their desperate search through promiscuity. Fidelity is difficult to achieve in even committed relationships. The *Advocate* survey revealed that only 52% of the gay couples were monogamous as far as they know in their current or previous relationship.[192] In a 1984 study of 156 male couples, only seven had been able to maintain sexual fidelity, none of which had been together more than five years.[193]

Make it work!

You can keep your behavior in line with gospel standards. The Apostle Paul promised, "There hath no temptation taken you but such as is common to man: but God is faithful, who will not suffer you to be tempted above that ye are able; but will with the temptation also make a way to escape, that ye may be able to bear it" (1 Corinthians 10:13). This scripture explains that there is no challenge beyond your ability to handle, and also that as you turn to God, He will provide a way for you to get through the trial.

The Lord said, "And if your eye be single to my glory, your whole bodies shall be filled with light, and there shall be no darkness in you; and that body which is filled with light comprehendeth all things" (D&C 88:67). Every time you do the things that are right, the light inside you increases and the darkness decreases. This light gives you the right to call upon the powers of heaven when you need help.[194]

For further reading

Willpower is Not Enough: Why We Don't Succeed at Change by A. Dean Byrd and Mark D. Chamberlain.

Homosexual No More: Practical Strategies for Christians Overcoming Homosexuality by Dr. William Consiglio, especially pages 88–93.

Eliminate Your SDBs: Self-Defeating Behaviors, by Johnathan M. Chamberlain.

Out of the Shadows: Understanding Sexual Addiction by Patrick
    Carnes.

Don't Call It Love: Recovery from Sexual Addiction by Patrick Carnes.
    Note especially the boundary worksheet on page 250 and the
    abstinence worksheet on pages 246–247.

Breaking the Cycle of Compulsive Behavior by Martha Nibley Beck
    and John C. Beck.

*Gentle Path through the Twelve Steps: A Guidebook for All People in
    the Process of Recovery* by Patrick Carnes

*Regaining Self-control: Conquering Obsessive-compulsive Behavior
    and Other Habits you Want to Break* by Archibald John Bennee,
    MD.

Putting on the Armor of God: How to Win Your Battles With Satan by
    Steven Cramer.

Conquering Your Own Goliaths by Steven Cramer.

Sexaholics Anonymous. Describes a twelve–step program for those
    who struggle with sexual addictions.

Chapter Eleven

Self-Perception

We are greatly influenced by our perception of our self and the world around us. Since these perceptions govern how we feel about ourselves and, ultimately, how we act, it is critical that we see ourselves for who we really are. When we better understand ourselves and expand our self-image, we expand the possibilities. This chapter discusses the concept of paradigms, then gives suggestions on how to improve your self-image and your feelings of self-worth.

Paradigms

A paradigm is simply the way you see the world. These perceptions are important because they are the basis of your attitudes, behaviors, and relationships. If you see the world in a distorted way, you may develop unrealistic expectations, behave in ways inconsistent with happiness, and have relationships that are unfulfilling. The good news is that paradigms can be changed. Stephen Covey explains that "the more aware we are of our basic paradigms, maps, or assumptions, and the extent to which we have been influenced by our experience, the more we can take responsibility for those paradigms—examine them, test them against reality, listen to others and be open to their perceptions—thereby getting a larger picture and a far more objective view."[195] Difficult circumstances in life often require us to reevaluate our paradigms and sometimes create a whole new frame of reference by which we see the world and ourselves. Albert Einstein observed, "The significant problems we face cannot be solved at the same level of thinking we were at when we created them."[196] Stephen Covey says that trying to "change outward attitudes and behaviors does very little good in the long run if we fail to examine the basic paradigms from which those attitudes and behaviors flow."[197] Therefore, it is important to look at your paradigms to determine (1) if they are correct and (2) if they are helpful. You may discover that your views are not correct—that your parents really *do* love you, you really *can* enjoy healthy, nonsexual relationships with other men, and you really *can* control your sexual urges.

Scott Peck, author of *The Road Less Traveled*, explains that "the more clearly we see the reality of the world, the better equipped we are to deal with the world. The less clearly we see the reality of the world—the more our minds are befuddled by falsehood, misperceptions and illusions—the less able we will be to determine correct courses of action and make wise decisions."[198]

The fact that you are attracted to men indicates that something happened during your developmental years to skew your thinking. Your attractions are caused, in part, by your perception of the world and your instinctive efforts to become a part of something you know you need. Homosexuality is the story we tell ourselves to explain what we don't understand. Our task, then, is to discover what we don't understand and adjust our perceptions to match reality.

Knowing that you are attracted to men, you may have labeled yourself a "homosexual" and with that label, taken upon yourself the extra baggage of society's definition of a homosexual. If so, you have likely taken on much more of a burden than you deserve. If you can find a way to divest yourself of these extraneous perceptions, you may find that your key issues are not as overwhelming as you thought. It is counterproductive to use terms such as "homosexual" or "gay" to describe yourself. Refer to your "homosexual problems" rather than referring to yourself as a "homosexual," a "recovering homosexual," or even a "former homosexual."

Stephen Covey explains that "paradigms are powerful because they create the lens through which we see the world. The power of a paradigm shift is the essential power of quantum change, whether that shift is instantaneous or a slow and deliberate process."[199] Therefore, make a careful evaluation of how you see yourself. If you have convinced yourself that you are a "homosexual," then even when you make the kinds of changes described in this book, you may still feel like a "homosexual." See yourself in a new light. Developing healthy male relationships and affirming your masculine identity will give you the evidence and confidence you need to change the perception you have about yourself.

Self-image and self-worth

Homosexual problems have little to do with sexuality, but a lot to do with self-image (how you think about yourself) and self-worth (how you feel about yourself). Many men who struggle with homosexual attractions have good self-images—they have good jobs and get along well in life. But they have low feelings of self-worth—their gut-level feelings tell them they are not worth much. Whether you believe you can change your self image or not, you are right. Your self image establishes your personal beliefs about what you can and cannot do. Consider the following suggestions to improve your perception of yourself:

Focus on principles and values

Stephen Covey believes that "a life of integrity is the most fundamental source of personal worth."[200] A life of integrity is one that is consistent with your personal values. Working toward being more centered on these principles and values can help you in many ways. A principle-centered person sees things in terms of his personal values, and all the decisions he makes are based on those values. Because of this, he acts in ways that support and strengthen those values. This solid, unchanging core gives him a high degree of stability and allows him to be powerfully proactive in life. Stephen Covey explains that "intrinsic security doesn't come from what other people think of us or how they treat us. It doesn't come from our circumstances or our position. It comes from within. It comes from accurate paradigms and correct principles deep in our own mind and heart. It comes from inside-out congruence, from living a life of integrity in which our daily habits reflect our deepest values."[201]

Get to know yourself

Some men have undeveloped feelings of self-worth because they do not know themselves; they have an undefined sense of self. In their attempts to be accepted by others, they may lose their unique sense of identity. In the Mormon culture, it is easy to fit into predefined molds and not be highly self-defined.

To improve your feelings of self-worth, it may help to define yourself better. Who are you as a person? What do you like? What do you dislike? Chris Austin, author of *Cleaning Out the Closet*, suggests that you take time to think about and write down your likes and dislikes regarding foods, television shows, movies, smells, colors, holidays, fears, memories, feelings, weaknesses, strengths, and values. This forces you to think about your preferences and make decisions. If you later decide you don't like what you have defined, you can change your mind, but make decisions for today and define yourself. During this process of self-exploration, name your feelings and your fears—the first step in learning to understand and deal with them. Ask your therapist for advice in this process.

See the eternal perspective

President Spencer W. Kimball wrote, "If we look at mortality as a complete existence, then pain, sorrow, failure, and short life could be a calamity. But if we look upon life as an eternal thing stretching far into the pre-earth past and on into the eternal post-death future, then all happenings may be put in proper perspective."[202]

You are not a mortal having a spiritual experience; you are a spiritual being having a mortal experience. Likewise, it may be helpful to think of yourself as a Christian who has a homosexual problem, and not as a homosexual who happens to believe in Christ. Don't define yourself by your present temptations. Bob Davies and Lori Rentzel explain that "our identity is not found by looking backward to our past or by looking inward to our fleshly nature. Both of these indicators will give us a false report about who we are."[203] To find your true identity, you must look to Christ.

If you have received a patriarchal blessing, read it again to give eternal insight into your potential and what the Lord has in store for you. If you have not received a patriarchal blessing, talk with your bishop or branch president about getting one. If you have received your endowments, take a few minutes to reflect on the promises and gifts you received in the temple. You will recall that you were promised great blessings if you are faithful to the covenants you made there. If you have not received your endowments, prepare yourself to enter the temple. President James E. Faust said, "As we mature spiritually under the guidance of the Holy Ghost, our sense of personal worth, of belonging, and of identity increases."[204]

Accept your true self

Stephen Covey wrote, "We are not our feelings. We are not our moods. We are not even our thoughts. The very fact that we can think about these things separates us from them and from the animal world. Self-awareness enables us to stand apart and examine even the way we 'see' ourselves—our self-paradigm, the most fundamental paradigm of effectiveness. It affects not only our attitudes and behaviors, but also how we see other people. It becomes our map of the basic nature of mankind."[205]

The popular advice to "accept yourself" is certainly good advice. However, it is the interpretation of "accepting yourself" that gets people into trouble. Should you accept yourself in your current condition and not try for anything more? The concept of personal growth tells us we should expect to be constantly improving and changing our conditions in life for the better. To say "I'm a homosexual and I'll always be a homosexual" is a defeatist acceptance of a changeable aspect of your current condition. As a child of God, you have the divine ability to continue to improve your station in life, to grow, and to continue to progress. To believe anything less is to deny the power of God and His promises to us.

In quiet moments, try to get in touch with your inner self. Something inside each of us is ancient, wise, and knows our true self—it is our eternal soul. We have always existed: first as intelligences, then as spiritual beings, and now with a physical body. Your eternal soul can help you decide what you must do to live with integrity.

As one man described it, "For many years I thought I was gay. I finally realized I was not a homosexual, but really a heterosexual man with a homosexual problem."[206]

Respect yourself

Many of us devalue ourselves and feel that we don't have much to offer. We are often our own worst critics. We put ourselves down physically and discount our personality traits. So what if you have a narrow chin, or a high forehead, or a sensitive temperament? Be grateful that you have a chin and a forehead and sensitivity.

In the darkest moments, you may feel you don't deserve the blessings you have. As you come to understand that your developmental problems can be corrected, your outlook on life can improve. You will realize that nothing is inherently inferior about you. Having been created in the image of God, you have great potential. And when you recognize your good traits and feel better about yourself, you will be in a better position to relate positively with other men.

Part of respecting yourself is to recognize that you are worthy of love. There is a difference between *being* loved and *feeling* loved. If you are like I was, you may need to learn to *feel* it. I used to worry about losing friends and missing opportunities to be with them such that I couldn't enjoy it when I was with them. During an outing with other guys, I would worry about when the next one would be, and when it was over I would be devastated by the realization that it was over. The more rewarding and fulfilling it was, the more devastated I would be at its conclusion, afraid that I would never have a good experience like it again. For some reason, I believed that having joy now meant misery and pain later. It took time to learn to enjoy experiences as they were taking place, then cherish the memories, but look forward with confidence to the next experience. I also had to convince myself that I was in control of my life and could plan and enjoy additional fulfilling experiences. I had to learn it is okay to be happy now and there didn't need to be a negative consequence later.

Don't compare yourself with others

Comparing ourselves with others can be damaging to our self-image because we usually compare our worst aspect against someone else's best. We can always find someone who is a little stronger, better-looking, or more outgoing than we are. And when we find this person, we may compare our whole selves against that one aspect and conclude that the other person is better in all respects than we are.

When we see someone laughing and having a good time in a social setting, we think their entire life is happy and carefree. Upon closer examination, we will likely discover that they have challenges and heartaches just like everyone else.

Consider the following excerpt from Spencer's journal: "On Monday, I found myself really looking at other men around me—not lusting after them, but comparing myself to them. Although I don't do it all the time, for a while I was really caught up in the comparison, and I was almost overwhelmed by how difficult and how depressing it is to always look at other men and compare yourself to them, and feel you are not as good as they are. I saw something in almost every man that I wished I had. I didn't consider the good in myself, but just noticed the things in others that I wished I had, and I felt sadly inadequate. I wished I could fit in, wished I were as together, as good-looking, or as tall as they were. I was comparing and wishing, but not feeling like I measured up."

It can be healthy to try to emulate the good traits in other people, but it is demeaning and degrading to always feel inadequate. Recognize that each person is unique and that you don't have to be like other people in every respect. We all have both good and bad traits. Recognize your good traits and work on improving the others.

Don't judge by superficial standards

Think about how you judge others. If you judge them superficially by the kind of car they drive or the clothes they wear or the people they know, it could be that you also judge yourself by the same outward standards, rather than looking at deeper, more meaningful character traits. Not only are the superficial things less important, but they are also often out of our control and are inconstant. By these standards, we feel good about ourselves when we are dressed sharply, but feel like losers when we are not. If we judge by these external barometers, we will always consider ourselves second class. We can always find someone who at the moment is more attractive, has a better car, or has a friendship with someone we wish to associate with.

As you define what is important, you may realize that what you have been chasing after is not what you really want after all, and the pursuit of it will no longer be important to you. As I looked at my value system, I identified what I wanted to do with myself and my life. For me, the choice was to grow up and to move on to other things. I discovered that the year-round tan wasn't as important to me. It didn't matter as much that I wasn't in perfect physical shape. Cars and clothes began to matter less. I looked at my long-term value system and decided that other things were more important to me.

Recognize that your worth is not tied to what you do

While it is important to do good things, your self-worth should not be tied to what you do. A friend of mine felt he was only deserving of love when he pleased his parents. He spent a good part of his life trying to live up to their expectations, and when he didn't, he felt he was worthless. If you strike out one day, it doesn't mean you are a bad player. It takes time to build and maintain feelings that you are inherently good and a lot of that comes from understanding your divine potential as a son of God.

Writing about his personal struggles, Randy Walters explained, "At times I pushed myself to excesses in my studies and Church work so I always seemed to excel. My successes brought praise and admiration from peers and family, which I used as a temporary fix to satisfy my craving for acceptance. But inside I never met the unrealistic expectations that I set for myself."[207]

Recognize your limitations

Respect your own limitations and strengths, as well as the limitations and strengths of others. The serenity prayer reads: "God, give us grace to accept with serenity the things that cannot be changed, courage to change the things which should be changed, and the wisdom to distinguish the one from the other."[208] You may not be able to change some physical aspects of your life. For example, if you are small of stature, no matter how hard you work out you will probably never be a great lineman on a football team. However, most things are changeable. If you are shy, you can learn to be more outgoing. If you are nervous speaking to people, you can gain more self-assurance. If you don't make friends easily, you can learn to be more friendly. Have the "wisdom to distinguish the one from the other" and the courage to take on the challenge.

Define success

It is important to define what success means to you. Camilla Kimball understood what is important in life. She said "It is a truism that the Lord does not judge us by what we have but by what we do with what we have. The rich may be haughty, the poor envious, the powerful cruel, the weak sniveling. And those between the extremes may well be complacent and lukewarm." She then continued:

"To be rich is good, if you can be humble.

"To be learned is good if you can be wise.

"To be healthy is good if you can be useful.

"To be beautiful is good if you can be gracious.

"There is, however, nothing inherently bad in being poor, unlettered, sickly, or plain.

"To be poor is good, if you can still be generous of spirit.

"To be unschooled is good, if it motivates you to be curious.

"To be sickly is good, if it helps you to have compassion.

"To be plain is good, if it saves you from vanity."[209]

Be honest with yourself

Dishonesty can be a real problem for men with homosexual attractions because most at one time or another have lived a life of dishonesty. Even otherwise honest men tend to hide the truth about their attractions, fearing how others might react if they knew their dark secrets. After a while, they become so clever at hiding the truth that they often can't even see it themselves.

Resolving homosexual problems demands a commitment to *absolute* honesty. You have to admit to yourself the full extent of your problems. You can't be open with your therapist or your support group if you aren't first honest with yourself. Holding back will delay your progress or stop it all together. Writing in your journal can be a way to reveal things to yourself. The more you write, the clearer will be your views and perceptions. Stories you write in your journal can be powerful opportunities to teach yourself things.

Overcome defeatist attitudes

Some people have developed a condition called "learned helplessness," a perception that they are unable to solve problems or manage events in their life.[210] Such people become passive and depressed. Instead, we need to turn our challenges into power and reject the notion that we are helpless victims. We can let challenges overwhelm, defeat and depress us, or we can turn our challenges into strengths (see Ether 12:27).

Don't collect a list of life's injustices. Everyone has problems and no one wins the game of "my problems are more difficult than yours." Rather than complain about them, take responsibility for making changes. You damage yourself by carrying grudges or chips on your shoulder. In his book *Homosexuality and Hope*, Gerard van den Aardweg writes about how to overcome feelings of self-pity by using "anti-complaining therapy," where he encourages you to laugh at your complaints and your self-defeating attitudes.

At times you may think that no one understands your "special situation" and that if they did, they would give you special concessions. Such feelings are self-defeating. They decrease your internal ability to help yourself and drive away other people who may be able to help you. For ideas on how to overcome self-defeating behaviors, read *Eliminate Your SDBs: Self-Defeating Behaviors* by Johnathan M. Chamberlain.

When faced with painful experiences, the normal reaction is to retreat and withdraw from relationships and activities. However, great personal healing can come from reaching out to others. Investing your energies in serving people can help you stay engaged in life and out of depression. Turning outward and filling the needs of people is actually one of the most healing things you can do for yourself.

Keep a positive outlook

Concentrate on your potential and not your limitations. If you focus too much on your problems and tell yourself that life is an endless series of trials and complications, you will surely feel stressed and depressed. But when you remind yourself that you are alive, you have the gospel, and everyone else has hardships just like you, then you are better able to keep things in perspective.

Be careful what you say to yourself. These automatic internal conversations with ourselves are learned responses and can be healthy or unhealthy. This self-talk is the way some people mentally review their actions. If your self-talk is negative and self-punishing, it provokes stress and decreases your feelings of self-worth. Become aware of what you say to yourself, especially when you are under stress. Negative self-talk in a traffic jam would be, "I hate this." Healthy self-talk would be, "I'm not going to let a traffic jam upset me. Now I can listen to that CD I just bought." Instead of saying "I'm rude," say "I'm trying to be kinder." Instead of giving yourself a negative message, label yourself as working toward and developing a positive quality. This can revolutionize your identity. A scripture in the book of Ephesians reminds us to "be renewed in the spirit of your mind" (Ephesians 4:23). That is part of the transformation. (For further ideas, you may read the book *From Stress to Strength: How to Lighten Your Load and Save Your Life*, by Robert S. Eliot.)

Keep a balanced perspective

Since you are more than your homosexual problems, don't give undo attention to them. Elder Richard G. Scott noted, "Sadness, disappointment, and severe challenge are events in life, not life itself. I do not minimize how hard some of these events are. They can extend over a long period of time, but they should not be allowed to become the confining center of everything you do."[211] Some people become so obsessed with their homosexual problems that their obsession is a bigger problem than their attractions. If you hold a basketball close to your face, it blocks out the rest of the world and all you can see is the ball. Similarly, if you focus too much on the problems caused by your attractions, keeping them foremost in your view, you may fail to see other good things about your life. You need to hold these problems back from your face far enough to see a panoramic view of the rest of the world so you can keep things in proper perspective. Working on these issues at the exclusion of other things in your life can create an imbalance and cause additional problems. There may be other unrelated things you can benefit from working on. You may need to take a break and spend time on a relaxing hobby or activity to reduce stress and keep life in perspective.

Be assertive

To be successful in life, you need to know how and when to be assertive. Being assertive means that you honor your desires, needs, and values. It does not mean that you throw your weight around or that you are demanding with inappropriate aggressive behavior. Assertiveness is the ability to be aggressive while being keenly aware of your behavior and its appropriate limits. Nathaniel Branden, a clinical psychologist and founder of the Branden Institute for Self-Esteem,[212] warns that "if you are aware of your needs and values but fail to express them, each act of suppression chips away at your self-esteem, thus eroding your sense of who you really are."[213] He says that self-assertiveness is linked to self-respect. "When you stand up for what you think and feel . . . when you clearly voice your opinions and reactions . . . when you openly reveal who you are—you treat yourself as worthy of respect and as someone who matters."[214]

Being assertive may be difficult for you because we are often taught that what we want is not as important as what other people want. You may want to please others so much that you suppress your own wants and needs—even to the point that you lose touch with your own wants and needs. You may also feel that if you express them, you may be rejected. Don't be timid in expressing how you feel. You have a right to your opinions. Although people may disagree with you, it does not mean they reject you because your opinions or needs differ from theirs.

It may be helpful to be assertive toward your fears. Run toward your fears. Rather than working around your fears, you may need to choose a path through your fears. It is easier to act yourself into new ways of thinking than to think yourself into new ways of acting.

If you feel you need to work on being more assertive, read *The Six Pillars of Self-Esteem* by Nathaniel Branden.

Develop a sense of humor

While many of our problems are not a laughing matter, we need to find humor in life's situations. A mature adult is able to laugh at his mistakes. Humor can be an effective method of easing tension and breaking out of ruts to see a new perspective. Watch for the fine line between taking a situation lightly and finding humor in the situation. Don't dismiss your mistakes as unimportant, but don't take things so seriously that life becomes drudgery. Read Gerard van den Aardweg's book *Homosexuality and Hope* for ideas on how to use humor as a therapeutic technique.

Be happy

I used to feel that I couldn't be happy until I resolved all the homosexual problems in my life. Then one day I realized that working on challenges like these is the essence of life. Our whole purpose for being on this earth is to have experiences and learn and grow from them. If we decide we won't be happy until we have mastered all our challenges, we will never be happy.

Many people respond to life as though unhappiness is caused externally. Have you ever caught yourself saying things like the following? "Everything will be fine when I graduate." "If I could only get married, all my troubles would be over." "Things would be better if my wife just wouldn't spend so much money." "If my boss would get off my case, I could enjoy my job." It is easy to blame unhappiness on something or someone else. But happiness and unhappiness are generated from within. Certainly, there is unhappiness in life and you have likely experienced your fair share and then some. But there is also a time to say "enough" and get on with your life. Happiness is an elusive goal. It doesn't come as a result of getting something we don't have, but rather in recognizing and appreciating what we do have. Consider the following steps on the pathway to happiness:

Don't dwell on past injustices.

Focus on the present. Research suggests that thinking too much about events far in the future or in the distant past leads to unhappiness.

Check your goals periodically. Many of us get so wrapped up in the means that we forget about the ends. Ask yourself from time to time, "Why am I doing this?"

Take advantage of what you already have.

Develop new interests. An active mind is never bored. Resolve to notice new things each day about nature, people, or anything else that interests you.

Make time each day for quiet reflection. Turn the radio off and let your thoughts drift to who you are, how you feel, what you are doing, and how your life is going.

Exercise. It's good for the mind.

Establish a daily regimen. It will give you a feeling of control. Anything that proves you can make changes in your own life will give you a positive sense of self.

Learn to like yourself. A good way to think positively about yourself is to think positively about others.

Don't wear too many hats. Focus on one thing at a time and set aside time for your family, yourself, your golf game, and for having fun. If you set your priorities in advance, you avoid the anxiety of making moment-to-moment decisions.

Keep your sense of humor. A good laugh goes a long way to make almost any situation bearable. It also lightens the impact of life's inevitable tragedies.

For further reading

The Seven Habits of Highly Effective People by Stephen R. Covey.

The Road Less Traveled by M. Scott Peck, M.D.

Get Out of Your Own Way: Escape from Mind Traps by Tom Rusk.

Honoring The Self: The Psychology of Confidence and Respect by Nathaniel Branden.

The Feeling Good Handbook by David D. Burns.

Unlimited Power: The Way to Peak Personal Achievement by Anthony Robbins.

The Self-talk Solution: Take Control of Your Life With the Self-management Program for Success by Shad Helmstetter.

Chapter Twelve

Masculinity

Many men who have homosexual problems feel inadequate in their masculinity. Having diminished feelings of masculinity does not mean you see yourself as feminine or wish you were a woman. There is a considerable difference between feeling inadequate as a man and feeling feminine. How you feel about yourself is crucial because these inner feelings of being incomplete or inadequate as a man can be a breeding ground for a number of personal problems, including homosexual ones. Not all males who have such conflicts have homosexual problems, but those who have homosexual problems commonly experience feelings of inadequacy in their masculinity.

This chapter presents the concepts of gender identity and gender role, then addresses some of the conflicts men experience in the world today. It shows how rites of passage can help a young man move into manhood. The chapter then suggests that you define what is masculine for you and gives example of male role models. It discusses masculine and feminine characteristics and gives suggestions on how to improve your feelings of masculinity.

The developmental process

In The Family: A Proclamation to the World, the First Presidency declared, "All human beings—male and female—are created in the image of God. Each is a beloved spirit son or daughter of heavenly parents, and, as such, each has a divine nature and destiny. Gender is an essential characteristic of individual premortal, mortal, and eternal identity and purpose."[215]

Development of gender identity

A child's identity as masculine or feminine is acquired in the early stages of life, usually by age three, and it is during this time that the foundation of sexual health is laid or sexual distress begins. Loving, consistent family relationships can help children accept themselves and their gender identity.

Development of gender role

After a boy identifies his gender, he needs to learn his gender role. It is usually from ages four to eleven that he comes to understand himself as a male and learns how to relate socially with others. The boy develops a healthy masculine gender role most effectively when he can use his father or another significant male in his life as a role model. Alan Mcdinger wrote, "Modeling is an essential part of this process. In a culture where the father's role is clearly defined, it is not difficult for the boy to seek to form himself with a very clear perception of what he is to become. If the father is uncertain and vacillating in his role, the model becomes blurred, the child confused."[216] Joseph Nicolosi explained, "The mother's attitude toward father—and men in general— is very significant. If she undermines his role in the family, this diminishes his status as a desirable model. If the mother does not reflect him as a model to strive for, she fails to demonstrate that there is esteem related to being masculine."[217]

The boy can admire his father and pattern his life after him. The father can reinforce and affirm the boy's masculine behavior. Through many interactions, the boy learns from his father how to do masculine things. The father also teaches the boy about femininity by demonstrating how men should treat women. It is important that the boy attaches and identifies with his father and that he doesn't perceive him to be absent or emotionally disinterested. He needs to feel that his father is actively and emotionally interested in his socialization. If the boy feels affirmed in these masculine qualities and roles, he accepts the masculine. If he feels rejected, he may develop a confused identity and detach himself from the masculine.

In earlier times, boys worked daily at the side of their fathers in the fields or in the blacksmith shop. They had close relationships and boys learned from their fathers what it meant to be a man. The industrial revolution took fathers out of the home and put them in factories, and later the information revolution put them in offices doing work that boys don't understand. Today, fathers spend little meaningful time with their sons and therefore boys don't have as many opportunities to learn concepts of masculinity from their fathers.

Sexual development

Adolescence can be a very confusing time. Just as the boy is trying to learn who he is and how he fits in with the world, his body begins the profound physical and emotional changes of puberty. Although he is physically becoming an adult, he may lack the experience and maturity to deal effectively with the social, emotional, and physical changes taking place.

The masculine conflict

It is difficult to be a man in the world today. In his book *The Hazards of Being Male*, Herb Goldberg explains that even from childhood, males are in constant conflict. He wrote, "the elementary school setting puts the young boy into more than his share of painful binds. While there is great peer pressure to act like a boy, the teacher's coveted classroom values are traditionally 'feminine' ones. The emphasis is on politeness, neatness, docility, and cleanliness, with not much approved room being given for the boy to flex his muscles. Teacher's greatest efforts often go into keeping the boys quiet and in their seats."[218] Dr. Goldberg further explained, "[T]he young boy in our culture is placed into countless such dilemmas. He is told he must become a boy but he has to do so with very limited male model availability. He is taught that 'real boys' are active and strong but then gets into trouble in school for acting like a 'real boy.' He is in constant conflict between his own restlessness and the desire to be active and his teacher's demand that he be quiet, submissive, and passive."[219]

Suppressing feelings

Young boys are taught to suppress their feelings. "From early boyhood on, his emotions are suppressed by others and therefore repressed by himself. In countless ways he is constantly being conditioned not to express his feelings and needs openly. Though he too has needs for dependency, he learns that it is unmasculine to act in a dependent way. It is also unmasculine to be frightened ('scared'), to want to be held, stroked, and kissed, to cry, etc. While all of these expressions of self are acceptable in a girl they are incompatible with the boy's sought after image of being tough and in control."[220]

Performance

Boys are taught from a very early age that they must perform. While it is okay for women to focus on relationships and be open emotionally, men learn to be more closed and competitive. As boys, they must run faster and jump higher. As teenagers, they must have the best cars and date the prettiest girls. As adults, they must have the highest-paying jobs and the most expensive houses. As a result, men learn to measure their success not in terms of happiness or fulfillment, but in terms of performance. They define themselves in external rather than internal terms. This performance-oriented view of masculinity is so focused on goals that close friendships become difficult. While such a focus may enable a man to build a career, it inevitably sets up emotional roadblocks to a fulfilling personal life.

Accepting help

Men are typically adept at denying their problems. They learn to be self-sufficient and feel inadequate if they ask for help. Therefore, they typically wait until their lives have fallen apart before they seek help. When they do seek help, they want quick solutions to complex problems. The good news is that there is a movement in America today for men to realize they should not judge themselves solely by performance standards, but can be more self-fulfilled, can show emotions, and can reach out to others for help. Men are reading books like *Fire in the Belly* by Sam Keen and *Iron John* by Robert Bly and going to self-discovery weekend retreats to try to understand their feelings and bond with other men.

Rites of passage

A rite of passage is an event that helps young people make transitions in their life. These ceremonies of manhood can be powerful, life-changing moments where, in the presence of dad and other men, a boy can mark either his progress toward or passage into manhood. Mormon culture has many rituals of passage, such as the blessing of children, baptism, priesthood ordinations, missions, and temple marriage. Anciently, Greek boys took an oath of allegiance to the city; today, LDS boys take the oath and covenant of the priesthood. In ancient cultures, men were given swords and shields to defend themselves;

temple rites today give the garment of the priesthood as a defense.

Today, people are beginning to recognize the importance of these ceremonies of manhood and are giving them increased emphasis. A number of Christian and Jewish organizations in the United States are incorporating new rites of passage to help young people make the transition from youth to adulthood. These rites include wilderness survival programs, reconstructed African rituals in churches, revitalized confirmations in Protestant churches, bar and bat mitzvahs in synagogues, and newly created rituals using mythology, art, music, and games in various settings.[221]

As a boy passes through these stages of life, the father should help his son recognize the attendant responsibilities and roles. A central function of fathering is to help the son identify and assimilate his roles in life, such as the role of a son, a boy, a priesthood holder, a man, and a father. If you missed out on these rites of passage, as an adult you may benefit from a rite of passage experiential program. Chapter six of *The Wonder of Boys* by Michael Gurian has more information on rites of passage.

Understanding masculinity

What does it mean to be masculine? Society dictates much of what we deem masculine. Our culture says that a man should be tough and not cry. Is your concept of a "manly man" one that builds sheds, fixes cars, drives trucks, drinks beer, watches sports by the hour, and ignores the feelings of others? We gain our concept of manliness from how we interpret the world around us.

Masculine virtues

It is important to define what is masculine to you. A better question to ask yourself may be "What is a godly man?" A man of God is sensitive, humble, and patient.

Men are often attracted to other men who appear to have the masculine traits they desire; they somehow feel they can make up for the deficiency through sexual contact with the "ideal man." In the book *A Place in the Kingdom: Spiritual Insights from Latter-day Saints about Same-Sex Attraction*, Garrick Hyde writes about the envy he felt toward high school athletes. "I wanted to consume the jocks' talents and personalities. I coveted their physical attributes, which I presumed were the source of their self-esteem and outward popularity. Fixating on their physical abilities quickly led to sexual fantasies."[222]

Male role models

Jesus Christ provided the perfect pattern of masculinity to follow. He led in humility and by example. He boldly stood up for what was right and did not shrink when it was necessary to clear the temple of those who sold animals and changed money. But He also demonstrated emotions of sorrow and pain. He was affectionate and tender with children and patient and loving with transgressors.

The Book of Mormon is full of examples of men who stood up for what is right, who were righteous priesthood holders and loving husbands and fathers. As you read the stories of Nephi, Captain Moroni, the 2,000 stripling warriors, Mormon, and Moroni, think about the masculine qualities they possessed and consider how you can display the same qualities yourself.

As I have studied the life of Joseph Smith, I am impressed by his combination of strength and tenderness. He stood up to some of the greatest challenges any man could face, but was also as loving and tender as any man. The prophets are men to be emulated and reading books about their lives can help you see how to be a man of God.

Masculine/feminine qualities

It is necessary for everyone to have both masculine and feminine characteristics. A man has mostly male qualities and a woman has mostly female qualities. But a woman needs some masculine character-istics to give balance to her feminine side and a man needs some feminine characteristics to smooth out the rough edges of his masculinity. Rambo needs a little culture, emotion, and sensitivity. It is important to develop both because being out of balance with either can contribute to personal problems. The problem with many men who experience homosexual attraction is *not* that they have too much of the female qualities, but that their male qualities are underdeveloped. If men see masculinity as self-centered and cruel, they may suppress their masculine side and develop only their feminine side (perhaps emulating the good qualities they see in their mother). It was helpful for me to learn more about masculine and feminine characteristics to better develop both within me. I found two books by Robert A. Johnson helpful: *He: Understanding Masculine Psychology* and *She: Understanding Feminine Psychology*. The book *Men are from Mars; Women are from Venus* by John Gray also helped me understand the physical and emotional differences between men and women. It helped me understand that my wife perceives things differently than I do and that she will have different emotional expressions of her needs.

Improving your feelings of masculinity

Many men come to realize that what they experience as a homosexual attraction is really an attraction for qualities of masculinity they feel lacking. The following are suggestions to help improve your feelings of masculinity:

Define and incorporate good masculine qualities. After you define what is appropriately masculine for you, develop a plan of action to incorporate the things you feel you are missing. Remember to keep a good balance of masculine and feminine qualities. If you have any mannerisms or dress that would alienate you from other men, you may decide to change them without detracting from your individuality. There are a variety of acceptable masculine styles. If you are not happy with your voice, practice using a voice with a low pitch, medium pace, and volume. If you are personally dissatisfied with any traits, decide if they are really worth worrying about. If they are, work to change them but don't concentrate on them so much that they distract you from other important pursuits.

Risk by extending yourself. If you are unhappy with your current situation, don't give in to who you are now and give up on what you could become. Take the risk to stretch yourself and do things you have not done before.

Interact with other men. Find ways to join groups of men at work or in the community. Join ward sports teams or find a group that enjoys a certain type of recreation. Join in conversations with other men. Study up on a sports team so you can interject an occasional "How about the Bulls?"

Keep physically fit. Your weight, nutrition, and exercise can all contribute to your self-image. Regular exercise can help reduce anxiety, tension, mental fatigue, and depression. But even more important, I find that when I am out of shape I don't feel like participating on the ward basketball team or doing other things that would make me feel like I fit in with the guys. When I am strong and physically fit, I feel in control of my life. I enjoy working out at the gym because I am doing something masculine and it gives me the chance to associate with other men in a masculine environment. However, the gym can be a two-edged sword, offering both hope and fear. As Joseph Nicolosi explained, "It is one of the few all-male environments that provides both temptation and the healing sense of contact with masculinity."[223] Do you go to the gym for a legitimate workout or do you have other motives? A friend of mine used to refer to his "executive workout," a triathlon consisting of the sauna, steam room, and whirlpool. If you go to the gym for the scenery and not the physical rigors of a legitimate workout, you shouldn't be there at all. If it is a tempting place for you, find other ways to get a good workout without going to a gym. When my old gym became a cruising place, I changed to another gym. If you know cruising happens at certain times, avoid those times. To avoid any possibility of temptations, I go with several friends and that makes it even more enjoyable with their company.

Sports

Society focuses on winners. Winners get the lion's share of attention and few people even remember who else was in the running. In this competitive environment, a boy who is ill-coordinated or weak tends to be labeled a loser and his self-confidence is severely put to the test. Although there can be healthy competition, an emphasis on winning at all costs may be the single greatest reason why some young people get turned off to sports and physical fitness. Years later, no one may remember who won or lost the game, but he will always remember if he was left out. If a boy has negative experiences with physical activities or sports, it may result in a lifetime aversion to sports, both as a participant and a fan.

Psychologist Gerard van den Aardweg said, "studies reveal that most of the men with [homosexual attractions] had an outspoken childhood aversion for soccer or other group games. Such games are more or less the embodiment of boyish activity in our culture; they require enjoying competition with other boys and some fighting spirit and indicate adjustment to the peer group."[224] Jeff Konrad wrote, "I wanted to overcome certain inhibitions and rid myself of the crippling envy I'd felt. . . . I also wanted to get in shape, so I joined a health club. And hating my lifelong feelings of being awkward and incompetent at sports while other guys seemed to have been born on the playing field, I learned how to play softball and then volleyball by taking morning classes at Orange Coast. Anything that I'd allowed to restrain me in the past I was now determined to overcome. Every root I could find to my negative self-image and homosexual behavior was regarded as a challenge."[225]

My father was not home much as I grew up, and I was never encouraged to participate in sports. I was never on a little league team nor do I recall ever playing backyard football with neighborhood friends. The closest I ever got to team sports was playing Red Rover. In college, it seemed that all that my roommates cared about was sports. So on Saturdays while they vegetated on the couch watching one game after another, I went to work or the library. The more they cared about sports, the less I cared, and the gulf between us grew wider. When they dragged me to a college football game, I found myself cheering at the wrong times, so I soon replaced "yea" and "boo" to "oh-h-h-h" which they could interpret as either good or bad, depending on how the play turned out.

Sports play an important role in masculinity because men in much of the world spend a great deal of time watching and playing sports. If you are not involved in sports at least to some degree, you will be left out of much of male life in society and feel more separated from other men. If you have never developed a skill at a sport, it is not too late to learn. There are sports groups that teach adults the basic rules of the game and provide opportunity to develop basic skills. (See the chapter Support Groups for more information on sports programs.)

For further reading

Desires in Conflict by Joe Dallas, especially pages 99–113 and 157–175.

You Don't Have to be Gay by J. A. Konrad, especially pages 25–44, 187–214, 236, 245–248, and 265–267.

Homosexuality: A New Christian Ethic by Elizabeth Moberly, especially pages 1–16.

Homosexuality and Hope by Gerrard van den Aardweg, especially pages 17–24.

The Hazards of Being Male: Surviving the Myth of Masculine Privilege by Herb Goldberg.

Return from Tomorrow by George G. Ritchie, especially pages 48–49.

Learning to be a Man by Kenneth G. Smith.

Manhood in the Making by David G. Gilmore, especially the summary at the end of the book.

Chapter Thirteen

Emotions

Emotions are probably the most maligned and misunderstood part of our lives. We all have emotions, but few of us know what to do about them. We know we must overcome homosexual behavior and change our perception of ourselves, but what do we do with our emotions? A friend of mine often said to me, "I know the truth in my head, but have fears in my heart." Although we understand things intellectually, we need to accept them emotionally. Since life-changing decisions are painful, it may not be enough to decide to change; we also have to accept it emotionally and endure through the pain that will inevitably come as our emotional child grows to an adult.

Most of us are adept at repressing issues we don't want to deal with. We may distract ourselves by keeping busy or we develop escapes to avoid dealing with our negative emotions. But sooner or later, we must confront them and get to the root of what makes us feel unhappy or anxious.

Lori Rentzel writes about two extremes in the way we mishandle our feelings. One extreme is to be ruled by our emotions, allowing them to dictate our actions. The opposite is to live as though our feelings don't exist. Since neither of these is a good option, what are we to do? "First, we can begin to take a more balanced view. Our emotions are not meant to lead us around by the nose. Neither are they to be squelched and stifled. God created our emotions as well as our minds and physical bodies."[226] Our emotional nature can become whole when we accept and understand our feelings, and deal with them in a healthy way.

Share your feelings with others

Lori Rentzel wrote, "Emotional honesty begins with ourselves, then with God and finally with other people. Opening ourselves up to others can be incredibly frightening at first. We're afraid of being rejected for our so-called negative feelings of anger, jealousy or lust, or even for positive feelings of tenderness or kindness."[227]

After you admit your feelings to yourself, the next step is to admit them to God in prayer and to other people. Opening up to other people is one of the values of a support group. It can be frightening at first because we may fear being rejected for our feelings, whether they are negative (such as anger, jealousy or lust) or positive (such as tenderness or kindness). Lori reminds us that "feelings which seemed so dark and controlling when we kept them hidden start to lose their power when we bring them out into the light."[228] Listen to the Holy Ghost to determine who you should share your feelings with, how much to share, and when to share them. Sharing feelings can help you develop closer relationships.

Open up emotionally

Most men who struggle with homosexual desires have learned to be closed emotionally. This is an understandable defensive reaction to pain. When you have been hurt, you learned to close yourself off to guard against further pain. You found that if you didn't open up to anyone, you were not vulnerable. However, the sad reality is that if you don't open up emotionally, you also miss out on a world of emotional joy.

Once you start to open up, it may be an emotional roller coaster as you learn to deal with your emotions. You may become overly sensitive to personal interactions and take offense where none is intended. Be aware of this, and get feedback from other people to help you see things objectively. At times, you may wonder if your efforts to open up are worth it. Life with a hard outer shell prevented emotional pain and now when you open your heart, you are vulnerable and experience hurt. If it hurts too much, you may want to go back to your old safe, but unfulfilling, ways.

When you are desperately needy, your feelings may be intense and urgent. Therefore, you need to be patient and recognize that all your needs cannot be met immediately. The old sexual "fix" may have seemed to satisfy the need right away, but the long-term "fix" of healthy relationships will take longer to develop, but ultimately will be much more satisfying.

Work out past trauma

A hurt experienced early in life may still be unresolved, and the emotional memory may need to be healed. As a child, you may have defensively detached from your father, which is essentially an unresolved "mourning" that still needs to be worked out. Whether or not your father was at fault, you experienced resentment toward him, and so forgiveness is important. There may be other feelings that need to be worked out, such as a sense of grieving at the apparent hurtfulness of your parents or a sense of inferiority or loneliness. If there has been an abusive situation, work out the effects of the abuse with your therapist.

Express and control your anger

Anger is an appropriate response to many situations, but it must be properly expressed and controlled. Unrestrained anger, or rage, is unproductive. But equally damaging is anger that is suppressed. This internalized anger can make you feel powerless and can lead to depression.

You also need to learn how to receive the anger of others. When people are angry at a situation, they often misdirect it at the person responsible for the situation, or at the most convenient person. However, this misdirected anger doesn't mean they are angry *at you*. And even if someone is angry about something you did, it doesn't mean they reject you as a person.

Anger is a normal, expected reaction to tragedy. When it comes, try to direct your anger at the situation rather than at (1) yourself, (2) God, (3) those who might have prevented the situation from happening, or (4) those who are trying to help you. Getting angry at yourself makes you depressed. Being angry at God erects a barrier between you and His sustaining, comforting presence. Being angry at other people drives them away and makes it harder for them to help you. But, as Harold Kushner explained, "being angry at the situation, recognizing it as something rotten, unfair, and totally undeserved, shouting about it, denouncing it, crying over it, permits us to discharge the anger which is a part of being hurt, without making it harder for us to be helped."[229] Colin Powell developed a number of rules or thoughts to live by. One of them is to "get mad, then get over it."[230]

Make up for missed emotional growth

Making up for missed emotional growth can be both fulfilling and frustrating. When I finally identified some of my emotional deficits, I realized I was chronologically an adult but emotionally still a teenager. As I began to fulfill these emotional deficits, I discovered it was difficult to fully experience adolescent things when I was in my thirties. I also found that time was compressed. I was growing up emotionally perhaps a year every one or two months. I was anxious to maintain communication with my friends, similar to how teenagers communicate with their best friends daily. When I had new feelings or experiences, I felt an urgency to process them with my therapist or a friend, and when I had to wait hours it seemed like weeks. Teenagers growing up emotionally at a normal rate often find it difficult to adjust to their changing emotional state, but since I was changing even faster it lead to quite an emotional roller coaster ride. I went through many new experiences and had to correct my interpretation of some things I had learned from a distorted viewpoint in my childhood and teen years.

If you are going through similar experiences, keep trying. At times it may seem more than you can take emotionally, but it is certainly worth it. When you have made up all the deficits, you will be grateful for these experiences—and probably amazed that you made it through alive!

For further reading

Strong at the Broken Places by Linda T. Sanford.

A Door of Hope: Recognizing and Resolving the Pains of Your Past by Jan Frank.

Stolen Childhood: What You Need to Know About Sexual Abuse by Alice Huskey.

The Wounded Heart: Hope for Adult Victims of Childhood Sexual Abuse by Dr. Dan B. Allender.

Responding to Abuse: Helps for Ecclesiastical Leaders, Church of Jesus Christ of Latter-day Saints (item number 32248).

Preventing and Responding to Child Abuse, Church of Jesus Christ of Latter-day Saints (item number 33196).

Chapter Fourteen

Relationships

Homosexual problems stem from relationship deficits and one of the keys to resolving the problems is to repair existing relationships and build new, healthy ones. Those who make the most progress in resolving their problems are those who build quality male relationships. The first part of this chapter gives suggestions on how to develop relationships, and the later considers key relationships in your life, such as your relationship with your Heavenly Father and Jesus Christ, your father, mother, wife, and other men.

How to develop relationships

In their book *Coming Out of Homosexuality*, Bob Davies and Lori Rentzel identify qualities of appropriate relationships.[231] They say that healthy friendships are free and generous; built over time; not self-serving; directed outward, not inward; not mentally or emotionally preoccupying; and built on strength rather than weakness.

Develop appropriate relationships

Part of the attraction you feel to men may be a healthy drive to become like other men. Once you recognize the reasons behind your attraction and interpret them correctly, you can use this drive to your advantage. Channel this energy into bonding and healing by developing strong, appropriate relationships with other men. As healthy friendships develop, inappropriate sexual attractions diminish. When you learn that your peers do love and accept you, the intensity of your need for same-sex closeness will diminish. It will not go away because you always need the love and brotherhood of other men, but when your needs are being met legitimately, homosexual behavior will hold less appeal—and that is a sign of real change.

Allow yourself to be loved

We often create our own isolation because we convince ourselves that we are unlovable and that others won't enjoy relating with us. It may be that you subconsciously avoid situations where other men could reject you. If you have experienced love or intimacy that turned into pain, your defense may be a way of avoiding true love and intimacy so you don't get hurt again. In response to a relationship that didn't work out, you may have begun to believe you are not worthy of their emotional attention. Since faulty perceptions develop from faulty interactions, you need to have good experiences to challenge the bad ones and change your beliefs. You can have loving, healthy relationships that are rewarding.

To meet important emotional needs, you must be willing to build and nurture healthy relationships based on love, honesty, and appropriate intimacy. Rather than running from the relationships you need most, you need to allow yourself to be loved. As Alan Medinger, a pioneer in the Christian "ex-gay" movement, explained, "[T]o allow ourselves to be loved, is to open all of the doors to pain that were so carefully sealed shut."[232] Taking the chance to be loved means that you also open yourself to the risk of hurt. It may be frightening. "Love is never safe, nor is dealing with our true inner selves."[233] It takes courage. In his book *The Road Less Traveled*, M. Scott Peck says that "courage is not the absence of fear; it is the making of action in spite of fear, the moving out against the resistance engendered by fear into the unknown and into the future."[234] Reaching out and growing in any dimension will bring pain as well as joy. A full life will be full of pain, but the only alternative is not to live life fully, and it is regretful to miss out on loving relationships because they can be very rewarding. You will find that when you have the courage to extend yourself a little, people will get to know you and will be interested in you.

Let others help you

Letting other people help me was a difficult lesson for me to learn—one that I continue to work on. I am very independent and sometimes need to swallow my pride and reach out to others for help. We are all brothers and sisters of a loving Heavenly Father, and we need to rely on each other to make it through the challenges of this life. Spencer W. Kimball said, "God does notice us, and he watches over us. But it is usually through another person that he meets our needs. Therefore, it is vital that we serve each other in the kingdom."[235] We are not expected to live our lives in a vacuum and there is no shame in receiving loving help from another.

Do you find it difficult to let others into your life enough to help you? Do you fear that if others knew more about your thoughts and struggles they would reject you? Kathy Koch taught a good principle using an analogy of a rose.[236] She explained that when you look at a rose, you notice the beauty of the flower. Although you are aware that it has thorns, and therefore handle it with care, you still focus on the petals and the beautiful blossom. Likewise, if you let other people know about your thorns, they will still focus on the beauty that you have. The thorns on the rose have a purpose—to protect the blossom. There are advantages of having certain thorns. The Apostle Paul had a "thorn in the flesh" for which he prayed would be taken away. The Lord told him, "My grace is sufficient for thee: for my strength is made perfect in weakness" (2 Corinthians 12:9). To this, Paul responded, "Most gladly therefore will I rather glory in my infirmities, that the power of Christ may rest upon me. Therefore I take pleasure in infirmities, in reproaches, in necessities, in persecutions, in distresses for Christ's sake: for when I am weak, then am I strong" (2 Corinthians 12:9–10).

Carefully choose those to whom you expose your thorns, but trust them to help you. Dare to let them help you? Give them permission to watch for your thorns and help you recognize when the thorns grow. Think about the people who currently influence your life. List their names and write a brief description of how each influences you. If that influence is not a positive one, find ways to make changes to eliminate that influence. The people you spend time with will influence you, so be sure there is a good reason for them to be there.

Overcome defensive detachment

Many of your fears in developing relationships may stem from your childhood. If you had difficult and hurtful relationships, you may have developed ways to keep an emotionally safe distance from other men. Once you realize how you distance yourself from other men, you can work to tear down those walls and open your heart to men who can become the friends you've always wanted. Ed Hurst said, "Frequently, in our search for our 'dream friend,' we pass up quality potential friendships without realizing it. We lament our friendlessness while a willing, capable, quality friend looks on—wondering what it takes to get our attention."[237]

Build relationship skills

People can benefit from improving their relationship skills. Together with your therapist, you may identify specific areas in which you want to grow. Many good books can help you develop specific skills in areas such as communication, reading people, and interacting with them.

Be patient

Ed Hurst explains that "relationships don't just happen, they grow."[238] Relationships take time to develop. Be patient and allow them to grow normally and gradually and don't become frustrated when things don't go as you would like. All relationships have their awkward moments.

Be friendly and positive

Don't be afraid to show to others you care. Look for nice things about people and give sincere compliments. If you make others feel good about themselves, they will feel good about you. If you see to it that others have a good time, you will have a good time. You don't always have to talk about your problems, even within your support group. Spend more energy talking about your strengths and successes than about your problems. When you act happy and extend yourself to others, they respond.

Consider the old story of a man who sat by the city gates. One day, a traveler approached and asked him if it was a friendly town. The man asked the traveler, "What was the town like that you just came from?" The traveler replied, "Oh, it wasn't very friendly. The people were just interested in themselves." The man then replied, "Well, this town is the same. You wouldn't enjoy your stay here." So the traveler went on to the next town. A while later, another traveler approached the man at the city gates and asked what the town was like. "What was the town like that you just came from?" the man asked. The traveler replied, "Oh, it was as a very friendly town. The people were caring and helped each other." The man then replied, "Then you will enjoy your stay here because this town is like that, too." This story illustrates that we get what we give. If we are introverted and don't extend ourselves to love and help others, then we don't get much in return. But when we reach out to others and show love and caring, we get the same in return.

Don't require the constant approval of others

I used to feel that I had to have the love and approval of everyone all the time. When I didn't, I felt I had failed. It bothered me if anyone in the room was upset. In social situations, I felt it was my duty to keep everyone happy and I would jump into conflicts that weren't mine in an effort to be the peacekeeper. I now realize that no one has the approval of everyone all the time. I now try to find the appropriate balance between being true to myself and being sensitive to others. If I get their approval, great. If not, I don't feel I have failed because I realize they have their perspectives and preferences, and I respect them.

Recognize that you will never be able to please everyone all the time. At the beginning of my career, my boss shared with me his advice on how to win friends and influence people. He said, "Try to please everyone a little, and don't offend anyone a lot." Be happy if you live in congruence with your internal values and don't worry about whether it happens to please everyone around you. Try to be your best self and show concern for others, but recognize that some people will like it and others won't.

Overcome anger

In your attempt to repair and build relationships, you may find some unfinished business in some of your relationships. If you find unresolved anger or hostility, you may need to forgive to move on with your life. Some people think they have dealt with anger when they replace it with dutiful numbness. If you feel numbness, you may need to back out of the numbness and feel the emotions again, work through them, and come to a reconciliation. Ignoring problems doesn't make them go away. You may need your therapist's help to be sure that you appropriately deal with your anger and bring closure to the situation.

Learn how to apply your experiences

Sometimes we learn specific relationship skills, but have difficulty understanding how to apply them in other situations. We may learn to relate well to men in our support group, but not recognize that we can use the same skills with men at work. If you have difficulty relating to men at work, look at how you relate with men in your support group and see if you can transfer those same skills to the work setting. You may be able to tell other men in your support group that you love them, but you may have trouble showing feelings of concern at work. Although you may not want to come right out and say "I love you" to other men at work, you could say, "I'm sorry about your wife's poor health. It must really be tough on you."

Like yourself and spend time with yourself

The first step in building relationships with others is to like yourself. If you don't enjoy being with yourself, others may not enjoy being with you either. Ed Hurst said, "I've noticed in recent years that I actually prefer being alone far more than I ever did before. Sometimes that's because I have finally become my own friend. Other times, it's just to be reflective. For me, this is both time alone and time with Jesus. Although it isn't marked by formal prayer, it is a time when I'm searching my thoughts and asking Him what He thinks of all that I'm thinking and planning."[239]

Learn to give in your relationships

It is difficult to maintain relationships if you are always taking but not giving. Healthy adult relationships are mutually-beneficial, give-and-take relationships where you treat each other as equals. Don't expect to give only when you receive. Think of what you can give without expecting anything in return. Since people reciprocate in different ways, you'll only get frustrated if you try to keep score. If you make others feel good about themselves, then you will feel good about yourself. When you meet someone, try to determine what he or she needs, then fulfill the need as much as you can.

A good way to grow is to lift another person. Be the strong one for others who are weaker than you. Rather than always looking for someone to be your mentor, become a mentor to others. Be for them the kind of man you wished you had met when you were hurting.

Recognize and avoid dependent relationships

A common misconception is that dependency is love. Different from love, dependency is when you require another individual for your survival. Dependency is beyond the normal need for friendship and intimacy. It is a virtual obsession with another person, where you cannot function without him. You need constant reassurance from him, consistent displays of affection, and large quantities of time.[240] In his book *The Road Less Traveled*, M. Scott Peck explains that people in dependent relationships "are so busy seeking to be loved that they have no energy left to love." He explains that "they tolerate loneliness very poorly. Because of their lack of wholeness they have no real sense of identity, and they define themselves solely by their relationships."[241] Two people really love each other "only when they are quite capable of living without each other but *choose* to live with each other."[242] You may need the help of a therapist to overcome relational dependency.

Recognize and avoid codependent relationships.

In her book *Codependent No More: How to Stop Controlling Others and Start Caring for Yourself*, Melody Beattie describes a codependent person as "one who has let another person's behavior affect him or her, and who is obsessed with controlling that person's behavior."[243] If you find that you are obsessed with controlling another person's behavior, or if someone else is obsessed with controlling your behavior, you are in a codependent relationship. I have a friend who has a very controlling mother who isn't happy unless she is involved in every aspect of his life. In order to grow beyond some of his identity problems, he had to confront his mother about her controlling influence. He had to cut the apron strings and help his mother see how her control affected him negatively. This was a difficult process, but very rewarding for him.

Recognize and avoid obsessive friendships

When you are needy, it is easy to become obsessive in your friendships. Obsessive relationships are marked by jealousy, possessiveness, and exclusiveness. If you find that you are preoccupied with a friend and cannot make plans that don't include him, you may need to release your "death grip" on him before you lose him as a friend. Keep your friendships within the bounds of moderation.

I used to look for one perfect friend who could meet all my needs. For some reason I thought it had to be an all-or-nothing arrangement and I became jealous if my best friend had friendships with other men. I later learned that I shouldn't expect to get all my needs met by just one man. I need to build friendships with several men to get all my needs met. When I put all my emotional eggs in one basket, I set myself up for devastating hurt when that person doesn't live up to my high expectations. It is better to look to several people for love and affirmation. Each can give me what he is capable of giving, and I can give to them what I am capable of giving as well.

If you try too hard to relate to the other person, you may also find that your own sense of identity becomes lost. It is common for men desperate for relationships to overlook the differences and see only the similarities. In my support groups, I cannot count the number of times I heard comments such as "We are just alike." "We think alike." "We like the same things." "We're soul mates." When I was most desperate in my relationships, I found I would even modify my tastes to match those of the person with whom I was trying to bond. When one of my friends didn't like raisin cookies, I stopped eating them and actually began to detest them. It wasn't until years later that I realized I really *did* like raisin cookies and started eating them again. If you find you are entangled in a dependent, controlling, or obsessive relationship, you may need the help of a therapist to understand and unravel the situation.

To understand more about the issues of dependency, co-dependency, and obsessiveness, read the booklet *Emotional Dependency: A Threat to Close Friendships*, by Lori Thorkelson Rentzel (available through Regeneration Books; see the Organizations section in this book).

Move out of your comfort zone

Building relationships is not always easy. Although you may be afraid at times, have the courage to work on relationships. Remember that *all* men have a certain fear of new relationships and certain difficulty maintaining existing ones. You may need to stretch and exert yourself more with associates at work and with men in your ward to build relationships with them. Spend more time talking with them and be more friendly toward them. You should always be a bit uncomfortable by stretching and extending yourself.

One Sunday in priesthood meeting, when they passed around a sheet for men to help in the nursery, I signed up because I noticed that Steve had already signed up. I had wanted to get to know Steve better, and figured this would be a chance to interact. I stretched with him. I was friendly and tried to make conversation, but he didn't respond much. Although we didn't build much of a friendship then, the experience was a success for me, because I realized that he was as uncomfortable around other men as I am. That gave me the confidence I needed to extend myself with another man in the ward with whom I became good friends.

Be appropriately intimate

Intimacy involves closeness in relationships and sharing of your true self. For hearts to bond, affections must be shared. In building healthy relationships, it is important to understand correct principles of both physical and emotional intimacy.

Physical intimacy

All men have basic emotional needs for affirmation, affection, attention, and approval. If these needs were not met as you grew up, deficits were created, and as you instinctively searched for ways to meet the emotional needs, at some point they became sexualized. The solution now is to back out of the sexual feelings, but not to the point of emotional indifference. You need to find ways to appropriately express your affections.

This can be tricky because male affection is limited in contemporary American culture. While women friends may hug each other upon greeting, men usually shake hands. Two women may even hold hands at particularly emotional times, while it is generally considered taboo for two men to do the same. For some men, this arms-length intimacy is sufficient for their needs, while others wish they could express more affection but are held back by cultural norms. It is interesting to note that when men's defenses are down (such as when they are drunk) or when they are particularly excited (such as at the winning touchdown in the Super Bowl), they tend to be all over each other, hugging and touching. Cultural norms guide a lot of what we do.

Traveling in different countries, it is easy to note different cultural norms that guide the physical expression of intimacy. In some cultures, men show more affection with each other by greeting each other with a kiss or by holding hands. These customs allow men to more easily meet their needs for physical affection and affirmation from other men. In some countries, males spend a great deal of time together in buddy activities. For them, it is not a social taboo to touch another man, to hold hands in particularly emotional moments, or to walk down the street with an arm around the other's shoulder. This level of male companionship can be very healthy if handled appropriately. It may be helpful for you to distinguish between cultural norms and gospel standards of chastity that are the same across all cultures.

When I began to really watch the men around my office, I was surprised to realize I was the least physical man in the office. I began to notice that men touched each other and I tried to follow their lead.

Emotional intimacy

Emotional intimacy includes the sharing of your true self and it increases the more you disclose yourself to others. Because of shame over your attractions, you may have learned to hide your true self from others, and maybe even from yourself. Once you come to understand and appreciate who you really are, you owe it to yourself to share that person with others. When you do, you will be in a position to support each other. Life and love are meaningless if they are not shared and men who find a way to open up with each other are more emotionally healthy.

My friend Todd describes what it felt like when he began opening up to friends: "For the first time in my life, I no longer felt like I was unacceptable because I started to find out that people could know everything about me and still want to be my friend. In fact, through the sharing of deep emotions, I gained some of my closest friends; and I continue to seek such relationships. It seems that the value and impact of the friendship is directly proportional to the emotional investment I make. The more I share and trust, the more sharing and trusting I receive—and I think there is more value in that simple truth than most of the things I learned in college or since."

How to meet your needs for intimacy

All your needs for intimacy will not be met perfectly all the time; there will be some disappointment. Don't become discouraged and stop trying to build relationships because disappointment does not mean rejection. Be confident in the fact that other men give you their time, even though you may wish they would give you more attention or verbal signs of affection. Learn to accept their intangible forms of affirmation. Remember that most men bond by *doing* things rather than *talking* about things. If another man is spending time with you doing things, recognize he is saying that you are worth spending time with. His smile may mean the same as a hug. To better understand how men express themselves, you may read the book *Men are from Mars; Women are from Venus* by John Gray.

Heavenly Father and Jesus Christ

Although we have a variety of friends, many of us search for a special friend with whom we can have a deep, meaningful relationship. We long for a friend who will believe and trust us—someone who understands and accepts us and won't reject us even when he knows our darkest secrets. Many of us search for a friend among the people we see each day, but seldom think that we already have two such friends who are waiting and willing.[244] One is your Heavenly Father and the other is your brother Jesus Christ. Your Heavenly Father already knows your darkest secrets and still loves you. Jesus cares so much about your pain that He gave his very life to take care of the consequences of your sins.

Your Heavenly Father wants you to do what is right so you can be happy. His unconditional love for you doesn't change from day to day depending on whether you made any mistakes that day. He *always* keeps his word and unlike other relationships you may have, He will *always* be there for you. You are the only one that can default in this relationship. There is no need for any defensive detachment from Him because He will never do you wrong. It is the safest relationship you can have. Draw your support and strength from Him. Elder Richard G. Scott explained, "Your Father in Heaven and His Beloved Son love you perfectly. They would not require you to experience a moment more of difficulty than is absolutely needed for your personal benefit or for that of those you love.[245]

Alma taught, "let the affections of thy heart be placed upon the Lord forever" (Alma 37:36). You cannot build a relationship without talking and interacting with the person. If you want a personal, emotional relationship with God, you must spend time talking and interacting with Him. You can do this by praying and listening. President Howard W. Hunter explained, "If prayer is only a spasmodic cry at the time of crisis, then it is utterly selfish, and we come to think of God as a repairman or a service agency to help us only in our emergencies."[246] President David O. McKay said, "When we pray we should have a consciousness that there is something within us which is divine, which is part of the Infinite, which is the offspring of God, and until we can feel that harmony with that Infinite, we have not sensed the power of prayer."[247] If you take the time to pray sincerely with a desire to know and love God, you will come to know Him and know that He loves you. You may wish to read Elder Richard G. Scott's conference address, "Learning to Recognize Answers to Prayer" (*Ensign*, Nov. 1989, pp. 30–32). Remember that your long-term goal is not just to get over your homosexual problems, but to become like your Father in Heaven. The first step in that process is to come to know Him and His attributes of faithfulness and unconditional love.

Your father

It is common for men who experience homosexual attraction to have poor relationships with their fathers. Even if you and your father get along, it is likely that you may not know him very well or particularly enjoy spending time with him. It is important that a boy have a healthy emotional relationship with his father. Even though you may now be an adult, those boyhood needs may still exist and an improved relationship with your father may help fill some of those needs. Even if you have since found a way to meet those needs through another male, you may want to work out things with your father to bring closure to certain unresolved issues. If you and your father have developed a defensive detachment from each other, you may need to understand these defensive mechanisms before you can build a better relationship. (To understand more about defensive detachment, read *Homosexuality: A New Christian Ethic* by Elizabeth R. Moberly.) Reconciling your relationship may require some forgiveness from both sides and acceptance of each other for who you are. Just as you want your father to recognize your worth, you need to respect and honor him.

If your relationship with your father is weak, work diligently but gradually to build it. If you don't have a habit of hugging him, start out gradually or you may scare him away. As I was beginning to extend myself to get closer to my father, I remember an incident when I was leaving his house after a Sunday dinner. After hugging my sisters, I walked up to dad and gave him a hug. It wasn't until I hugged him that I realized that we usually just shake hands. In fact, I couldn't remember the last time we hugged each other. He was stiff, and didn't put his hands on my back. It felt uncomfortable to both of us, but I'm glad that I did it, because it was the beginning of an improved relationship. Today we are closer than we have ever been, and the hugs are natural and plentiful.

Your mother

It is important to have a good relationship with your mother. If there are relationship difficulties, work to resolve them. If your mother is controlling, you may need to confront her about the controlling influence and help her see how it affects you negatively.

Reconciling with your parents

If you have developed a defensive detachment from your parents, you may need to understand your defensive mechanisms before you can establish a connection with them. To understand more about defensive detachment, read _Homosexuality: A New Christian Ethic_ by Elizabeth R. Moberly. Your therapist can also help guide you through these emotional mine fields. To reconcile with your parents, forgive them and accept them for who they are. Chances are the deficits you experienced in childhood were through no conscious choice on their part. If you are carrying grudges, get rid of them. They do no good and only hold you back. Recognize your parents' worth. If you want them to be interested in you, then show interest in them. This can open new lines of communication and emotions can be shared on a deeper level. Don't try to change your parents. Accept and honor them for who they are. Have compassion on them for the pain they have experienced. Learn to relate with them as an adult and not as a child.

Your wife

If you are married, it can be both a blessing and a challenge. It is a blessing because you have a companion who loves you and can be a support to you. It is an additional challenge because you have to care for your wife and perhaps children while you work on your issues, which may take large amounts of time and energy for individual therapy, group therapy, support group meetings, and reading books. At times, these obligations may seem overwhelming, but rather than consider your family a burden, turn it into a strength. The truth is you need your family as much as you need the interactions with other men. You need to keep your life in balance. As you work on new male relationships, you still need to pay attention to your wife and family. The following ideas may help you give priority to them. (If you are not married, consider how the following ideas may apply to your parents or other family members.)

Keep your wife informed about what you are doing. Help her understand why you need to be involved in so many meetings and why you need so much time for interaction with other men. Help her understand how it will help you become a better husband and father. Although you can't divulge confidential details of things discussed in your group meetings, let her know in a general way what goes on in those meetings. Help her feel a part of what you are doing. She needs to have a level of understanding and trust, and that comes from information. If she has no idea what you talk about and what you do, it is likely that her fears will multiply. But when she understands what you are doing and why, she can be a support by encouraging you to go to the meetings. Also, if she knows what things you are working on personally, she can be more helpful in her support and encouragement.

Consider how your wife is affected by your problems. What are her needs? You are not the only one struggling with difficulties because of your attractions. Consider your wife's needs and be as considerate to her as you wish her to be to your needs. She may feel hurt and rejected by your attractions toward other men, and may even feel that she is to blame. Even if she understands the issues intellectually, she may inwardly feel that there was something she could have done. She may feel she could have been more attractive physically or emotionally, in which case she needs your reassurance that she is feminine and has great worth. She may feel betrayed in the marriage, particularly if you have been involved in sexual activity. Have you specifically told her you are sorry that she hurts? You may have to go to significant efforts to reestablish her trust in you and this may be difficult when you are attending many meetings away from home. You may need to volunteer a great deal of information about your activities so there will be no question as to your whereabouts. As you attend meetings and receive therapy, you will come to understand yourself and find ways to deal with your problems. Your wife may need the same help to come to terms with her feelings, hurts, and doubts. She may need counseling herself or may want to join a support group for wives.

As you learn to open up emotionally to men in your group, apply it also to your wife and family. Be open and available to them emotionally. When you are with your wife and family, pay them the full attention they deserve. Be there emotionally as well as physically and make the time count. Remember that you are in a covenant relationship with them.

Be a good father to your children. I find as I interact with my son in being a father to him, not only does it fill his needs, but it also helps me in two ways. First, I feel affirmed in my role as a father in being for him the kind of father I always wanted. Secondly, as I play with him, I am able to relive my childhood vicariously through him and feel through him the connection with my father that I did not feel when I was a child.

Don't compare your relationships with men with your relationship with your wife. The needs involved and the affirmations you receive are different. Because these new male relationships fill needs that have long been unmet, they may be very fulfilling and some men mistakenly begin to think that these relationships are more important than their marriage relationship. Men in your support group will be able to relate to your feelings better than your wife can, simply because they are male, because they are going through the same experiences as you are, and because you share more information with them. Appreciate your male friends, but don't let them take priority over your wife. Remember your wife is the one who will always be there for you and you are in a covenant relationship with her that cannot simply be put aside. Some men also try to compare sexual experiences with men with the sexual experiences they have had with their wives. This is an unfair and unnecessary comparison. Since illicit sex with a man is counterfeit love, Satan is anxious for it to be intense and seem fulfilling. But like illegal drugs, it produces an abnormal high that does not last.

If you do not yet have a wife

If you are not yet married, you may wonder if you will ever marry. Although marriage is an important goal, don't make it your immediate, short-term goal. Speaking in a general conference, President Gordon B. Hinckley counseled, "Marriage should not be viewed as a therapeutic step to solve problems such as homosexual inclinations or practices, which first should clearly be overcome with a firm and fixed determination never to slip to such practices again."[248] Getting married will *not* solve your current homosexual problems, and in many cases may only intensify them. Work first on resolving your immediate problems and on developing a secure sense of self and male identity.

Even if marriage does not seem like an option to you now, keep an open mind about it. I personally know several men who thought they would never marry in this life. Over the years, however, they resolved their homosexual problems, found themselves more attracted to women, and the day came that they married and are now happily raising families. Brad wrote, "As my self-confidence increases, and my relationship with my father and other men improves, SSA continues to diminish in strength. I now find myself less and less attracted to men, they, now being the familiar. A curious interest in women is developing. It is a new phenomenon in my life, strange and interesting to experience, as I continue to step forward with faith as my guide. Women are now the unfamiliar and attraction occurs to that with which we are unfamiliar."[249] Don't get married until you feel you are ready, and if you listen to the Holy Ghost, you will know when the time is right.

Other men

Every man has legitimate emotional and social needs that should be met through loving, validating relationships with other men. Elizabeth Moberly wrote, "Homosexuality is the kind of problem that needs to be solved through relationships. The solution to same-sex deficits is to be sought through the medium of one or more non-sexual relationships with members of the same sex. . . . It is the provision of good same-sex relationships that helps to meet unmet same-sex needs, heal defects in the relational capacity, and in this way, forward the healing process."[250] Relationships or social contacts with women are not the solution to your problems, since contact with women does nothing to fulfill same-gender needs. Healthy relationships with women, however, may support your sexual identity and encourage appreciation of the opposite sex.

In his book *Desires in Conflict*, Joe Dallas wrote, "Relationships are your most valuable resources. You've got to know that you are significant to somebody else, appreciated for your gifts and uniqueness. And you've got to know that you have people to lean on, people interested in your life and rooting for you as you grow."[251] An important benefit of friendships is the effect they have on your self-perception. They can correct false concepts you may have grown up with.

Everybody needs a buddy. In his book *The Hazards of Being Male*, Herb Goldberg explained that although men need close male relationships, "many men have come to view the need for a buddy as a remnant of immaturity, or an adolescent need."[252] But through your openness and friendliness, you can help another man come out of his emotional shell and become your buddy. Dr. Goldberg explained, "the capacity for what I term 'buddyship' is a genuine social skill, an area of competence that needs to be learned. I have chosen the word 'buddyship' because of its connotations of youth and of spontaneity. This, combined with adult maturity contains the potential for the ultimate in masculine friendship."[253] If you want to learn more about developing a buddyship, read *The Hazards of Being Male: Surviving the Myth of Masculine Privilege* by Herb Goldberg, particularly chapter nine.

Consider the following suggestions as you develop relationships with other men:

Don't judge other men. Allow others the same consideration you ask of them. I used to judge other men by external criteria (how they looked, how they dressed, how they carried themselves), and I thought they judged me by the same superficial standards. I expected that other men would reject me if I wasn't properly dressed or if I wasn't good-looking. But I have come to realize that most men don't care how attractive I am. Although these criteria fit in the gay world, they don't in the world at large.

Don't make sweeping generalizations of other men. Although you may have experienced some men as insensitive or uncaring, not all men are. On the other hand, don't expect that all men will share your zeal for male bonding. Recognize the limitations in each person and accept what each has to give.

Don't feel rejected if others don't recognize your needs. The truth is that most men don't recognize the developmental needs in others. You also may have created such a good exterior that they feel you don't need them or even want them. (There's the defensive detachment again.)

Be verbal. Comments like "nice shot," "great-looking suit," or "we missed you at the game last week" will show your genuine interest.

Diversify. A healthy way of investing financially is to diversify. That way, if some of your investments go bad, the others that turn out good will carry you through. The same is true with relationships. Not every relationship you try to develop will flourish, so don't be discouraged when one doesn't turn out the way you wished it would. Spread yourself out and work on several relationships at once.

Group relationships

A good way to ease into relationships with other men is to get involved with groups. The first and easiest group may be your support or therapy group. As you build relationships with these men, you will gain confidence in your ability to develop and sustain relationships and then be ready to branch out to other groups of men who do not struggle with homosexual attraction. You may need to take some initiative to find groups of men that come together for some purpose you are interested in. This may be a community or ward softball team, a reading club, a group of hobbyists, or a computer club. Look through the phone book or a listing of community organizations. You may want to join a service organization such as the Rotary Club or groups that provide services to the disadvantaged.

The most important group to be involved with is your priesthood quorum. If you feel distant from the men in your quorum, it may be your defensive detachment. If you feel they are not interested in you, it may be because you don't show much interest in them. The priesthood quorum is God's established plan for brotherhood and bonding, and it is important that you be involved in the quorum. No other group, including your support group, should take priority over the quorum. If your quorum is not functioning as it should, take the initiative to suggest activities and projects that will bring the quorum together and develop good relationships. As a community of Saints, we must be "willing to bear one another's burdens, that they may be light; yea, and are willing to mourn with those that mourn; yea, and comfort those that stand in need of comfort. . . ." (Mosiah 18:8-9).

Don't give up if relationships don't form immediately. Your active presence in the group sends a message. Some men may not respond immediately, but if you keep trying, eventually your investment of time and emotional involvement will pay off.

Individual relationships

Developing relationships with men in groups can help you have the courage to develop individual relationships. This may grow out of the group as you relate with some of the men individually or you may develop nurturing relationships with other key people in your life—family members, your bishop, your quorum president, or a man in the ward or at work who is accessible and warm. To be in a trusting, intimate relationship with a man who does not experience homosexual attractions is perhaps the most healing thing you can do.

For me, the ultimate challenge was to develop relationships with straight men to whom I was initially attracted. Sure, it took courage to approach them and get to know them, but the rewards were certainly worth it. As I came to understand the mystery of these formerly distant men, my attractions toward them disappeared. As Joseph Nicolosi explained, "While aesthetic appreciation for the man's good looks and masculine qualities may always be present, it will become increasingly evident that sexual fantasies do not fit within the mutually respectful friendship. As the [person] experiences increasing acceptance and familiarity, over time this grows into identification, and the original sexual feelings naturally diminish. This transformational shift from *sexual to fraternal* . . . is the essential healing experience of male homosexuality."[254] I used to look away when I saw an attractive man so I could avoid the tempting feelings, and I think that was necessary in the beginning to break my old compulsive cycles. But now I can look upon an attractive man and reframe the significance of what I see. I see him (and myself) as a child of God and realize that he could be my friend.

I used to divide the entire male world into two categories: those who had homosexual attractions and those who did not. Whenever I met someone, I used to try to figure out which category he fit in. Somehow I thought I needed to know so I could know if I could trust him and relate with him. Now it is not important to me to know because I can build relationships with all men.

Scriptural examples of good relationships

Perhaps the most unselfish friendship we read about in scripture was that of Jonathan and David. Jonathan was the son of King Saul and was the heir apparent to the throne, but it was given to David. Although Jonathan could have regarded David as his rival, they developed a most impressive friendship. The biblical account says "the soul of Jonathan was knit with the soul of David, and Jonathan loved him as his own soul" (1 Samuel 18:1). Accounts in 1 Samuel 13–23 describe the love these two men felt for each other. David's lamentation when Jonathan and King Saul were killed is one of the most beautiful of Bible poems (see 2 Samuel 1).

For further reading

Healing the Shame that Binds You by John Bradshaw.

Your Inner Child of the Past by W. Hugh Missildine, M.D.

The Road Less Traveled: A New Psychology of Love, Traditional Values and Spiritual Growth by M. Scott Peck.

Dealing With the Dad of Your Past by Maureen Rank.

How Will I Tell My Mother?: A True Story of One Man's Battle with Homosexuality and AIDS by Jerry Arterburn

Quality Friendship: The Risks and Rewards by Gary Inrig.

If the Gospel Is True, Why Do I Hurt So Much?: Help for Dysfunctional Latter-day Saint Families by Carroll Hofeling Morris.

When Victims Marry by Don and Jan Frank.

Chapter Fifteen

Spirituality

Of the hundreds of men I have met in support groups, I have been impressed that many of them are deeply spiritual men. Satan also recognizes this spiritual sensitivity and tries to use it against them. Tragically, their emotional needs are misdirected to homosexual feelings which divert them from developing higher levels of spirituality. They sometimes fall away from the Church all together and thus Satan has robbed the priesthood from the elect. Because the armies of hell are waging their final battle, we must be strong, have faith, and draw on the powers of heaven.

This chapter addresses the importance of spirituality in your efforts to resolve your homosexual problems. It treats basic gospel principles such as faith, the atonement, repentance, and forgiveness. The chapter then addresses the influences of the Holy Ghost and Satan and discusses other gospel subjects that relate to your ability to succeed in resolving your struggles.

The need for spirituality

Spirituality plays a major role in your ability to resolve your homosexual problems. Frank Worthen, a pioneer in Christian groups that minister to people with homosexual attractions, explained, "Our deliverance from homosexuality comes from a Person, rather than a method."[255] Commitment to and faith in Jesus Christ is the key to applying the healing power of the atonement in your life. Facing homosexual problems will force you to answer one of the most basic questions of life: Where does the power come from to deliver us from human sin and confusion?

Faith in Jesus Christ

The first principle of the gospel is faith in the Lord Jesus Christ (see Articles of Faith 1:4). King Benjamin declared, "Salvation cometh to none . . . except it be through repentance and faith on the Lord Jesus Christ" (Mosiah 3:12). Do you believe that Christ can save you? If

Christ is powerful to save you, can He change you? With faith, Christ can heal you not only physically, but also mentally and emotionally. Christ has the power not only to change you personally but also to heal the wounds of sin. President Ezra Taft Benson taught, "It matters not what is our lack or our weakness or our insufficiency. His gifts and powers are sufficient to overcome them all."[256] The Lord has promised, "And if men come unto me I will show unto them their weakness. I give unto men weakness that they may be humble; and my grace is sufficient for all men that humble themselves before me; for if they humble themselves before me, and have faith in me, *then will I make weak things become strong unto them*" (Ether 12:27, italics added). This is an amazing promise! The very source of our troubles can be changed into a strength and source of power. The Lord says that his grace is sufficient for *all* men, even those who have homosexual problems. (For an excellent discussion on how healing comes through Jesus Christ, you may read Elder Richard G. Scott's conference address "To Be Healed," *Ensign*, May 1994, pp. 7–9.)

Elder Richard G. Scott taught, "To produce fruit, your trust in the Lord must be more powerful and enduring than your confidence in your own personal feelings and experience. To exercise faith is to trust that the Lord knows what He is doing with you and that He can accomplish it for your eternal good even though you cannot understand how He can possibly do it."[257] There is nothing two men can't do if one of them is God. As Elder Robert E. Wells reminded us, "Personal peace and our level of spirituality will increase as we focus on studying and thinking about Christ every day; by loving and thanking Christ more each day for his atoning sacrifice. . . . In spite of all the problems in the world today, peace can come to the hearts of each of us as we follow the Savior."[258]

Equally yoked together

Christ wants to help us. He pleads with us, "Come unto me, all ye that labour and are heavy laden, and I will give you rest. Take my yoke upon you, and learn of me; for I am meek and lowly in heart: and ye shall find rest unto your souls. For my yoke is easy, and my burden is light" (Matthew 11:28–30). He offers us a yoke, not to encumber us, but to help us. When you are in the yoke with Christ, it means that Christ is pulling right along with you. And, in fact, when you don't have the strength to pull your share, He will make up the difference. What a comforting assurance! All you have to do is your very best. If you try with all your strength, then Christ will make up the difference. (To better understand this beautiful concept, I strongly recommend you read the book *Believing Christ* by Stephen E. Robinson.)

The Book of Mormon prophet Alma taught, "And he shall go forth, suffering pains and afflictions and temptations of every kind; and this that the word might be fulfilled which saith he will take upon him the pains and the sicknesses of his people. And he will take upon him death, that he may loose the bands of death which bind his people; and he will take upon him their infirmities, that his bowels may be filled with mercy, according to the flesh, that he may know according to the flesh how to succor his people according to their infirmities. Now the Spirit knoweth all things; nevertheless the Son of God suffereth according to the flesh that he might take upon him the sins of his people, that he might blot out their transgressions according to the power of his deliverance; and now behold, this is the testimony which is in me" (Alma 7:11–13).

The atonement

The Bible Dictionary explains the atonement: "The word describes the setting 'at one' of those who have been estranged, and denotes the reconciliation of man to God. Sin is the cause of the estrangement, and therefore the purpose of atonement is to correct or overcome the consequences of sin."[259] Jesus Christ "came into the world . . . to be crucified for the world, and to bear the sins of the world, and to sanctify the world, and to cleanse it from all unrighteousness; that through him all might be saved" (D&C 76:41–42). In the book *Gospel Principles*, we read, "The great sacrifice he made to pay for our sins and overcome death is called the *Atonement*. It is the most important event that has ever occurred in the history of mankind."[260] Because of the atonement, all mankind will be resurrected. The atonement also makes it possible for us to repent of our sins and be forgiven. Christ made this sacrifice for us freely because He loves us. The atonement applies to each of us as we try to improve little by little and overcome our challenges In addition to the sins we commit, the atonement can also compensate for things that are committed against us—the wounds we suffer as a result of another's sins or misdeeds. Thus the atonement has the power not only to heal us of the sins we commit against others but also of the impact of sins committed against us. It can heal all inadequacy and mortal sorrow regardless of its cause. There is no problem for which the atonement is not sufficient.

One of the greatest healing experiences for me was to gain a greater understanding of the atonement and a deeper appreciation for it. For me, that began by reading two small books by Stephen E. Robinson, *Believing Christ* and *Following Christ*. Such a small investment in time produced a tremendous dividend toward my eternal future. It is critical to understand the atonement and our role in it. You may also wish to read the article "Beauty for Ashes: The Atonement of Jesus Christ" by Bruce C. Hafen (*Ensign*, April 1990, pp. 7–13).

Repentance

Faith in Christ naturally leads to repentance. The Bible Dictionary gives the following definition of repentance: "The Greek word of which this is the translation denotes a change of mind, i.e., a fresh view about God, about oneself, and about the world. Since we are born into conditions of mortality, repentance comes to mean a turning of the heart and will to God, and a renunciation of sin to which we are naturally inclined. Without this there can be no progress in the things of the soul's salvation, for all accountable persons are stained by sin, and must be cleansed in order to enter the kingdom of heaven. Repentance is not optional for salvation; it is a commandment of God. . . ."[261]

President Ezra Taft Benson taught that "repentance means more than simply a reformation of behavior. Many men and women in the world demonstrate great willpower and self-discipline in overcoming bad habits and the weaknesses of the flesh. Yet at the same time they give no thought to the Master, sometimes even openly rejecting Him. Such changes of behavior, even if in a positive direction, do not constitute true repentance. Faith in the Lord Jesus Christ is the foundation upon which sincere and meaningful repentance must be built. If we truly seek to put away sin, we must first look to Him who is the Author of our salvation."[262]

What do you need to repent of?

Joe Dallas wrote, "You never asked for homosexual attractions. You never decided to incorporate them into your sexual makeup. Given the choice, you might have picked any number of problems before choosing this one. As for the conflicts creating your homosexuality, we know you didn't choose those, either. . . . [Y]ou didn't choose to respond to early events in a given way, and you certainly didn't have anything to say about those responses when they became sexual. You are, in many ways, a victim of circumstance. As far as the development of your attractions to the same sex is concerned, you're blameless. God does not and will not hold that against you. It is not a sin to be homosexually inclined. It's what you *do* with those inclinations that condemns or commends you."[263]

The steps of repentance

The book *Gospel Principles* identifies the steps of repentance as follows.[264]

Recognize your sins. You don't need to repent of same-sex attractions over which you have no control, but you do need to repent of conscious homosexual expressions.

Feel sorrow for your sins. President Ezra Taft Benson taught, "Godly sorrow is a gift of the Spirit. It is a deep realization that our actions have offended our Father and our God. It is the sharp and keen awareness that our behavior caused the Savior, He who knew no sin, even the greatest of all, to endure agony and suffering. Our sins caused Him to bleed at every pore. This very real mental and spiritual anguish is what the scriptures refer to as having 'a broken heart and a contrite spirit.'"[265]

Forsake your sins. Alma counseled, "Yea, I say unto you come and fear not, and lay aside every sin, which easily doth beset you, which doth bind you down to destruction, yea, come and go forth, and show unto your God that ye are willing to repent of your sins and enter into a covenant with him to keep his commandments. . . ." (Alma 7:15).

Confess your sins. This is discussed later in the chapter.

Make restitution. As much as possible, you must we must make right any wrong that you have done.

Forgive others. This is discussed in the next section.

Keep the commandments of God. True repentance means that you not only ask for forgiveness of past sins, but that you are willing to give them up in the present and the future. You may have favorite sins that you have used to escape painful situations or gain a certain amount of temporary satisfaction. You must recognize these "comforting sins" (now that's an oxymoron!) and be willing to lay them aside. (See Alma 7:15.) When you sincerely repent, you turn to Christ and don't look back. Homosexual behavior is no longer an option for you.

For excellent counsel on repenting and overcoming bad habits, you may read Elder Richard G. Scott's conference address "Finding the Way Back" (*Ensign*, May 1990, pp. 74–76). President Spencer W. Kimball's book *The Miracle of Forgiveness* is also very helpful.

Forgiveness

Ask to be forgiven

"Behold, he who has repented of his sins, the same is forgiven, and I, the Lord, remember them no more" (D&C 58:42). To me, this is one of the sweetest verses of scripture. It inspires hope and tells of the love our Heavenly Father and Jesus Christ have for us.

President Harold B. Lee explained how to know when you are forgiven. "If the time comes when you have done all that you can to repent of your sins, . . . then you will want that confirming answer as to whether or not the Lord has accepted of you. In your soul-searching, if you seek for and you find that peace of conscience, by that token you may know that the Lord has accepted of your repentance."[266]

Forgive others

The most important aspect of being forgiven is to forgive others who may have done injustices to you. Some may be perceived injustices, such as if you felt your father should have been less authoritarian or if you felt another male should have been more accepting. Others injustices may have been real and caused you great harm, such as cases of rape or other abuse. But regardless of the reality or the seriousness of the injustice, you need to forgive because withholding forgiveness can be a great hindrance to your healing. Regardless of the hurt you feel, release them from the penalty you would impose on them and leave it in the hands of God. The Lord explained, "I, the Lord, will forgive whom I will forgive, but of you it is required to forgive all men" (D&C

64:10). And he gives this warning, "But if ye forgive not men their trespasses, neither will your Fathers forgive your trespasses" (Matthew 6:15). An unforgiving heart is a serious problem. "Wherefore, I say unto you, that ye ought to forgive one another; for he that forgiveth not his brother his trespasses standeth condemned before the Lord; for there remaineth in him the greater sin" (D&C 64:9).

Roderick Linton wrote, "To have a forgiving heart is to see the world in a different light. It is to forsake the tendency to judge, condemn, exclude, or hate any human soul. A forgiving heart seeks to love and to be patient with imperfection. The forgiving heart understands that we are all in need of the atonement of Jesus Christ."[267]

President Joseph F. Smith taught, "It is extremely hurtful for any [person] holding the gift of the Holy Ghost to harbor a spirit of envy, or malice, or retaliations, or intolerance toward or against his fellow man. We ought to say in our hearts, 'Let God judge between me and thee, but as for me, I will forgive.' I want to say to you that Latter-day Saints who harbor a feeling of unforgiveness in their souls are more censurable than the one who has sinned against them."[268] Forgiving others frees us from anger and disappointment. It also opens the way for God to forgive us. Rather than blaming others, ask yourself what you learned from the experience. Ultimately, that is the more important eternal question.

Forgiveness and trust

If you are guilty of wrongdoing, it may take time to reestablish trust with your wife, parents, or friends. Trust is like a bank account that is built up over years of trustworthy experiences. When questionable experiences happen, you can rely on the high balance in the account. But when that trust is broken, the balance may drop—in some cases all the way to zero. Forgiveness means that they don't close the account, but allow you to build the account balance back up by showing time and time again that you are worthy of their trust. To do that, you may need to offer generous explanation as to your actions and whereabouts as you work to re-establish higher levels of trust. Trusting and forgiving are not the same thing. It is always appropriate to forgive, but may not be appropriate for others to trust you again right away.

Confession

Although God already knows our sins, we need to own up to them and admit that we have problems. Admitting problems and accepting responsibility for them is the first step in solving them. "By this ye may know if a man repenteth of his sins—behold, he will confess them and forsake them" (D&C 58:43). ". . . I, the Lord, forgive sins unto those who confess their sins before me and ask forgiveness" (D&C 64:7). Sexual sins, in particular, thrive in the darkness of secrecy and denial. The first step to freedom is to bring the sins to light. Confession shows humility toward the Lord. It shows you know your actions were wrong and you are willing to do all you can to make up for them.

Confession is a necessary step in the process of repentance. All sins should be confessed to the Lord, and serious sins should be confessed to your bishop or branch president. President Spencer W. Kimball explained, "The confession of [one's] major sins to a proper Church authority is one of those requirements made by the Lord. These sins include adultery, fornication, other sexual transgressions, and other sins of comparable seriousness. This procedure of confession assures proper controls and protection for the Church and its people and sets the feet of the transgressor on the path of true repentance. Many offenders in their shame and pride have satisfied their consciences, temporarily at least, with a few silent prayers to the Lord and rationalized that this was sufficient confession of their sins. 'But I have confessed my sin to my Heavenly Father,' they will insist, 'and that is all that is necessary.' This is not true where a major sin is involved. Then two sets of forgiveness are required to bring peace to the transgressor—one from the proper authorities of the Lord's Church, and one from the Lord himself."[269]

You may be embarrassed to talk with your bishop about homosexual behavior. But remember you are not the only sinner in your ward and the bishop has likely heard far worse tales than those you will tell him. Forgiveness cannot come without proper confession to the appropriate Church authorities. If you participate in a support group and disclose a misdeed to the group, it does not take the place of a proper confession to the appropriate priesthood leader.

Bishops are appointed to be common judges in Israel (see D&C 107:72–76) and have power and resources far beyond their personal experience. Bishops are given the gift of discernment (see D&C 46:27).

Although they are loving men who sincerely want to do what is right, remember they are also imperfect, human men who have their own opinions and perspectives that come from their experiences in life. Be tolerant and understanding of them just as you hope for compassion and understanding from them.

It was a great experience when I admitted my homosexual struggles to my bishop. We talked for two hours about my feelings and the drives behind my attractions. He was surprisingly understanding and willing to learn about it. We talked about gender identity and the need for male relationships. He asked about my relationship with my wife and encouraged me to build it stronger. Initially, he was concerned about my therapist and the support group until we talked about it and he understood better how they are helping me. Finally, during the last half hour we talked about my actions. He put me on informal probation and set up weekly interviews with me. He expressed his love for me and thanked me for voluntarily confessing to him. It felt good to have finally gotten things off my chest. I couldn't have asked for a more helpful experience.

Satan's influence

Satan is anxious to deceive even the most elect. The fullness of times also means that the fullness of evil is on the earth. Elder Dallin H. Oaks wrote, "[Satan] seeks to undermine the principle of individual accountability, to persuade us to misuse our sacred powers of procreation, to discourage marriage and childbearing by worthy men and women, and to confuse what it means to be male or female."[270] Elder Russell M. Nelson warned, "[W]e need to remember that the adversary sponsors a cunning plan of his own. It invariably attacks God's first commandment for husband and wife to beget children. It tempts with tactics that include infidelity, unchastity, and other abuses of procreative power. Satan's band would trumpet choice but mute accountability. Nevertheless, his capacity has long been limited, 'for he knew not the mind of God' (Moses 4:6)."[271]

Take comfort in the fact that Satan cannot force us to do evil. We are free to choose Satan's way of captivity and death or to choose God's way of liberty and eternal life (see 2 Nephi 2:27). The Prophet Joseph Smith taught that Satan has "power over us only as we permit him."[272]

James E. Faust explained, "Certainly he can tempt and he can deceive, but he has no authority over us which we do not give him."[273] Don't befriend Satan or his lies; steer a course that is comfortably within the safety zone.

The Holy Ghost

The Holy Ghost can help you understand things you could not otherwise understand. Draw on the Holy Ghost to get insight on resolving your problems and guidance through every step of the way. President James E. Faust taught, "By the power and gift of the Holy Ghost, we can know what to do and what not to do to bring happiness and peace to our lives."[274] The Holy Ghost can be your constant companion (see D&C 121:46).

You may have a battle raging within you. A part of you may want to respond sexually to the homosexual feelings within, but something else within reminds you of the moral principles you have always believed and points you back to the gospel. Which do you listen to? They both may feel right, but they are at odds with each another. This battle is one of Satan's most clever tricks. He wants you to lose hope because he knows that disbelief will trap you in your homosexual problems. Writing about homosexuality in *A Letter to a Friend*, President Spencer W. Kimball explained, "There are two forces working with every individual—one is the spirit of evil, the powers of darkness with a desire to enslave and destroy. . . . The other influence is the Spirit of the Lord striving to lift and inspire and build and save. If one lives all of the commandments of the Lord, then he has the power to withstand the temptations of the devil. If he yields to the evil one, then he gets weaker and weaker until he is unable to cope with the strength of the powers that afflict him."[275] He further explained, "Now let us assure you that you are not permanently trapped in this unholy practice if you will exert yourself. Though it is like an octopus with numerous tentacles to drag you to your tragedy, the sin is curable and you may totally recover from its tentacles."[276]

When this battle rages, listen carefully to distinguish Satan's influences from the Light of Christ within you. Although the whisperings of Satan may feel natural, they will steer you away from the gospel, from truth, and from peace. They may give you momentary gratification but no lasting joy or peace. President Spender W. Kimball said, "No one . . . was ever sublimely happy unless he was righteous. There are temporary satisfactions and camouflaged situations for the moment, but permanent, total happiness can come only through cleanliness and worthiness."[277] Satan's biggest lie is that you are born a homosexual and cannot change and thus he tries to lead you "carefully away down to hell" (see 2 Nephi 28:21). On the other hand, the whisperings of the Holy Ghost will uplift and inspire hope. They will always support gospel truths and will lead you to eternal joy. The art of listening takes concentration and effort, but it is worth it because when you listen to the Holy Ghost you can learn things that are vital to your salvation.

There is always hope

Moroni tells us that despair comes because of iniquity (see Moroni 10:22) and the greater the iniquity, the greater the sense of despair and hopelessness. One of Satan's tactics is to persuade a person who has transgressed that there is no hope of forgiveness. But there is always hope because of the gospel of Jesus Christ "which is quick and powerful, which shall divide asunder all the cunning and the snares and the wiles of the devil, and lead the man of Christ in a strait and narrow course . . . [to] the kingdom of heaven" (Helaman 3:29-30). We are saved by hope and the Lord Jesus Christ is our hope (see Romans 8:24 and 1 Timothy 1:1).

Hope is a great incentive to repentance. If you have made wrong choices and find yourself in a vicious habit, remember that because of the atonement there is a way out. Elder Russell M. Nelson said, "Each one who resolves to climb that steep road to recovery must gird up for the fight of a lifetime. But a lifetime is a prize well worth the price. This challenge uniquely involves the will, and the will can prevail. Healing doesn't come after the first attempt to change. The road to recovery must be followed firmly, bearing in mind that it often takes as long to recover as it did to get to the place you want to recover from. But correct choices can cure if they are made consistently and persistently."[278]

Live the gospel

Peace of mind comes from living your life in harmony with gospel principles. You cannot be content when you live differently from what you believe. C. S. Lewis wrote, "the right direction leads not only to peace but to knowledge. When a man is getting better, he understands more and more clearly the evil that is still left in him. When a man is getting worse, he understands his own badness less and less. A moderately bad man knows he is not very good: a thoroughly bad man thinks he is all right. This is common sense, really. You understand sleep when you are awake, not while you are sleeping. . . . You can understand the nature of drunkenness when you are sober, not when you are drunk. Good people know about both good and evil: bad people do not know about either."[279]

A mighty change of heart

After I had been in therapy for a while, had read extensively, and participated in support groups, I felt I had made good progress. I had unloaded some childhood baggage, had my behavior under control, and was growing emotionally. But somehow that wasn't enough. I kept thinking about Alma's crucial questions, "have ye spiritually been born of God? Have ye received his image in your countenances? Have ye experienced this mighty change in your hearts?" (Alma 5:14). When King Benjamin taught the people, they responded by saying, "Yea, we believe all the words which thou hast spoken unto us; and also, we know of their surety and truth, because of the Spirit of the Lord Omnipotent, which has wrought a mighty change in us, or in our hearts, that we have no more disposition to do evil, but to do good continually" (Mosiah 5:2). I wanted to feel that way myself. I wanted to reach the state where I had no more disposition to do evil. I wanted a change of heart. So I studied about the atonement and the grace of God. Great things can happen in therapy, but the ultimate healing comes through the power of the Savior.

Some people know the principles of the gospel in their heads, but don't feel them in their hearts. A key to making profound changes in your life is to move the gospel from your head to your heart. Many scriptures talk about change originating in the heart. A mental change, such as gaining new knowledge and changing perceptions, is important but not as critical as a change of the heart. Once you understand things in your mind, you still need to feel them in your heart and soul. A change of mind can come of yourself, but a change of heart comes from God. Although learning self-management and behavioral principles can certainly be helpful, the ultimate goal is the spiritual journey that ends in a change of heart.

President David O. McKay said, "No man can sincerely resolve to apply in his daily life the teachings of Jesus of Nazareth without sensing a change in his whole being. The phrase 'born again' has a deeper significance than what many people attach to it. This *changed feeling* may be indescribable, *but it is real.*"[280] To gain eternal life, there must be a rebirth and transformation. Alma taught that all mankind "must be born again; yea, born of God, changed from their carnal and fallen state, to a state of righteousness, being redeemed of God, becoming his sons and daughters; and thus they become new creatures. . . ." (Mosiah 27:25–26).

President Ezra Taft Benson taught, "The Lord works from the inside out. The world works from the outside in." He continued, "The world would mold men by changing their environment. Christ changes men, who then change their environment. The world would shape human behavior, but Christ can change human nature."[281]

Having a mighty change of heart and "no more disposition to do evil but to do good continually" does not mean that you'll never make a mistake again. We all struggle to overcome our carnal natures. Stephen Robinson explained, "That our disposition is *good* is proven by the fact that when we occasionally act otherwise, we feel bad about it, repent, and return to our previous heading toward righteousness. Like a compass needle that may swing this way or that but always comes again to point north, so are the believers who may make this or that temporary misstep but always correct their course and return to their original heading. That is a clear disposition to do good. 'The mighty change' is a change of heart, a change of desires, and a change of disposition concerning our goals. It is not a complete victory of the Fall or over our carnal natures all at once."[282]

The heart is the seat of your emotions, but it is also the house of the Spirit. Emotions don't have the calming and directing influence of the Spirit; they easily turn carnal. Work to keep the Spirit resident in your heart to guide and temper your emotions. "Cast away from you all your transgressions, whereby ye have transgressed; and make you a new heart and a new spirit. . . ." (Ezekiel 18:31). This is a process of daily renewal to keep our hearts clean, aligned, and properly directed by the Spirit. (You may wish to read "A Mighty Change of Heart" by President Ezra Taft Benson, *Ensign*, October 1989, pp. 2–5.)

In the Beatitudes, we read, "And blessed are all they who do hunger and thirst after righteousness, for they shall be filled with the Holy Ghost" (3 Nephi 12:6). Elder H. Burke Peterson explained, "The scripture does not say 'blessed are the righteous for they shall be filled.' That's obvious. But the scripture says blessed are they who want to be—blessed are they who want more than anything else to be righteous."[283] You can be filled with the Holy Ghost—even in the midst of difficulties.

Pride

In a general conference address, President Ezra Taft Benson spoke about pride. He said, "Pride is essentially competitive in nature. We pit our will against God's. When we direct our pride toward God, it is in the spirit of 'my will and not thine be done'. . . . The proud cannot accept the authority of God giving direction to their lives. They pit their perceptions of truth against God's great knowledge. . . . The proud wish God would agree with them. They aren't interested in changing their opinions to agree with God's."[284] He further explained, "Disobedience is essentially a prideful power struggle against someone in authority over us. It can be a parent, a priesthood leader, a teacher, or ultimately God. A proud person hates the fact that someone is above him. He thinks this lowers his position. Selfishness is one of the more common faces of pride. 'How everything affects me' is the center of all that matters—self-conceit, self-pity, worldly self-fulfillment, self-gratification, and self-seeking."[285] The antidote for pride is humility, meekness, and submissiveness. Alma reminded us, "And now I would that ye should be humble, and be submissive and gentle; easy to be entreated; full of patience and long-suffering; being temperate in all things; being diligent in keeping the commandments of God at all times; asking for whatsoever things ye stand in need, both spiritual and temporal; always returning thanks unto God for whatsoever things ye do receive" (Alma 7:23).

A friend of mine never sought the help of a therapist because he was afraid confidentiality could be broken and someone would find out about his homosexual problems. His pride and concern for outward appearances got in the way of getting the help he needed to resolve his problems.

Submitting to the Lord

Do you accept life on the Lord's terms or do you insist that things be on your terms? King Benjamin taught, "For the natural man is an enemy to God . . . and will be, forever and ever, unless he yields to the enticings of the Holy Spirit, and putteth off the natural man and becometh a saint through the atonement of Christ the Lord, and becometh as a child, submissive, meek, humble, patient, full of love, willing to submit to all things which the Lord seeth fit to inflict upon him, even as a child doth submit to his father" (Mosiah 3:19). Being submissive and humble means that we surrender ourselves to God's terms. We must give up everything to Him. Half promises only result in half successes.

President Ezra Taft Benson explained, "Men and women who turn their lives over to God will discover that He can make a lot more out of their lives than they can. He will deepen their joys, expand their vision, quicken their minds, strengthen their muscles, lift their spirits, multiply their blessings, increase their opportunities, comfort their souls, raise up friends, and pour out peace."[286]

President Howard W. Hunter warned of the consequences if we do not submit to the Lord. "Indifference to the Savior or failure to keep the commandments of God brings about insecurity, inner turmoil, and contention. These are the opposites of peace. Peace can come to an individual only by an unconditional surrender to him who is the Prince of peace and who has the power to confer peace."[287]

Randy Walters wrote, "For several years my fear of rejection kept me from reaching out for help. I continued to use my own sheer willpower to try and slay my enemy. I was convinced that with enough righteous living I could do it on my own. Yet as much as I tried to eradicate my SSA [same-sex attraction], it would not die. Only after I humbled myself and acknowledged that I could no longer trust in my arm of flesh did I receive the help I needed once I surrendered my will to the Lord."[288]

In daily prayer, admit to God that you don't have the power to overcome your problems by yourself. Ask Him to provide the additional help you need. My friend Todd wrote, "I believe that we have a loving Heavenly Father who is deeply concerned for our welfare, and when we ask Him to help us with a problem, He helps. The help can sometimes be frustrating, because we must often wait for the help to come in His way rather than ours; and often the process to achieve the desired goal can be lengthy. I believe that the waiting period is often to help us develop and exercise faith and . . . almost always provide some learning experience."

Spiritual activity

Be spiritually active, which includes more than just going to meetings. Adversity either makes us complacent so we drift away from the Church and what is important to us, or it makes us dig in and grow closer to things of eternal worth. What you have accomplished in the past matters little compared to who you are today. If you have served a mission or accomplished great things in the past, congratulations! But what are you doing now? If ten years after your mission, you are still relying on the spiritual experiences you had then, ask yourself why you are not having spiritual experiences now.

Studying the scriptures

Take seriously the counsel to read the scriptures daily. It can be one of the most helpful things you can do, not only to find the answers you need, but to maintain a level of spirituality to help you overcome temptations and keep working on your plan of action. Take the scriptures personally. For example, think of John 3:16 as follows: "For God so loved *me* that he gave his only begotten Son, that if *I* believe in him *I* will not perish, but have everlasting life." Or substitute your own name. "For God so loved *Jason* that he gave his only begotten Son, that if *Jason* believes in him *Jason* will not perish, but have everlasting life." The scriptures apply to you personally. The promises in them were meant for you individually. Christ did not just die for the sins of the world, He died for *your* sins.

God considers us individually

In his book *Following Christ*, Stephen Robinson explained, "We forget that God, in his perfect judgment, adjusts credit and blame to allow for the circumstances of the individual in question. The gospel is not a 'one-size-fits-all' arrangement in that regard. God puts us all in different circumstances in this life and judges us accordingly. In the Parable of the Talents, it didn't matter that one servant had been given five talents and the other only two. What mattered most was what both servants did with what God gave them. The Master said to *each* of them, 'Well done, thou good and faithful servant' (Matthew 25:21)."[289]

Brother Robinson also teaches a parable of the divers.[290] In this story, a particular diver won even though other divers had better form. Although outwardly it appeared that the other divers did better, he won because he performed a dive of greater difficulty. Because of the difficulties we experience in life, we may feel—like the diver—that our scores are less than perfect, but God will bless us for the difficulty we had to go through. We will be blessed for making righteous responses to difficult situations. I recommend that you read the entire parable in the book *Following Christ* to understand this important concept. It helped me gain the insight I needed to stop judging others—and myself—by my limited perspective.

Elder H. Burke Peterson stated, "Each one of us came to this earth with our own unique and different package filled with enough positive strengths to overcome the personal challenges that are also a part of our makeup. We must never forget that the number of gifts as well as the challenges we each have does not categorize us as being better or worse than another How we *handle* our package is what makes the difference."[291] He further explained, "A person more gifted than another is not necessarily a better person than another; and, conversely, an individual who has received fewer endowments from the Lord is not less qualified for godhood than another. Remember, the Lord gave the very same commendation to the servant who magnified two talents as to the servant who increased five talents."[292]

Plan of Salvation

Elder M. Russell Ballard observed, "Life's most challenging questions seem to be those that begin with the word why. 'Why is life so hard?' 'Why is there so much sorrow, hate, and unhappiness in the world?' 'Why does death take the young?' And 'Why must the innocent suffer?'"[293] These are the deep questions of mortality and satisfying answers come only when we understand the plan of salvation. Alma called it "the great plan of happiness" (see Alma 42:8). We are the spirit children of heavenly parents with whom we lived before coming to this earth to receive our bodies of flesh and bone. This mortal life is also a test for us to prove ourselves. Since we all make mistakes that would prevent us from returning to our Heavenly Father, Christ agreed to pay the penalty for them if we will repent. Jesus also made it possible for everyone to be saved from physical death and be resurrected. Thus we continue to live and progress eternally.

Elder Ballard reminded us, "By focusing on and living the principles of Heavenly Father's plan for our eternal happiness, we can separate ourselves from the wickedness of the world. If we are anchored to the correct understanding of who we are, why we are here on this earth, and where we can go after this mortal life, Satan cannot threaten our happiness through any form of temptation. If we are determined to live by Heavenly Father's plan, we will use our God-given moral agency to make decisions based on revealed truth, not on the opinions of others or on the current thinking of the world."[294]

Elder Dallin H. Oaks said, "To the faithful, spirituality is a lens through which we view life and a gauge by which we evaluate it." He reminded us, "To be spiritually minded is to view and evaluate our experiences in terms of the enlarged perspective of eternity."[295]

Enduring to the end

Stephen Robinson explained, "Enduring faithfully to the end does not just mean 'coping' successfully with our problems or suffering affliction with stamina, although some have been called upon to do these things in order to endure. Certainly it has little to do with overcoming personal obstacles or achieving personal goals. Rather it means *staying put* in the kingdom by holding on to Christ and to his church without altering our commitment—no matter what. Neither 'enduring' nor 'being faithful' means being perfect or living from our baptism until our death without sinning. . . ."[296]

Enduring does not always mean *overcoming*. Many people do not overcome physical or other disabilities in this life. God does not always answer our fervent prayers by taking away the challenge. God may not take away your homosexual desires, but He will stand by you as you overcome the desires of the flesh by learning to control the homosexual actions.

Covenants

As a member of Christ's Church, you have made sacred covenants with him. You have taken upon yourself the name of Christ and have promised to always remember him and keep his commandments. In return he gives you his Spirit to guide and help you. If you have received the priesthood of God, received your temple endowments, or been married in the temple, you have made additional covenants. Covenants should not be taken lightly. We draw strength from making and keeping covenants. Set a goal to get worthy or stay worthy of a temple recommend. Regularly attending the temple can be a great help to keep your thoughts pure and stay focused on eternal truths.

You may wish to read the conference talks "Covenants" by President Boyd K. Packer (*Ensign*, Nov. 1990, pp. 84–86) and "Choices" by Russell M. Nelson (*Ensign*, November 1990, pp. 73–75).

Service

A good way to overcome your own problems is to help someone else overcome theirs. The best cure for self-absorption is to serve others. In fact, it is through serving others that you learn how to love—a key element in your healing. When you reach out to help someone else, your own problems don't seem so great. When you volunteer to help other people, you feel better emotionally and physically. Helping others causes you to focus outside yourself. Elder Richard G. Scott taught, "The power of your worthy example is increased as you help others caught in the web of transgression and guide them into a harbor of safety."[297]

My friend Garrick explained the benefit of serving as the leader of a support group in the Evergreen organization. "As great as all the lessons and books and therapy sessions and videos and conferences are, they couldn't teach me nearly as much as quiet service to others does. The more I give, the more I get. Instead of viewing Evergreen as some panacea that will cure my every ill just because I'm occupying a chair, I came to appreciate Evergreen the same way I appreciate our weekly church services: yet another opportunity to practice Christianity."[298]

For further reading

Gaining a greater understanding of gospel principles will give you greater power to make changes in your life. Even if you feel you know the gospel well, I suggest you read the book *Gospel Principles* (The Church of Jesus Christ of Latter-day Saints, Salt Lake City, UT, 1992, item number 31110). It is easy to read, but yet powerful because it teaches the core principles in their simplicity.

Many excellent books written by General Authorities and others on gospel subjects may also be helpful.

Chapter Sixteen

Adversity

When faced with challenges in life, it is helpful to keep a proper perspective. This chapter explains the purpose, origins, and benefits of adversity, then gives suggestions on how to successfully deal with our struggles.

Why there must be adversity

The scriptures teach that there must be opposition in all things (2 Nephi 2:11–14). There must be wickedness to understand the good, there must be misery to appreciate happiness, and there must be suffering to enjoy good health. But simply understanding that adversity will come does not make it easy to face.

Righteous living does not guarantee an easy life

Living a righteous life does not mean that bad things will not happen to you. A common misbelief among members of the Church is that if we strive with all our might to live the commandments, nothing bad will happen to us. We may believe if we are married in the temple our marriage will be heaven on earth, or if we live the Word of Wisdom we will enjoy good health throughout our lives. But the truth is, bad things may happen to the best of people. Elder H. Burke Peterson explained, "We must remember that all rewards for doing good do not come in this life. All penalties for doing wrong are not meted out in this life either."[299]

Lowell Bennion wrote, "The gospel of Christ is not an escape from the hard realities of life. . . . Both the person who follows Christ and the person who mocks Him live in the world among the same men and where the same laws of nature operate. Many things happen alike to saint and sinner. Cancer takes over in the human body with no regard for a person's spiritual or moral worth. . . . Innocent children suffer from it, and some of the most wonderful Christians we have known are not spared its merciless attack. Death itself . . . appears to be without discrimination. Clean-living Christian boys fall on the battlefield with those who curse God. A young and beloved husband and father is taken while a mean and feared husband and father is left to curse his wife and children. On the highway, death takes the careless, the sleepy, and the innocent victims alike with no regard for their Church attendance, tithing records, or love of neighbor that we can observe. The wicked prosper as well as the righteous, and sometimes more quickly. Individual prosperity is no proof of Christian discipleship; neither is poverty. . . . Living the gospel of Jesus Christ does not necessarily bring with it physical health, freedom from accident and misfortune, freedom from pain and suffering, prosperity and long life. As a matter of fact, some who have lived it best with great devotion have shortened their lives and brought considerable suffering upon themselves."[300]

The Savior came to heal broken hearts, not to prevent them from being broken. Living the gospel will not shield us from pain, but it is a resource to help us deal with pain. Robert L. Millet wrote, "The Savior may not take away our problems, and he certainly will not shield us from all pain, but he will provide us perspective and strength to bear up under them."[301]

Tragedy is not always a punishment for sin

"And as Jesus passed by, he saw a man which was blind from his birth. And his disciples asked him, saying, Master, who did sin, this man, or his parents, that he was born blind? Jesus answered, Neither hath this man sinned, nor his parents: but that the works of God should be made manifest in him" (John 9:1-3). Tragedy does not always come as a punishment for sin. Of course there are times when we do cause sorrow in our lives and we ought to take responsibility for it. But there are also many misfortunes that come through no fault of our own for which we have no right to blame ourselves. If we do, not only are we victims of the injury or unfortunate circumstance, but we make a bad situation worse by seeing ourselves as bad people who had it coming to us. When things go wrong, it is tempting to assume that if we had been more worthy, or had made a different choice, things would have turned out like we wanted them to. In his book *When Bad Things Happen to Good People*, Harold Kushner wrote, "A sense of our inadequacies and failings, a recognition that we could be better people than we usually are, is one of the forces for moral growth and improvement in our society. An appropriate sense of guilt makes people try to be better. But an excessive sense of guilt, a tendency to blame ourselves for things which are clearly not our fault, robs us of our self-esteem and perhaps of our capacity to grow and to act."[302] Therefore, we should take responsibility for things that are the direct result of mistakes or sin but not believe that every misfortune is our fault or is a punishment for wrongdoing.

The origins of adversity

Adversity vs. sin

When a bad thing happens in life, we often ask ourselves what we could have done to prevent it. We tend to blame ourselves and search for answers. "If only I could have been more careful." "If only I could have made a different decision." Some things are the result of our actions and others simply happen because of the world we live in.

Bruce Hafen wrote, "We might think of the degree of our personal fault for the bad things that happen in our lives as a continuum ranging from sin to adversity, with the degree of our fault dropping from high at one end of the spectrum to zero at the other. At the 'sin' end of the continuum, we bear grave responsibility, for we bring the bitter fruits of sin fully upon ourselves. But at the other end of the spectrum, marked by 'adversity,' we may bear no responsibility at all. The bitterness of adversity may come to us, as it did to Job in the Old Testament, regardless of our actual, conscious fault."[303]

Sin	Adversity
High degree of fault	No fault

It is important that we distinguish between the things that are our fault and those that are not because it is important that we accept responsibility for things that are our fault. On the other hand, it is unfair that we carry the burden of guilt for things that are not our fault. At times, this may be difficult to judge because between the poles we find such things as unwise choices and hasty judgements. In these cases, it may be difficult to determine how much personal responsibility we bear for the pain we feel or cause others to feel.

Problems because of sin

Much of the suffering in the world is the direct result of sin. Elder M. Russell Ballard said, "Much adversity is man-made. Men's hearts turn cold, and the spirit of Satan controls their actions. In foreseeing the day of suffering in our time, the Savior said, "The love of men shall wax cold, and iniquity shall abound" (D&C 45:27). Violence, immorality, and other evils run rampant on the earth and much adversity has its origin in the principle of agency."[304] Elder Ballard then explained, "The plan of happiness is available to all of his children. If the world would embrace and live it, peace, joy, and plenty would abound on the earth. Much of the suffering we know today would be eliminated if people throughout the world would understand and live the gospel."[305]

Problems because of nature

Many of the problems we face in life are a natural result of the world we live in. Elder M. Russell Ballard said, "God has put his plan in motion. It proceeds through natural laws that are, in fact, God's laws. Since they are his, he is bound by them, as are we. I recognize that for purposes we mortals may not understand, the Lord can control the elements. For the most part, however, he does not cause but he allows nature to run its course. In this imperfect world, bad things sometimes happen. The earth's rocky underpinnings occasionally shift and move, resulting in earthquakes. Certain weather patterns cause hurricanes, floods, tornadoes, and drought."[306]

The atonement heals all suffering

We often think of the atonement only in terms of relief from sin and guilt. But the atonement is more. Alma taught that Christ would "go forth, *suffering pains and afflictions and temptations of every kind*; and this that the word might be fulfilled which saith he will take upon him the *pains and the sicknesses* of his people. And he will take upon him death, that he may loose the bands of death which bind his people; and he will take upon him their *infirmities*, that his bowels may be filled with mercy, according to the flesh, that he may know according to the flesh how to succor his people according to their infirmities. Now the Spirit knoweth all things; nevertheless the Son of God suffereth according to the flesh that he might take upon him the *sins of his people*, that he might blot out their transgressions according to the power of his deliverance; and now behold, this is the testimony which is in me" (Alma 7:11–13, emphasis added).

Regardless of the source of suffering, the atonement can heal the effects of all pain.[307] When suffering is our fault, we can be cleansed through repentance, and "after all we can do," it can compensate for the consequences of our sins. The atonement can also compensate for the harmful effects of our ignorance or neglect and also for the pain and suffering caused by the willful actions of others.

The benefits of adversity

If a tree grows with much water but little wind, it develops shallow roots, and when the winds come it will topple over. People can also be shallow. Adversity can help you develop strong roots. You came to this earth knowing there would be trials and adversity and that they would refine you and help you develop character and strength.

One of the survivors of the ill-fated Martin Handcart Company said, "We suffered beyond anything you can imagine and many died of exposure and starvation, but did you ever hear a survivor of that company utter a word of criticism? Not one of that company ever apostatized or left the church, because everyone of us came through with the absolute knowledge that God lives for we became acquainted with him in our extremities."[308]

Orson F. Whitney said, "No pain that we suffer, no trial that we experience is wasted. It ministers to our education, to the development of such qualities as patience, faith, fortitude and humility. All that we suffer and all that we endure, especially when we endure it patiently, builds up our characters, purifies our hearts, expands our souls, and makes us more tender and charitable, more worthy to be called the children of God . . . and it is through sorrow and suffering, toil and tribulation, that we gain the education that we come here to acquire and which will make us more like our Father and Mother in heaven"[309]

How to deal with adversity

Since adversity will come to us all, consider the following ideas that can help us deal with adversity.

Recognize that God loves you

God knows you personally. He knows your needs and he loves you more than you have the capacity to understand. You can face adversity much easier when you understand who you are, who your Father is, and who your Savior is, and the relationship you have with Them. You chose to come to an unjust world where you would suffer. Christ died to atone for your sins. Although Christ died for all of us, He died for each one of us individually. He would have died for you if you had been the only one. He would have suffered in the garden for your sins if yours had been the only ones.

Recognize that others love you

Family and friends also love you. Rely on them. President Ezra Taft Benson said that heavenly hosts are also pulling for you. He called them "friends in heaven that we cannot now remember who yearn for our victory."[310]

Trust that the Lord is in control

Elder Richard G. Scott said, "This life is an experience in profound trust—trust in Jesus Christ, trust in His teachings, trust in our capacity as led by the Holy Spirit to obey those teachings for happiness now and for a purposeful, supremely happy eternal existence. To trust means to obey willingly without knowing the end from the beginning (see Proverbs 3:5–7). To produce fruit, your trust in the Lord must be more powerful and enduring than your confidence in your own personal feelings and experience. To exercise faith is to trust that the Lord knows what He is doing with you and that He can accomplish it for your eternal good even though you cannot understand how He can possibly do it."[311]

Camille Fronk observed, "No one can tell you just how your life will evolve, nor how to avoid misfortune. You can design your most hoped-for life and painstakingly work to achieve it. But I would dare say that fortunately for you and me, it may not unwind as we have planned. There will be surprising turns that we never could have anticipated. The Lord is in control. He is the Potter. And as a result, we have richer, more meaningful lives. As you look at your own past, you can recognize the obvious guidance of the Lord. . . . Why should we question that he will continue to direct us in the future?"[312]

Elder Richard G. Scott explained, "Your Father in Heaven and His Beloved Son love you perfectly. They would not require you to experience a moment more of difficulty than is absolutely needed for your personal benefit or for that of those you love.[313] You may wish to read Elder Scott's conference address "Trust in the Lord" (*Ensign*, Nov. 1995, p. 17).

Elder Scott also said, "The Lord is intent on your personal growth and development. That progress is accelerated when you willingly allow Him to lead you through every growth experience you encounter, whether initially it be to your individual liking or not. When you trust in the Lord, when you are willing to let your heart and your mind be centered in His will, when you ask to be led by the Spirit to do His will, you are assured of the greatest happiness along the way and the most fulfilling attainment from this mortal experience. If you question everything you are asked to do, or dig in your heels at every unpleasant challenge, you make it harder for the Lord to bless you."[314]

Accept that life is difficult

M. Scott Peck begins his book *The Road Less Traveled* with the following insight: "Life is difficult. This is a great truth, one of the greatest truths. It is a great truth because once we truly see this truth, we transcend it. Once we truly know that life is difficult—once we truly understand and accept it—then life is no longer difficult. Because once it is accepted, the fact that life is difficult no longer matters. Most do not fully see this truth that life is difficult. Instead they moan more or less incessantly, noisily or subtly, about the enormity of their problems, their burdens, and their difficulties as if life were generally easy, as if life *should* be easy."[315]

Dr. Peck explains that "it is in this whole process of meeting and solving problems that life has its meaning. Problems are the cutting edge that distinguishes between success and failure. Problems call forth our courage and our wisdom; indeed, they create our courage and our wisdom. It is only because of problems that we grow mentally and spiritually."[316]

Remember that everyone has challenges

When we consider the challenges that other people have, ours may not seem so difficult. I know a man who was just a few months old when he lost sight in both eyes. He could have let his disability ruin his life, but instead empowered his hearing and became a concert pianist. He has developed the ability to recreate on the piano any music he hears. Since he can't read the scriptures, he could have become spiritually dormant. But instead, he developed a spiritual sensitivity by listening incessantly to the scriptures on tape.

A colleague of mine has a disabled child who needs total care. They must lift her out of bed, feed her, and change her diaper. She is now seventeen years old and has grown so large that her mother cannot lift her, but has to wait until her husband comes home to move her. Their daughter requires physical therapy, special chairs, and daily medication. As my friend goes about his daily work, I seldom think about the extra emotional energy he gives at home to deal with his daughter's special situation. He is sometimes fatigued by the late nights and the financial pressures, but somehow finds the strength to go on. He does it because he loves her. And he doesn't regret the inconvenience or the extra money it requires, money he could otherwise spend on his other children or on things for himself. I am not sure that my trials with homosexual feelings are any more emotionally taxing than the trials he goes through. When I talk with parents of disabled children, they always say that their capacity to love has been increased and they have been blessed in many ways. They often seem to be the ones who have been able to develop strong character traits of sensitivity, integrity, and endurance that perhaps they would not have been able to develop without the trials. We all need to take the trials we have and use them to our advantage.

I know another woman who fought a battle with cancer.[317] Although she endured pains and heartache that few people understood, she remained cheerful and optimistic. She lost her hair from radiation treatments and after spinal surgery had to wear a metal brace around her head and chest to immobilize her head. As embarrassed as she must have felt by her appearance, she still came to church meetings and smiled and tried to cheer up everyone else. She wrote her own obituary which, in part, reads "Today at the young age of 33 I left this mortal existence to a holier sphere. I was born . . . to wonderful parents . . . who taught me to live life well. . . . We have three sweet children who I will miss greatly. At the young age of 29, I was introduced to something called cancer. Cancer was my great adversary but I have learned that in this life our enemies can become our choicest friends; the secret is in learning what to do with the conflict." She came to earth and suffered, and through it learned a little about her nature. An important mystery of life is to discover who we are, and who God is, and a little about our relationship with Him. It is critical to know in our hearts who we really are.

Let adversity strengthen you

Adversity effects people in different ways. For some, it becomes a challenge to overcome, for others an excuse to fail. Harold Kushner observed, "We may not ever understand why we suffer or be able to control the forces that cause our suffering, but we can have a lot to say about what the suffering does to us, and what sort of people we become because of it. Pain makes some people bitter and envious. It makes others sensitive and compassionate. It is the result, not the cause, of pain that makes some experiences of pain meaningful and others empty and destructive."[318]

When you face challenges, draw closer to God, even if conditions are not resolved as you would want. Dean Conlee said, "We pray earnestly and emotionally for the Lord to strengthen us and lift us, to prepare a way for us to endure, even to remove the bitter cup if it be his will, and then we release those things into his hands and believe within us that our prayers are heard, and the stress of the condition will be transferred to Him. I have a strong testimony that the Lord accepts our stress and blesses us with strength and courage and hope to continue the fight."[319]

Since you have to endure adversity, will you bear it through the bondage of bitterness or through the freedom of forgiveness? When hurt happens in your life, you can either keep it inside and become bitter about it or you can choose to grieve, let the emotions surface, feel the pain, then give it to the Lord.

Let God carry your burdens

When Alma and his people had come under the oppression of the

Lamanites, they cried "mightily to God" for deliverance. The Lord did not remove their persecution, but promised to help them carry the burden. "And it came to pass that the voice of the Lord came to them in their afflictions, saying: Lift up your heads and be of good comfort, for I know of the covenant which ye have made unto me; and I will covenant with my people and deliver them out of bondage. And I will also ease the burdens which are put upon your shoulders, that even you cannot feel them upon your backs, even while you are in bondage; and this will I do that ye may stand as witnesses for me hereafter, and that ye may know of a surety that I, the Lord God, do visit my people in their afflictions. And now it came to pass that the burdens which were laid upon Alma and his brethren were made light; yea, the Lord did strengthen them that they could bear up their burdens with ease, and they did submit cheerfully and with patience to all the will of the Lord" (Mosiah 24:13–15).

God can ease your burdens and make them light. When you turn to God, you will not only find the comfort you seek, but in so doing gain an increased testimony of the reality of the Savior and the atonement. In the words of Dean Conlee, "This is the higher purpose of trials in God's plan: to bring his children to the knowledge of him and his son."[320]

Don't expect quick solutions

We live in a day of instant gratification. We want fast food and instant fixes to our problems. If we can't solve a problem in minutes or days, we become frustrated. We also think that we should be instantly emotionally comfortable. President Boyd K. Packer said, "it was meant to be that life would be a challenge. To suffer some anxiety, some depression, some disappointment, even some failure is normal." He said, "There is great purpose in our struggle in life."[321]

Don't expect perfection in all things right now

For some reason, many people in the Church feel they need to be perfect now. While perfection is our ultimate goal, we need to realize that in this life we can only be perfect in some things. We may be able to pay tithing perfectly or avoid drugs and alcohol perfectly. But when we expect perfection in all aspects of our lives, we ask for frustration.

We feel ignorant when someone talks about a subject we don't know. We judge ourselves as too fat, too skinny, too short, or too tall. We need to stop believing that we are failures if we don't reach 100% all the time. Mistakes are understandable as long as we learn from them and do better the next time. Even the best of us will repeat some mistakes many times. Continue to learn, to grow, and to move toward your goal. People will accept and love you even though you have faults. All people have faults.

Maintain balance

Learn to keep things in balance. When you are asked to make a dessert for a ward dinner, you could spend half a day making it to perfection, but you need to evaluate what it is worth, considering all your other responsibilities, and spend the appropriate amount of time on it. When I built a shed in my back yard, I had to evaluate how much time it was worth, then built it to that level of perfection. Learn to balance your time and energies among the many things that are important. If you spend excessive amounts of time with your male friends, for example, you may be ignoring the eternal relationships found in your family.

Know there is a time for everything

When I was in high school, my father and I were hooked on genealogy and at times spent fifteen hours a week doing research. One year, we submitted thousands of names for temple work. At this point in my life, I cannot spend that much time on family history work because I am working and raising a family. I need to go to the temple as often as I can. However, I should not expect to go as often as my father who is retired and does ten to fifteen sessions a week. I look forward to doing a lot of temple work when I am retired, but I am not going to beat myself up now because I cannot go more often than I do. We are usually our own worst judges. Perhaps when all is said and done, God may not beat us with stripes so much for what we did not do, but bless us for what we did do.

Make the best of your situation

People who succeed in life don't waste time looking for the right circumstances. They *make* the right circumstances. Take the challenges you have been given, and use them to your advantage. It's always too soon to quit, but never too late to keep trying. You can choose to complain and drown in your problems or you can make the best of the situation and choose to grow through your problems.

Recognize that happiness comes from within

We generate our own happiness and we generate our own unhappiness. Many people say things like, "Everything would be fine if I just didn't have to work such long hours," "If my boss would get off my case. . . ," or "If my children would show me more respect. . . ." We tend to blame unhappiness on someone or something else. The truth is that unhappiness is generated internally. Although life can be brutal, relationships can fail, and families can go through crises, it is still *you* who decides how to react. This doesn't mean that you should be happy in the face of a crisis, because there is legitimate unhappiness at times. But there is a time to say "enough" and get on with life. That is what repentance is all about. Focus on what can be changed and not how bad things are. We all think we have it worse than someone else. But if everyone could take all their troubles and put them in a bag and place them on a table, and we could choose any bag we wanted, we would probably pick our own again.

Acknowledge there is more good than bad

God has created a world where there are many more good things than bad. Harold Kushner explained, "We find life's disasters upsetting not only because they are painful but because they are exceptional. Most people wake up on most days feeling good. Most illnesses are curable. Most airplanes take off and land safely. Most of the time, when we send our children out to play, they come home safely. The accident, the robbery, the inoperable tumor are life-shattering exceptions, but they are very rare exceptions. When you have been hurt by life, it may be hard to keep that in mind. When you are standing very close to a large object, all you can see is the object. Only by stepping back from it can you also see the rest of its setting around it. When we are stunned by some tragedy, we can only see and feel the tragedy. Only with time and distance can we see the tragedy in the context of a whole life and a whole world."[322]

Serve others

We heal ourselves of pain when we reach out to help others. Service to others is the great healer. Harold Kushner writes about the old Chinese tale of the woman whose only son died. "In her grief," he wrote, "she went to the holy man and said, 'What prayers, what magical incantations do you have to bring my son back to life?' Instead of sending her away or reasoning with her, he said to her, 'Fetch me a mustard seed from a home that has never known sorrow. We will use it to drive the sorrow out of your life.' The woman set off at once in search of that magical mustard seed. She came first to a splendid mansion, knocked at the door, and said, 'I am looking for a home that has never known sorrow. Is this such a place? It is very important to me.' They told her, 'You've certainly come to the wrong place,' and began to describe all the tragic things that had recently befallen them. The woman said to herself, 'Who is better able to help these poor unfortunate people than I, who have had misfortune of my own?' She stayed to comfort them, then went on in her search for a home that had never known sorrow. But wherever she turned, in hovels and in palaces, she found one tale after another of sadness and misfortune. Ultimately, she became so involved in ministering to other people's grief that she forgot about her quest for the magical mustard seed, never realizing that it had in fact driven the sorrow out of her life."[323]

Overcome discouragement

Read the following story about the inventor Thomas Edison and note his attitude during a trying time. "Thomas Edison devoted ten years and all of his money to developing the nickel-alkaline storage battery at a time when he was almost penniless. . . . One night the terrifying cry of fire echoed through the film plant. Spontaneous combustion had ignited some chemicals. Within moments all of the packing compounds, celluloids for records, film, and other flammable goods had gone up with a whoosh. Fire companies from eight towns arrived, but the heat was so intense and the water pressure so low that the fire hoses had no effect. Edison was 67 years old—no age to begin anew. His daughter was frantic, wondering if he were safe, if his spirits were broken, how he would handle a crisis such as this at this age. She saw him running toward her. He spoke first. He said, 'Where's your mother? Go get her. Tell her to get her friends. They'll never see another fire like this as long as they live.' At 5:30 the next morning, with the fire barely under control, he called his employees together and announced, 'We're rebuilding.' One man was told to lease all the machine shops in the area, another to obtain a wrecking crane from the Erie Railroad Company. Then, almost as an afterthought, he added, 'Oh, by the way, anybody know where we can get some money?'"[324] Virtually everything we now recognize as a Thomas Edison contribution came after that disaster. Some of his most famous inventions include the electric light bulb, the phonograph, motion pictures, the electric voting machine, the stock ticker, and the mimeograph machine. How would the world be different today if Mr. Edison had become discouraged and given up?

Others who have gone before you have experienced discouragement and have overcome it. Noah was discouraged when everyone was against him, but he followed through and built the ark. Moses initially resisted his destiny, saying that he was slow of speech, but gained courage and led the children of Israel out of bondage. It was difficult for President Spencer W. Kimball to speak, yet he traveled around the world delivering powerful sermons that are still widely quoted today. Job experienced extraordinary trials. He lost is family, his health, and his wealth, yet he never cursed God. Although Paul suffered much, listen to the positive attitude he expresses in his second epistle to the Corinthians: "We are troubled on every side, yet not distressed; we are perplexed, but not in despair; persecuted, but not forsaken; cast down, but not destroyed" (2 Corinthians 4:8–9).

When you feel discouraged, admit your weaknesses to the Lord and positively work at solving the problem at hand. The following scriptures may provide encouragement: Alma 26:27; Joshua 1:9; Proverbs 3:5–6; Romans 5:3–5; D&C 68:6; D&C 121:7–8; D&C 61:36; 2 Nephi 4:30.

Accept adversity

Ultimately, you have to come to grips with the fact that there will always be adversity. Remember that you are not left alone. Accept the reality of the atonement and its power to compensate for the effects of injustice. It may come in a quiet room after you have thought, and wondered, and become angry, and prayed, and pleaded, and finally, come to peace with yourself. Remember, something inside you is ancient and wise and knows what needs to be done. It is a combination of the Light of Christ, the Holy Ghost, and our own eternal spirit. It is the eternal part of you. Rely on it. You are tougher than you think.

"But that ye have patience, and bear with those afflictions, with a firm hope that ye shall one day rest from all your afflictions" (Alma 34:41). Trust in the greatness of God and believe that "he shall consecrate thine afflictions for thy gain" (2 Nephi 2:2).

Elder Richard C. Edgley said, "For the faithful, the normal tests and trials of life need not be the enemy of faith. While we don't necessarily look forward to these obstacles and challenges, we accept them, and we build our lives and faith from them. To the faithful, the very obstacles that we overcome draw us closer to our Heavenly Father by helping us develop a humble, submissive spirit and causing us to be grateful and appreciative of those blessings that flow from a loving Father. In short, these experiences can and often do increase our faith. The faithful do not pray to be spared the trials of life but pray that they may have the strength to rise above them."[325]

Conclusion

In the gospel of Jesus Christ we can find comfort in the face of adversity. Remember that the fruits of righteous living are spiritual, not material. Lowell Bennion wrote, "The religion of Jesus does not enable us to escape tribulation, but it does fortify the spirit of man to accept and face it when it comes. . . . The life founded in the gospel can suffer with patience, can meet adversity with hope, can take malice with forgiveness, can recompense hate with love, and can face death with equanimity. The religious person can find himself in no circumstance . . . in which his religion is not a source of strength to him. In weakness, he knows where to turn for strength; in strength, he remains humble; in poverty he knows whereof his riches consist; in wealth he remembers his brethren in mercy; in health, he is grateful; in illness, he exercises faith."[326]

Each of us has hope because of who we are and who God is and who we are together. Don't pray that God will make your life free of problems, but pray for hope, strength, and courage to bear them.

Adversity can bless our lives if we let it purify us and teach us.

President Spencer W. Kimball taught, "Is there not wisdom in His giving us trials that we might rise above them, responsibilities that we might achieve, work to harden our muscles, sorrows to try our souls? Are we not exposed to temptations to test our strength, sickness that we may learn patience, death that we might be immortalized and glorified? If all the sick for whom we pray were healed, if all the righteous were protected and the wicked destroyed, the whole program of the Father would be annulled and the basic principle of the gospel, free agency, would be ended. No man would have to live by faith."[327]

For further reading

The Road Less Traveled by M. Scott Peck, M.D.

When Bad Things Happen to Good People by Harold Kushner. (Although the author does not believe in the omnipotence of God, his advice on how to cope with tragedy and personal pain is thought-provoking and helpful.)

When All You've Ever Wanted Isn't Enough by Harold Kushner.

If the Gospel Is True, Why Do I Hurt So Much?: Help for Dysfunctional Latter-day Saint Families by Carroll Hofeling Morris.

Chapter Seventeen

Gay Identity and the Gay Rights Movement

In addition to the personal battle raging within you, there are external challenges that may add to the difficulty of resolving your homosexual problems. This chapter explains that if a person has developed a gay identity and assimilated into a close-knit gay community, he may find it difficult to leave it behind. The chapter discusses the origins and objectives of the gay rights movement, including its efforts to normalize homosexuality and limit the options available to those who want to resolve their homosexual problems.

Development of a gay identity

The personal conflict over homosexual feelings creates a difficult internal struggle. After years of trying to find answers and no success at trying to change their feelings, some people become convinced that their homosexual feelings are inborn and unchangeable and they accept a gay identity which finally ends the internal struggle that has caused them so much frustration and pain. Accepting a gay identity has far-reaching implications because being "gay" includes not only personal feelings, but also describes a social and political identity. As they associate with other gay people, they find a great deal of acceptance and feel—perhaps for the first time in their life—that they fit in. Since they often feel that the world has let them down or they feel rejected by the world, they turn to each other for support. There they feel safe, comfortable, and at home.

Moving out of a gay culture

Larger cities have distinct areas where gay people tend to live or congregate for entertainment. Gay-identified people often move to major cities where they can find a larger gay community. They tend to trust and give preference to each other in personal and business dealings and find comfort in the gay community because they feel the acceptance they never found among their family, ward, friends, or classmates.

If you have lived as part of a gay community, you may have additional lifestyle challenges to overcome, in addition to the homosexual problems themselves. If your emotional support system is tied to a gay community and gay friends, you may need to move and find new friends who will support you in resolving your homosexual issues.

The plight of gay people

Gays and lesbians suffer, often unjustly and unfairly. In addition to their difficult internal struggles, they also encounter the ignorance and prejudice of others. Instead of receiving love and support from their families, they are often ostracized. Rather than being involved in supportive church groups, they find themselves on the outside because even good Christians often don't know how to react to someone with homosexual attractions.

Gay people are evicted by landlords, fired by employers, and even face violent physical attacks. Hate crimes are increasing and some people use AIDS as an excuse to show their hatred.[328] Less than 2% of the gay population survives to age sixty-five. They are 116 times more likely to be murdered and twenty-four times more likely to commit suicide than the average person.[329] It is a difficult lifestyle where AIDS and other factors cause suffering and premature death.[330] The collective anger over mistreatment and the frustration caused by their internal struggles are powerful forces behind the gay rights movement.

Elder Dallin H. Oaks wrote the following in the *Ensign* magazine: "Our doctrines obviously condemn those who engage in so-called 'gay bashing'—physical or verbal attacks on persons thought to be involved in homosexual or lesbian behavior. We should extend compassion to persons who suffer from ill health, including those who are infected with HIV or who are ill with AIDS (who may or may not have acquired their condition from sexual relations). We should encourage such persons to participate in the activities of the Church."[331]

The beginnings of the gay rights movement

Gay people finally became sick and tired of being mistreated and began to fight back. In the 1960's, they simply wanted the public to leave them alone. They didn't want to be called names and didn't want to be arrested for going to gay bars. When dialog and reason didn't get results, they began to form organizations and develop protest strategies.

Following the social protest strategies of the era, they turned social issues into political issues. Although homosexual behavior is as old as history itself, there had not previously been a social identity based entirely on sexual behavior. The pro-gay strategy was to take the behavioral definition and expand it to become a definition of a class of people. (Some say that ancient Greece had a gay culture. And while it is true they had a more naturalistic view of life, including homosexuality, there was no gay identity. In fact, the Greek language had no word meaning "gay."[332] The concept of a "homosexual person" was created in the nineteenth century.[333] Although homosexual behavior was certainly practiced before that time, it was seen as something you did, and not who you were.)

The watershed event of the gay rights movement in America happened in 1969 at a gay bar called the Stonewall Inn in Greenwich Village, New York, where gay patrons fought police in clashes that continued sporadically for two days.

Over the years, organizations have been formed to further various gay causes. Many are well-meaning and some are over the edge. A number of highly organized, well-funded organizations attempt to mold public opinion in favor of homosexuality as a normal, alternative sexuality. In 1997, over $75 million will be donated to these organizations.[334] For fiscal year 1997, the National Gay and Lesbian Task Force had a budget of $2.3 million and the Lambda Legal Defense and Educational Fund had a budget of $3.1 million.[335] These significant resources are massed toward achieving multiple discrete and troublesome objectives, such as those that follow.

Political issues

Gay activists turn social and cultural issues into political ones and through various means attempt to achieve a minority status. They define themselves as a class of people, an oppressed minority fighting for civil rights. They merge *being gay* with *gay rights* so that those who oppose gay rights are seen as bigots who hate gay people. This civil rights approach takes on a feel of a racial equality movement and gives the collective gay community a tremendous amount of power. They support gay or pro-gay political candidates to introduce legislation to help move their causes forward.

You have the right to let your legislators know your position on social issues and vote on referenda that come to ballot. Vote for representatives that will uphold the standards you believe. The National Association of Research and Therapy of Homosexuality (NARTH) or The Lambda Report can help keep you informed of current issues. (See the Organizations section of this book.)

Legal issues

Seeking gay rights protection, activists focus on the courts—not the polls. Rather than permitting the voters to decide whether to legitimize gay marriage, they seek to have judges dictate that society will have gay marriage—whether society on the whole wants it or not. They have obtained many changes by nondemocratic, nonpolitical means. "Gay rights" have been created by state and federal judges although there is nothing in the express wording, text, or structure of the Constitution that suggests a fundamental—let alone constitutional—right to sexual expression (whether that expression be heterosexual or homosexual).

See the Organizations section of this book for information on contacting organizations that are addressing these concerns.

Social issues

The pro-gay agenda seeks not only for the right to practice and celebrate homosexuality openly, but wants the endorsement of society. Although gay couples already receive some benefits of marriage through domestic partnership laws, activists seek to legalize homosexual marriage and redefine the traditional family. They work toward more favorable child custody and visitation rights as well as the right to adopt children. They promote moral relativism, saying in effect, "it might be wrong for you, but not for me." They also seek a redefinition of gender, with the goal of giving humans five genders from which to choose instead of two. When freed of traditional biases, a person can then decide whether to be male, female, homosexual, lesbian, or transgendered.[336]

These efforts present a real threat to traditional family values. President Boyd K. Packer spoke about this danger in a general conference address in October 1990.[337] In 1994, the First Presidency issued a letter that stated, "The principles of the gospel and the sacred responsibilities given us require that The Church of Jesus Christ of Latter-day Saints oppose any efforts to give legal authorization to marriages between persons of the same gender."[338] Speak up for traditional family values and the divinely-appointed roles of men and women. See the Organizations section of this book for information on organizations that support families.

Educational issues

Gay activism pushes for an increase in gay and pro-gay school teachers and counselors who are in positions to influence children's values. Boys are often confused about sexuality during their adolescent years, and a gay counselor's attempts to help them come to grips with their "gay identity" may add to their confusion and lead them down the wrong path. Project 10 is a pro-gay counseling program in the Los Angeles Unified School District that helps teens accept their gay, lesbian, or bisexual identity. The program uses exclusively gay-identified counselors and sexually-explicit literature with students at large in an aggressive search for the mythical 10% of the teens that are gay. In New York schools, first-graders were required to read books such as *Heather Has Two Mommies* and *Daddy's Roommate* to counter the more traditional values taught in the home. Deborah Glick, New York state assemblywoman and a lesbian, explained why first grade is the new front line of the pro-gay movement: "Most of the parents themselves have tremendous prejudice and bigotry that have been passed on for generations . . . and the reality is that we as a society, if we are to remain free and just, must provide a counter-balance to what kids are obviously learning at home."[339] Pro-gay school programs promote sex education that includes acceptance of homosexuality as a healthy lifestyle and encouragement to explore alternative sexualities. AIDS education is often an avenue for pro-gay indoctrination. Such programs teach "safer sex" but rarely teach abstinence.

If a teenager is confused about sexuality or his gender identity, it is important that he have a safe person or group to talk with. However, pro-gay school counselors and gay clubs are seldom safe. The counselors, club advisors, and guest speakers are not usually supportive of gospel values. They typically encourage students to "come out of the closet" and accept a gay identity rather than to grow past it.

A natural response to these alarming situations may be to confront the pro-gay movement directly. However, experience shows it is generally a waste of time to try to argue with pro-gay advocates in an attempt to come to middle ground. You may therefore want to be proactive rather than reactive and work with your school principal and school board on these issues. File formal grievances against teachers that don't follow state laws on curriculum. School programs should be balanced and should not belittle traditional values of sexuality. The Focus on the Family organization (see the Organizations section of this book) offers programs with Christian principles.

Religious issues

The gay agenda encourages the ordination of homosexual ministers and a redefinition of theology to accommodate homosexual lifestyles. Gay advocates teach that religious opposition to homosexuality is bigotry that must be stopped. Unfortunately, they are beginning to establish a legal precedence for granting gay rights over religious rights. The following news item appeared in the April 1988 issue of the *Intercessor's for America Newsletter*: "The Washington, D.C. court of appeals has ordered Georgetown University [a private Catholic institution] to support homosexual groups on campus. The court ruled that Georgetown's policy which denies support to gay organizations because homosexual practice is contrary to Catholic doctrine to be discriminatory on the basis of sexual orientation and is a violation of the Washington, D.C. area's Human Rights Act. The court also declared that 'homosexual orientation tells nothing about a person's abilities or commitments concerning religion. The compelling government interest to eliminate discrimination against homosexuals outweighs the freedom of religion.'"[340]

The response of some Christians is to join anti-gay crusades which do nothing to reduce the incidence of homosexuality, but simply convince gays there is no place for them in religion. The most effective thing you can do is teach others about homosexual issues in their proper gospel context. Evergreen International (see the Organizations section of this book) sponsors educational conferences and other programs. Remember that the fight is not against people who experience homosexual attractions, but against the propaganda that is being taught.

The media

Gay activism seeks equal time and space in the media and encourages writers and producers to include more gay themes and present a positive image of gays. Since there are many liberal, pro-gay producers and journalists, there is a great deal of media exposure.

As a concerned citizen, you can express your opinion to media owners and operators to encourage traditional, family-oriented values. You can also encourage local libraries to have books that present all sides of the issue of homosexuality, including the fact that homosexual problems can be resolved.

Inborn homosexuality

Gay advocates state that homosexuality is inborn and unchangeable. The proposition that a person could change questions the very concept of a gay identity. In addition, recognizing that anyone would *want* to change is to admit there are those who believe it is wrong and does not make them happy. Gay advocates may go to great lengths to try to disprove anyone who claims to have changed. They may say that such people were never gay in the first place or that they have been brainwashed into believing they have overcome homosexuality and some day will realize they are just suppressing their true homosexual nature. It is ironic that gay advocates have no problem believing that a straight man may discover his latent homosexuality, but they cannot tolerate the idea that a man with homosexual desires may discover his heterosexual nature. Jeffrey Satinover also noted, "There will always be people who seek to change but are not successful, even after many years of effort. Understandably perhaps, some of these relapse into a vocally gay-activist posture and become hostile toward the ministries they perceive as having failed, or even deluded, them."[341]

The conservative response from society is to ignore homosexual issues and hope they will go away. This leaves gay activists as the only ones speaking on the subject, giving distorted views of the problems and the solutions. Don't be afraid to speak up and tell others what you know about homosexuality. In appropriate settings, tell others about the changes you have made in your own life and the changes you have seen in others.

The normalization of homosexuality

The American Psychiatric Association (APA) is the organization that determines for the professional community what is normal and what is abnormal. Their *Diagnostic and Statistical Manual of Mental Disorders* (DSM) is a handbook widely used by clinicians to assist in diagnosing and classifying mental, emotional, and sexual disorders. The first edition of the DSM, published in 1952, listed homosexuality as a mental disorder, a severe form of psychopathology.

By 1968, the gay community had a few organizations in place and one of their first targets was the APA. Over the next few years, protestors interrupted APA conferences, shouting at the speakers and taking control of meetings. After three years of disrupted conventions, the APA agreed to let gay activists be involved in the decision-making process, even though the activists were not professionals in psychiatry or psychology. Finally in 1973, the board of trustees agreed to redefine mental illness in a way that accommodated homosexuality. Previously, disorders had been determined by deviations from an objective norm, but this redefinition said that the norm should be more subjective, that people should not be considered disordered if they do not experience distress over their condition and if they show no major impairment in social functioning. With this redefinition, homosexuality was removed as a disorder from the DSM-III.

The decision by the APA board was not based on data and clinical reasoning nor did it represent the professional opinions of the practitioners the APA represents. Surveys show that a majority of mental health professionals believes that homosexuality is not normal.[342] In his book *Homosexuality and American Psychiatry: The Politics of Diagnosis*, Ronald Bayer describes how clinical decisions are made and the factors that influence those decisions. This subjective standard of normalcy set a dangerous precedent, because without an objective standard nearly any deviation can be considered normal as long as the person is not seriously disturbed by his condition. For example, in the DSM-IV, one of the criteria for diagnosing pedophilia (a disorder in which children are the preferred sexual objects) states, "The fantasies, sexual urges, or behaviors cause clinically significant distress or impairment in social, occupational, or other important areas of functioning."[343] Such changes were also made in the criteria for diagnosing sexual sadism and masochism, transvestitism, voyeurism, and exhibitionism. In their attempt to be politically correct, the psychiatric community has lost the distinction between what is normal and what is right.

Today, a growing number of professionals are dissatisfied with the APA's political commitments and have formed organizations that oppose the APA's advocacy of social issues such as abortion, the environment, affirmative action, gay rights, support of special interest groups, and other issues irrelevant to the profession of psychology. (For more information, write to Psychologists For a Free APA, 1807 North Elm #321, Denton TX 76201.)

The elimination of homosexuality as a disorder in the DSM has also had a negative effect on clinical research in the area of homosexuality. It is difficult to get funding or recognition for research in an area not listed in the *Diagnostic and Statistical Manual*. One of the few organizations currently promoting research and documenting clinical successes in treating homosexuality is the National Association for Research and Therapy of Homosexuality (see the Organizations section in this book).

The movement to deny treatment

Gay activists seek not only to declare homosexuality to be normal, but also to block a person's attempts to change his homosexuality. They believe that such attempts are simply manifestations of the person's internalized homophobia and self-loathing, and that the only healthy response to homosexual feelings is to accept a gay identity. They seek to make it professionally unethical for therapists to help people grow out of homosexuality. Although homosexuality is no longer classified as a disorder, clinicians who treat those who seek treatment for homosexuality are treating within the guidelines in the DSM-IV, section 302.9, "sexual disorders not otherwise specified," "persistent and marked distress about sexual orientation." However, proposals have been presented in both the American Psychiatric Association and the American Psychological Association to make it unethical for a therapist to offer treatment to those who seek treatment for their distress over homosexual desires. Such therapists would have their licenses revoked and be liable for punitive damages.

Since such proposals are gaining increasing support, it is important to take proactive measures to preserve the right to receive professional help. Therapists who have seen how people can be helped are organizing to find ways to protect the rights of patients who seek treatment as well as the rights of the therapists who treat them. For more information, contact the National Association of Research and Therapy of Homosexuality (see the Organizations section in this book). While it is true that no one should be coerced into treatment, the reverse is also true that no one should be denied treatment if they want it. Ultimately, it is an issue of personal freedom and self-determination.

Militant gay groups

A small number of political-activist groups have become militant in their tactics. Feeling wronged and oppressed, they are now fighting mad and fighting back with vocal, in-your-face tactics. They have been known to threaten or cause property damage or physical injury. Although most gay people are respectable, law-abiding members of society, these militant gays get media attention and give the impression that gay people are on the fringe of society, feeding incorrect stereotypes.

ACT UP is a civil disobedience organization dedicated to confronting the issues of discrimination against people with HIV infection or AIDS. It has more than a hundred chapters in the United States and abroad. Queer Nation was organized by several members of ACT UP who wanted to focus their energy specifically on gay and lesbian rights issues. According to one of the group's founders, "We wanted to do direct action, to get out on the streets, to scream and yell, to stage very visible protests against anti-gay violence and discrimination."[344] Such groups go to radical extremes to shock the public, such as putting up pornographic signs or painting "We're queer; we're here" on businesses they target as homophobic. Since words like "queer" and "fag" have been used derogatorily against gay people, these radical groups have reclaimed the words and now use them pro-actively for their shock value.

Some groups have the purpose of "outing." They take it upon themselves to identify a person who is gay and force him out of the closet by informing employers, families, and friends that he is gay. Although they do it against the person's wishes, sometimes ruining careers and breaking up families, they feel it benefits the greater cause of the gay movement by showing that greater numbers of people are gay. Identifying successful, prominent people as gay seems to lend credibility to the cause.

Gay activism promotes stereotypes

When we have little experience with something, we tend to stereotype. Although many people think that all gays are alike, the truth is that the gay population is about as heterogeneous as the heterosexual population. Unless a person knows a relative or friend who is gay, the only experience they have to draw on is what they see in the media. When they watch a gay parade in New York City and see men and women flaunting their sexuality with lewd costumes and behavior, they only see the extremes of the gay population. And when the population at large begins to think that all gays are riotous and lewd, it seems reasonable to ban gays from serving in the military. A gay sailor parading around in drag propositioning other sailors would certainly not strengthen a cohesive fighting unit. While this obviously is not a fair representation of most gay people, it is the stereotype people form in their minds when they see the extremists of the gay movement in the media. They don't see the average man or woman who is a responsible and productive member of society who only asks for reasonable rights and respect. Gay activism gives gay people a reputation they don't deserve.

Latent homosexuality

Gay advocates would like you to think that there is latent homosexuality in all men because it gives credence to their position that homosexuality is natural and occurs to some degree in everyone. What they call latent homosexuality is nothing more than the natural, right desires for companionship, acceptance, and healthy relationships. The only thing potentially homosexual about it is that if not fulfilled through healthy relationships, it could lead to homosexuality.

Homophobia

Homophobia is defined as an irrational hatred or fear of homosexuality. Although there are legitimate cases of homophobia, the use of the term has been expanded to take on social and political meanings. Gay advocates use it widely to refer to those who are hostile toward gay people and even those who disagree with the pro-gay perspective. They consider homophobic those who want to resolve their homosexual problems as well as therapists who try to help them. Some activists have an almost neurotic attitude toward all "straight" people and blame all their suffering in life on either social or internalized homophobia.

The truth is, those who are hostile toward gay people are usually *prejudiced*, meaning that they have an opinion against it without adequate basis, but not homophobic. Those who disagree with the pro-gay perspective may also do it legitimately out of *conviction*, which is a strong belief. Those who object to homosexuality on religious or moral grounds do so out of conviction, not because of a phobia or prejudice.

For further reading

Unforgiven Sins by Joe Dallas. This novel about the gay rights movement teaches powerful lessons about facing potentially explosive situations with sensitivity and wisdom.

Homosexuality in America: Exposing the Myths (American Family Association, P. O. Drawer 2440, Tupelo, MS, 38803). This twenty-four–page booklet responds to the reality of homosexuality from a traditional family-values perspective.

Desires in Conflict: Answering the Struggle for Sexual Identify by Joe Dallas. Chapter sixteen gives an insightful description of the genesis of rage in gay activism.

Testimonials

My Challenge Has Become a Blessing
Todd Daniels

Everyone is faced with challenges in life, without exception. Although the specific nature of the challenges does not necessarily define who we are, how we deal with those challenges does. When we give in to the impulses brought on by our struggles, we accept the consequences of a life out of harmony with our personal beliefs and, possibly, with the plan of happiness that God has laid out for us. Conversely, when we face the challenge and fight against the urges to forsake what is right, we are molded and sculpted by that battle. It is not likely that we will escape from such battles without a few scars; but we will be stronger and have a greater understanding of our specific purpose and destiny because of the rigors of the fight. Most important, we will have a greater appreciation and humility for the love of a God who is surely the only way out of many of these struggles.

One such challenge for me has been same-sex attraction. It is a battle that no one chooses, nor is it easily won. I remember same-sex attractions since childhood, and as I entered adolescence, those attractions became sexual. For many years I constantly struggled with feelings which I did not understand or want. I felt terribly alone in the world and was terrified that my secret would get out and that people would find out how sick and perverted I was. As I struggled with this internal turmoil, the battle began to manifest itself in my actions. I got caught in an ongoing cycle of loneliness, homosexual fantasies, pornography, and masturbation, and I eventually found myself engaging in sexual indiscretion with others—thinking that this was somehow a solution to my problems.

Of course, just as an alcoholic finds that a drug does not solve his problems, I found that my addictions did not solve mine. That realization, however, was not enough to alter the behavior. I sought out therapists who I hoped would help me with this dilemma. One of these therapists was not helpful. Although her intentions were good and she wanted me to be happy, she had "swallowed the lie" which has been so carefully propagated by the pro-gay community which encourages people not to abandon homosexual behavior, but to abandon a system of beliefs which does not condone such behavior. Unfortunately, this has become a common approach in the mental health profession. Other therapists were very helpful, however, helping me understand how my struggle had caused me to close out the world to "protect" myself and how I needed to let other people become a part of my life on a close, emotional level. The most helpful therapist was one specifically acquainted with homosexual issues and with the knowledge that the pathway out of homosexuality revolves not around problems with the opposite sex, but in coming to terms with my own masculinity, and in feeling and being included and connected in the male world rather than feeling different and isolated. I also found many friends within the Evergreen organization with whom I could share my successes and failures. I am still close friends with many of those people, and several of us have made successful transitions out of the homosexual lifestyle.

I believe there are some challenges we can plow through alone in life, simply by putting our mind to it and pushing forward. I do not believe, however, that homosexuality is one of these challenges. Indeed, the battle rages on as to what causes homosexuality—is it genetic, or is it environmental? Gay rights advocates desperately grasp for any evidence that it is somehow inborn; for them, they insist, it is meant to be and it is pointless for us to attempt to alter "who we are." Outside this political rhetoric, however, many scientists and therapists believe there are probably a variety of causes which all interact to create a propensity toward homosexuality. However, regardless of the cause, most who have struggled with same-sex attraction deal with issues which have been part of their lives for many years and the thought patterns and ways of reacting to stimuli tend to become part of them.

For this reason, I found that the homosexual struggle cannot be won overnight. Indeed, the slow and painful process of recovery convinces many that the challenge is not worth it and they accept the homosexual lifestyle rather than the fight. I have known good friends who were fighting the battle by my side several years ago who have since given up. I would argue they have also given up true happiness in the process.

Because of the difficulty of impacting such deeply imbedded feelings and habits, although the therapy and personal interaction is critical, reliance on God is essential. I am convinced that without His help, I would never have been able to make a transition out of the lifestyle which I hated, but from which I could not escape. Different organizations talk about "surrendering" your problems to God, and I found that this was the only way to truly get past homosexual attraction. I can't describe exactly how it works, because I think it is probably impossible for me to understand. All I can say is that it does. That does not mean that the change is easy or fast, it just means it is possible, and that God will be by our side as we learn and change.

Many people, particularly those currently struggling with same-sex attraction issues, have difficulty finding any possible good that can come from such struggles. In retrospect, I can say that the struggles and the painful process out of homosexuality taught me much. I learned to rely on God, and that He has put us here to develop faith and there is no better way to do that than to realize that we are completely dependent on Him for everything. The challenge also taught me compassion for my fellow man. We live in a world that tells us so much about taking care of ourselves and tending to our own needs that we often overlook the pain and needs of our brothers and sisters. After having battled with homosexuality for so many years, I can never again look at someone struggling with problems in life without a greater degree of compassion and understanding for them.

Today my sexual attraction is primarily heterosexual, whereas it was clearly homosexual previously. That does not mean that I absolutely never have a homosexual thought anymore. However, those thoughts are now simply lingering reminders of the pathways developed in my consciousness over so many years and the real key is that I am no longer troubled by such thoughts and they fade as quickly as they appear. It is a dramatic difference from my former struggles where I would literally spend hours of the day locked in homosexual obsessions which impacted my work and social life. Now, I am happily married and have a wonderful child. I have never been happier, and I no longer experience the chronic depression which was once associated with homosexuality. I feel no deficits with respect to my own masculinity, nor do I feel compelled to compare myself to other men.

God has truly showered His infinite grace on me because of what I have learned and experienced. I thank Him for the change I have experienced, along with understanding Church leaders who were patient with my long struggle and the periodic setbacks, and who sought to find the resources to help me with my problem. I thank the therapists who challenged me and encouraged me to take some frightening steps toward recovery. I thank my friends in Evergreen who stood by my side and helped me maintain the strength to continue. Finally, I thank my wonderful wife for her understanding and her patience with someone who has a few lingering quirks. Indeed, I think that although it is possible to get past the sexual attraction issues, many who deal with homosexuality never lose the sensitivity which they so often possess. However, that sensitivity, although sometimes annoying, can ultimately be a great strength to families and friends if focused properly.

Change is possible. Life has options and God does not leave us to fend for ourselves. His primary purpose is our happiness, and He will fight our battles if we will rely on Him and constantly trust in His plan of happiness rather than seeking the fleeting happiness the world has to offer.

I Finally Found Answers
Daniel Packard

I went on a mission hoping it would solve my homosexual problems, but it didn't. I came home and became friends with another LDS man who also had homosexual feelings and connected with him because for the first time there was someone who understood my feelings. Neither of us knew how to reconcile homosexual feelings with God's eternal plan or even His mortal plan of the Church. We knew we were supposed to get married but couldn't imagine being sexually involved with a wife. We had no idea how to change these feelings. Trying to be faithful didn't change them. Going on a mission didn't change them. It didn't take long before we started hanging out at gay bars because there we felt accepted and loved and understood. We stopped going to Church because by then our behavior was contrary to Church standards.

This story has a happy ending, however, because six months ago I found an LDS support group called Evergreen. There I am finding in a positive way the love and acceptance I had been seeking at the gay bars. I am also finding answers to questions I thought had no answers. I know it will take a long time to completely overcome my problems, but I have made tremendous progress already. I am working on changing my attitudes and the way I feel about myself. I'm also working on how I relate to and bond with other men. As I do that, I can see changes in my sexual feelings starting to take place already.

Even though at times I stumble off the path, I now know what I need to do and I won't give up. I know I have a long way to go. I've gone through some dark days and not always with flying colors. But that's the down side; the most important thing is that it has been worth every moment. I'm honestly happier than I've ever been. I'm leaving my worldly value system and becoming a spiritually-oriented person in Christ. Everyone needs to do this, whether they have homosexual feelings or not. We just need to have faith. If Jesus was able to heal the sick and raise the dead, certainly he can heal my homosexual problems.

He Will Help If We Ask
Susan Parkinson

I am thankful for the chance to write about my experiences and hope that the testimony that has developed from it can help others, specifically spouses, help find your way.

Jack and I have been married ten years and we have three beautiful children. I did not know Jack's struggle with homosexuality until two years ago when he began spending excessive time with a family friend and I began to suspect, but not accept, that he was involved with another man. Finally, a family member confided in me, and I could no longer deny the inconceivable situation I had prayed was not happening.

We have fought long and hard over the past two years to keep our marriage in tact. Those of you who have been through this experience understand the heartbreak, the mistrust, and the damage this kind of revelation can bring. I wrote in my journal shortly after "D-day" (as we call it in our home) that I felt as though a big, dark cloud had wrapped itself around my heart and wouldn't stop squeezing until my heart quit beating. This period of blackness was not something I would recommend for anyone. But something unexpected happened in the midst of it. What I was not prepared for was the growth and the lessons that I could not have learned any other way. I would never have dreamed that there would come a day we could both say that this experience has been a blessing and has brought us closer together as a couple. I am learning that the experiences that cause the most pain also teach the most long-lasting lessons and can bring with them a proportionate amount of joy, if we choose to let them.

Orson F. Whitney's words have been a great strength to me. He said: "No pain that we suffer, no trial that we experience is wasted. It ministers to our education, to the development of such qualities as patience, faith, fortitude and humility. All that we suffer and all that we endure, especially when we endure it patiently, builds up our characters, purifies our hearts, expands our souls, and makes us more tender and charitable, more worthy to be called the children of God . . . and it is through sorrow and suffering, toil and tribulation, that we gain the education that we come here to acquire and which will make us more like our Father and Mother in heaven."[345] I have found this to be true and through it, I have gained a testimony of many things, a few of which I'd like to share.

I believe in the power of prayer. For someone like myself, personal revelation did not come second nature. It has been perhaps the weakest link in my chain. But it has strengthened with practice, and I am learning to listen to the whisperings of the spirit that I ignored a few years ago. I am starting to listen to spiritual feelings, acknowledge them, and the hardest part, confront and talk about them. In our nightly prayers, we ask continually for the power to be faithful under all circumstances. And in times of difficulty, I have felt the help of our Heavenly Father.

The Lord said, "I will be on your right hand and on your left, and my Spirit shall be in your hearts, and mine angels round about you, to bear you up" (see D&C 84:88). I have felt this power when I thought I couldn't walk in the door one more time and be the supportive wife, the nurturing mother, and the hundred other things I was supposed to be. I have felt it when I didn't think I could get up one more morning and pretend my life was ok with coworkers or relatives. And the angels have certainly been there for me on days I'm jolted into remembering that just because we have found Evergreen doesn't mean Jack is "cured."

I have an unwavering belief that our Father in Heaven loves each and every one of us, regardless of our inadequacies. He does not reserve revelation for only the perfect or the prophets of the Church. Each of us is entitled to personal revelation, if we will *listen* and allow it in our lives. I know we all have times we feel unworthy to receive inspiration. But let me suggest that it is at this time we need it the very most. Our independent two-year-old doesn't ask for help until it is long overdue. She'll work on getting dressed for 15 minutes and still end up with her head in the arm hole of her shirt and both legs in one side of the pants, which are backwards, and mismatched shoes on the wrong feet. I have to impatiently wait for her, until exhausted, she finally cries for help.

Unfortunately, this is how I behaved with my Heavenly Father, waiting until I was far into the danger zone and completely exhausted before asking for His guidance. I am learning to seek out His help every day in the little things, so that I don't find myself all tangled up in the big things. When D-day hit, there I was, both legs in one side of my pants, mismatched shoes and all, saying "*Help!* Get me out of this mess." He is there and waiting to help if we but ask.

In life, sometimes we feel like we can take Satan on in a one-on-one game of basketball and win. One thing is certain, Satan will always win unless we employ the Lords help.

I spent many hours agonizing over "Why me?" "Why am I going through the agony of this trial?" "Is the Lord just trying to measure my inadequacies?" Finally, I am realizing that the Lord does not give us tests to measure us. Just as I give each of my children gradually more and more responsibility to teach them, our Father in Heaven gives us adversity so we can grow and gain spiritual strength.

I love my Heavenly Father. I appreciate His faith in me to overcome the trials I have been given. I am especially grateful for our elder brother Jesus Christ and the atonement that provides us with a way back home, for me and couple of friends I know that weren't born perfect. We are all working toward the same goal whether a spouse, a friend, family or struggler. We are striving to become more like Christ, to overcome our own weaknesses and to someday reach the Celestial Kingdom. I have a long way to go, but I am grateful for the chance I've been given.

A Letter to a Brother

Dear Frank,

I really enjoyed seeing you at the family reunion last week. It's a shame that brothers have to live so far away. I had hoped to find some time to talk in private, but before I knew it, it was time for your flight. There are a few things I wanted to explain. A lot has happened in my life since we first talked about homosexuality four years ago and we discovered that we both have the same problem!

Confronting homosexuality is not easy. There are no easy answers and no single way of dealing with it. I've spent these last four years trying to figure out what to do about it in my life. I've explored the options and made some choices.

During these four years, I have developed close relationships with several men. With three of them, I considered seriously the possibility of a long-term relationship, but as I considered a life with them, I always came to the conclusion that I couldn't give up my family. I just wouldn't be happy without my family even if I found Mr. Right. I also realized that I can't in good conscience live a double life, having both a family and a lover on the side. So I had to make a choice between the two, and the decision was always to stay with my family. The gospel also means a lot to me, and I know that happiness only comes by living righteously.

I've discovered the roots of my homosexual feelings. I don't have time to go into all of it here, but one of the big problems is that I used to sexualize my emotional feelings for other men. I now realize that what I really wanted all along was closer, more meaningful relationships with them, and not sex at all. With some of the good, close friendships I have now, I find that I seldom have homosexual desires anymore.

As for my behavior in the past, repentance is real, and I feel I have been forgiven. I want you to know that I'm not living a double life. My bishop and stake president know all about my past behaviors and they have confidence in me—and I do in myself—that I can live worthily. It's been about a year now that I feel I've settled my struggle with homosexuality. I no longer feel torn between homosexuality and my family or the gospel. One friend of mine tells me that I'm just suppressing it. But I don't think so. I've thought out carefully what I want from life and have made some conscious choices. My closer friends can see that I've made some significant changes and really am a different person now. I had to look within my heart to see who I really wanted to be. And most important, I feel at peace with the conclusions I've reached.

I love having you as my brother. I look forward to seeing you in September and talking about this some more.

Love, Spencer

A Husband's Perspective
Mark

I believe that my struggle with same-sex attraction started long before the day that a thirteen-year-old boy lost his innocence. I grew up feeling different than I expect most of the guys felt. Small for my class and a step behind in my physical coordination, it was difficult to compete. Terrified that I would be the last one picked for games at school, it seemed like I usually was. I loved my family. My parents worked hard to raise us well. Yet, in a lot of ways, home was not the haven that I wanted it to be. Dad was strict, though I hardly remember a single spanking. I walked in fear of his short temper and the constant threat of discipline. I don't recall being teased in school. I learned early that both image and reputation last a long time and I worked hard to do everything right. I tried to act "normal" even though I felt quite odd.

Always active in the Church and scouting, I advanced through the priesthood, received my Eagle Scout, and filled leadership positions in all my Aaronic Priesthood quorums. I enjoyed the social aspects of school. I was fortunate to have a close group of friends at school and at work, but I always discounted their friendship because I was sure they would reject me if they knew the struggle I faced.

I became sexually active at the age of thirteen after having been abused by our dentist. I craved the attention from a man that said "you are someone." I remember praying with all my heart that God would intervene and save me from this man. There was no miracle. For the first time, I believed that God had let me down when I really needed him. From that point on, things were different. It was difficult for a teenager's imagination of heterosexuality to compete with the reality of same-sex experiences. The gap between me and the men I admired widened. I confided in my bishops as I advanced through the priesthood. They were always kind and supportive, but never seemed to know what to do about my struggles.

I dated in high school. All of my friends did and it was important to maintain my image. I really enjoyed double dating, not so much for the girl I was with, but because it was a legitimate way to bond and associate with male friends. At eighteen, I read about LDS Social Services and asked my bishop if I could go. I had high hopes that I would finally find some answers. I remember kneeling countless times and praying, pleading that God would take this struggle from me. I fasted, I exercised, I studied the scriptures, attended church regularly, offered service, and even dressed right. I did everything I could think of, yet the feelings remained. After several sessions of talking about my relationships with my Heavenly and earthly fathers, I saw little progress and stopped going.

At nineteen, I wasn't worthy to go on a mission, but I really wanted to go. I worked hard for an extra year, had consistent interviews with my priesthood leaders, and finally an interview with a general authority. I loved my mission. I even loved the MTC. I gained a testimony and finally learned to recognize the companionship of the Spirit. God finally answered my prayers. I was a good, hard-working missionary; that is, until the last month when as a zone leader, a transfer left me alone for three days. I crossed the line and in a way, acted out. I called my mission president and he informed me that the last twenty-three months of my life had been a complete waste. I tried not to believe him, but he was my mission president.

While there was no romantic attachment, I had dated Becky for two years before my mission. She was fun to be with and her mom was a great cook. We became great friends. I looked forward to my mission as a time to break away from the relationship. To my surprise, it grew stronger. One day while walking along a dirt road in South America I realized that I loved her and we were married one year after I got home. Finally, I was cured! During our engagement, I mentioned my past struggles to Becky. I also assured her that it wasn't a problem anymore. I learned the truth within months of our wedding. Marriage didn't make it go away. I didn't know it at the time but I would eventually learn that same-sex attraction is not a sexual problem. It is a problem of the heart with sexual symptoms.

Becky found out two years later. We sought counseling with an LDS Chaplain who told Becky that I was damned and told me that I had been sexually abused. I didn't believe him. After a few months of counseling, I once again had the problem under control. But a few months later it was out of control and I was afraid to confide in Becky.

Another couple of years passed before I got caught again. We went to the bishop and then the stake president. Luckily we had a renowned therapist in our stake. We started therapy again with the express knowledge that if I ever acted out again, there would be a disciplinary council. The first visit was very intense. Within ten minutes of leaving his office, I had acted out. I couldn't tell him—he was on our high council. The next two years of therapy were helpful, but they were also a sham. He seemed to have no specific knowledge about same-sex attraction and I didn't dare tell him the truth about my continuing struggles. I asked about some sort of support group or at least a person that understood what I was going through. I knew I couldn't be the only Mormon struggling. I was told there were none. I finally decided that I would just have to find a way to cure myself, then some day in the distant future I would clear my conscience by admitting to my wife and bishop that I used to have a problem but I had taken care of it some ten years earlier. I swore to myself that until that day, I would never confess again. Ten years did pass, but I never found a way to cure myself.

Eventually I became two different people. One was a religious, loving father and model husband. The other was a desperate man seeking validation by making sexual contact with other men at any opportunity. It was the only time I felt truly accepted, in spite of my deepest secret. I acted out more and more. The more I did, the more I needed. Like salt water, no matter how much I drank, my thirst increased. My contacts grew more intense and more risky. The more people I could act out with, the more worthwhile I felt, and the number of partners multiplied again and again. I needed it so bad that I was willing to sacrifice my own life as well as the health of my wife and children—whatever it took to get the next fix.

My two conflicting lives continued for the next eight years. I always seemed to be in therapy for one of a thousand things: anxiety, stress, time management, fear of success, or depression, but never for same sex attraction. I tried the spiritual approach without success as a teenager and as an adult. A dozen therapists proved that the psychoanalytical approach didn't work either. I hated myself. I spent my life comparing my weaknesses to a thousand other people's strengths and I always came up lacking. Eventually the burden became too heavy to carry. I felt emotionally paralyzed and unable to succeed at anything. It seemed hopeless. I could feel myself starting to snap. I had four wonderful children and a great wife. Yet, I could barely get out of bed. One day I realized that I couldn't shrug off the thoughts of suicide anymore and I got scared. With no other way out, my therapist finally convinced me to tell Becky what was happening. It took another six months to build up my courage, but the truth finally came out. She was devastated. After the initial shock had passed, we went to see the bishop. I didn't have much faith in the ability of the priesthood; I had confessed too many times with little effect. I was wrong. My bishop gave me a book to read called *Born That Way*. I read the book and in many ways, I felt like I was reading my own story. Finally there was hope. Someone did share my struggle and they had found answers. When I got to the end of the book there was a phone number for Evergreen International. I nervously called and my life began to change even faster.

Evergreen offered me the answers I had searched for during twenty years of struggle. I learned that there were others struggling just like I was and they were succeeding. It offered an approach that combined the power of faith and the hope of reparative therapy. I quickly learned to love going to group meetings. I had found a safe place where I could talk, share my fears and struggles, and be myself without rejection.

Since my introduction to Evergreen, the process of recovery has been a jagged one. It is paved with many successes and many failures. Most important, I have learned about myself and what I can do to succeed. Evergreen has helped me learn how I can address the real problem rather than just the symptoms.

My stake held a disciplinary council in March As I walked in to meet with the stake presidency prior to entering the high council room, they had tears in their eyes. They hugged me and told me that they loved me. Although I was disfellowshipped, I never felt more love from other men than I did that night. My journey home had begun. A life of broken promises and repeated falls left little self confidence. I saw a very long journey. I did not dare to even hope that I would leave the council and not act out again because I had made and broken that promise a thousand times before. I did believe I could be honest. I made two promises that night: that I would be honest and that I would never give up.

There are a lot of things that strengthen me as I journey home chipping away at my same-sex attraction. I would like to share how I learned just a few of these things.

I believe that dealing with same-sex attraction is much like dealing with heart disease. When a person learns that to go without treatment means certain death, he usually goes to great lengths to save his life. He begins by going to a heart specialist. It usually requires surgery, specialized medications, and an aggressive rehabilitation program of exercise and a restricted diet. It takes time and a lot of effort, but it usually works. More important, it offers hope. Something can be done to fight the disease of the heart. When I learned there was hope for my struggle, I decided I needed a special program. I didn't want to be like a critically-ill patient that goes to the hospital for treatment and wanders aimlessly from floor to floor, and room to room, picking up whatever medicine happens to be available. For me, the alternative to suicide was an intense program of study, bishop's interviews, and exercises in risk, honesty, and faith. I also learned the hard way that I needed a specialist. I needed to make sure that my treatment gave me the tools I needed to get well. I sought a counselor that knew the struggle better than I—one who could offer a realistic perspective and a workable plan. I cannot afford to fail.

I have learned that if I want to get well, I must accept responsibility to get the help I need. I cannot afford to leave my healing up to chance. I study and learn. Becky and I talk for hours at a time trying to sort out the contributing factors. We make the journey a priority. I find that our struggle is often misunderstood and the challenges we face go unrecognized. I generally must educate my priesthood leaders about what my needs are, what realistic expectations are, and explain the process I must go through to get well. I believe that Heavenly Father helps us understand those needs as we seek His Spirit. He makes it possible for us to successfully address those needs. Accepting responsibility also means that I made a commitment to go to Evergreen every week. If I disagree with my therapist's opinion, I tell him. If I don't think I am progressing, I seek change. If my bishop forgets that we have an appointment, I call him.

Pornography plays a major role in my same-sex attraction. It was a stepping stone that led me to acting out and became one of my greatest addictions. I got to the point where I needed pornography so badly that I would drive for several hours just to buy it. Pornography fueled my addiction without the complications of cruising or acting out with someone else. It became a major stumbling block in my battle to set my life straight. In the beginning, it was not an issue that I felt comfortable discussing with Becky. I did address it with the bishop. At first, I simply could not imagine surviving without it. I told him that I had to have it. It was my safety valve. As I progressed, the bishop often encouraged me to get rid of it. One evening, while meeting for our weekly interview, I took advantage of a moment of strength and committed to get rid of it. I left his office with new resolve. It felt good. The very next day I took my stack to a friend's house. We talked. I left the stack with him, and brought home a new one. Rather disappointed with myself, I related the incident to the bishop when we met the following week. Again he encouraged and strengthened me and finally after about six weeks of effort, I got rid of it for good. I used to think that I would shrivel up and die without it. Now I thank my Father in Heaven that I don't have to struggle at that level any more. Oddly enough, each time I left the bishop's office, I was confidant that I would succeed. Four times I tried. Four times I failed. It was the fifth time that I finally succeeded.

I don't believe that we can overcome same-sex attraction alone. I think Heavenly Father expects us to trust in others to help us. It seems that trust is one of the fundamental concepts we must learn so we can heal. I learned that the more people I can trust and rely on, the better I do. Parents, spouses, family members, bishops, stake presidents, therapists, and friends have all helped. This can be an overwhelming challenge and the more support I have, the better I progress. When I share my challenges with these people and they know my struggles, their acceptance is unconditional. I don't have to discount their love for me anymore by thinking that they would reject me if they really knew me.

Because of the years of failure and constant comparison with other men's strengths, I could not love myself. I hated myself. I am learning to love myself as I open up to Becky time and time again. I tell her of my successes and, more important, of my failures. She loves me regardless. She often tells me she is proud of me and my efforts even after painful failures. Eventually, I began to believe her and I began to feel I might be able to learn to love me, too.

For me, it is often a difficult and long process as I try to relearn a lifetime of inaccurate thinking. I have made several mistakes in my healing journey that have broken hearts and even caused me to lose some of my friends. But true friends don't turn their backs. They weep with me, pray with me, and continue to love and support me. They strengthen me and encourage me, and I am learning to trust.

I have given my bishop several heart attacks and my setbacks have been frustrating for both of us. I expected rejection and condemnation, but he has always responded with unconditional love, support and encouragement. My association with him teaches me to rely on the Spirit for healing. He teaches me about the atonement. He helped me to finally believe that it even applies to someone like me. He blesses me through the Spirit. I progress faster when I meet with him regularly. I can imagine the Savior's love for me because I see it and feel it when I meet with the bishop.

I firmly believe that all progress we make is based on taking risks. Once, a long time ago, I took risks and got hurt. It hurt so badly that I eventually stopped venturing out to new ground. I found safety by hiding within myself. Evergreen sports has been a great addition to my life. The long drive is worth the opportunity to associate with other great guys doing what guys do—sports. It means a lot to finally learn how to shoot or dribble a basketball, how to bat, and why not to slide in softball while wearing short pants. It gives me the chance to risk and to address a fear that has bound me for as long as I can remember. I have met some very intimidating people on the basketball court and resented their boldness and strength. But as I learned to play and started to compare our similarities, I found that we held a lot in common and friendships were easily formed.

My therapist teaches me about honesty. I am learning to be openly honest with Becky, with God, with myself, and with others. It isn't easy after spending most of my life trying to deceive everyone around me. When we deceive people in hopes of being accepted, we cheat ourselves out of the very thing we seek. We tend to reject their acceptance based on that little phrase, "If they really knew me, they wouldn't have accepted me." I am also learning to recognize when things are in balance or when I am tipping toward disaster. For me it is like riding a bicycle. When I first learned to ride a bike, I crashed a lot before I really felt comfortable. Then I learned to make the continuous fine adjustments necessary to keep my balance. As I practiced, keeping my balance became instinctive and I could keep my balance without even noticing. Then I could spend more time riding my bike and less time falling off. Now, many of my emotional corrections are becoming a matter of instinct. I still struggle every day, but the struggle is different. I work at keeping my balance rather than picking myself up off the ground.

Open honesty means I share my struggles in their infancy. I tell others about risky places and risky situations before I find myself in them. While I am strong, I constantly build fences for possible times of weakness and I express my concerns before they become actions.

Becky also taught me about the power of faith. Day after day as we held our morning prayer she would ask Heavenly Father to carry my burden and remove my desires to act out until I was strong enough to carry them myself. Having prayed for a similar blessing for years, I expected no relief. But there was relief. My desires were almost completely eliminated. Through Becky's faith, for the first time I experienced the joys that come from obedience to the laws of chastity. The burdens of guilt are lifted and replaced by a new peace of mind and a greater sense of self control. I had never understood what it felt like to be chaste.

My relationship with Becky has grown immeasurably. We have learned to trust one another, have broken that trust, and rebuilt it more times than I would like to admit. We have learned to talk without judgement and have learned how to be supportive. I feel like I finally have the marriage and friendship I have always wanted—one where I can express my fears and weaknesses and where I receive support and understanding that strengthens me. It makes me more than I would ever be by myself. Becky has also learned to let go. It seems like it would be a lot easier if she could meet all of my needs, but she cannot. I must go back and address the insecurities of a little boy who felt alone, rejected, and even betrayed by other men. She does help me to keep it all in perspective, and even to notice the need to address specific issues. But we both realize that ultimately I am responsible for my success.

Our physical relationship has also grown. Although we have been married 14 years, most of those years I resented the need to have sex. I avoided it and responded only out of a sense of duty. Although I never thought I would look forward to a normal relationship or find it emotionally satisfying, I can honestly say that I now love the physical relationship we share. It exceeds anything I have experienced in the past, both emotionally and physically.

I believe there are many ways we can experience a change of heart, especially when the powers of heaven are invoked by our faith in God and our works in righteousness. I decided never to return to the disciplinary council until I was sure I was ready. The thought of another broken promise was too much to bear. In June, I returned to the high council, confidant in the Lord's confirmation to me that it was time for the next step. A few new faces had joined the high council in the past sixteen months, including my next-door neighbor. Once again, I was treated to a strong witness that God loves me. The leaders of my stake love me as well. That single night reflected months of work, frustration, faith, and tears. My blessings were restored, and on the fourth of July the entire nation celebrated as I led my eight-year-old son into the waters of baptism. Once again, I thanked God for His mercy, His love, and His priesthood.

I have a personal testimony of this work. I know that it is ordained by God. He has provided a plan that demonstrates His love for us. I know that He watches over each one of us and longs to help us if we will believe in Him. Several times I find myself struggling with all of my strength to succeed. The more I struggle, the more difficult it becomes. When I finally let go and place my burdens before the Lord, He lifts me up. Try as we may, we cannot win this battle alone. I am grateful for the knowledge that He is there for me if I will let Him in.

There are so many areas that I can feel the hand of God working in my life to help me overcome. I have also seen it working in the lives of others. While there are many facets to the progress we make, I have found two essential elements: the hope of reparative therapy and the power of the Savior's atonement and unconditional love. Never have I felt the Lord's influence so strongly in my life as I do now. My mission president was wrong. My mission to South America was a success. I gained a testimony, learned to recognize the companionship of the Spirit, developed a foundation of faith, fell in love with Becky, and influenced thousands of people for good. I have a new mission now and perhaps this calling is greater than the first. And perhaps the results will be more important and significant as well.

I have no doubt that the Lord lives and, more important, that He loves me. He loves each one of us just the way we are. There is hope. We can be happy. He wants us to succeed. He will help us. I believe this struggle tries the faith of some of God's most valiant souls. I also believe He holds a special place in His heart for each one of us. We did not ask for this challenge which in many ways requires effort and sacrifice akin to that of the pioneers who crossed the plains. Yet, we too shall arrive at our journey's end purified and strengthened as we walk with God. May He bless your every step and lighten your burdens as you seek the mighty change of heart He has promised.

Your Brother in Faith, Mark

A Wife's Perspective
Becky

The day before Mark and I were engaged, he told me that he had been sexually molested by a family friend as a young boy. I reassured him that I loved him and that it did not change the way I felt about him. I told him how sorry I was that he had to go through such an ordeal. We didn't discuss the subject again. I didn't think to ask about any lingering problems or really understand that there could be other associated issues.

We were married in the temple and I felt it was the beginning of a perfect life together. We struggled with the normal problems of young married couples, but all my dreams were coming true and I knew that with Mark by my side we could overcome them all. I often joked with Mark that my only sin was loving him too much.

We had been married just over two years when the first bombshell fell. I found some pornography Mark had hidden. I confronted him and the continuing issues of same-sex attraction were revealed. I heard it, but could not or would not accept it. We went to the bishop and had some counseling from an army chaplain, but the chaplain seemed angry when the Church didn't take any action. He told me to divorce Mark while I could still salvage my life. The bishop, on the other hand, told me that Mark really loved me and if I did everything I could to help him, we would make it. Our first child was four months old and I chose to believe my bishop. Thus, began my quest to be the perfect wife, mother, lover, companion, and Church member. The list was endless, but if I could do it all, I would save my marriage and, more important, my husband.

Mark assured me that things were better and that somehow things had fallen into place. I thought my plan was working. If I were perfect, or if I could just prove to him that I was enough and loved him unconditionally, all would be well. Once again, while never really knowing much about the problem, the subject became a closed issue and stayed closed for two years.

A few days before Christmas, I was looking for something, opened his briefcase, and found another magazine. This time I took our son and left. Mark immediately went to the bishop who sent him to the stake president. I went with Mark to his appointment with the stake president expecting the worst—a Church council. The stake president decided against a council and placed Mark on probation. He advised him to see a counselor in our stake, an authority on sexual abuse and problems. He told me he was sure that Mark truly loved me, wanted to repent, and get better. He said that I could help him by staying with him and loving him and that I should never give him any reason to "act out." If I would do these things, our marriage would be saved. The stake president told Mark that if anything happened again, there would be a Church council. I told Mark if anything ever happened again, our marriage was over. I returned home and tried even harder to be enough to make Mark "be good," determined to never give him any reason to "act out" again. We went to counseling with the expert that our stake president recommended, which proved to be a very painful experience for me. I was told that because I was a prudish Mormon woman, I could not expect to make my husband happy. But he seemed to be helping Mark. We finished up our counseling sessions and Mark was taken off Church probation. Things seemed a lot better and again the subject was closed.

Eight years passed. They were pretty good years, although we seemed to always be having bad luck. Mark couldn't seem to get through school. I became very dependent or codependent on Mark. I lived in fear of making a mistake and causing him to "act out," and wanted to be with him all the time. Eventually, Mark confided to me that school was a difficult place for him to be. When he said he was having a hard time, I would encourage him to stay home with me. That way he was safe and so was I. We loved being together and we had some really good times, but we weren't making progress.

One day I suggested to Mark that he might need some counseling. I felt that he didn't feel worthy to succeed and would unconsciously set himself up for failure. Mark did begin some counseling and for a while things got a little better, then the old patterns became apparent again: financial trouble, not doing well in school, and depression I didn't understand. I told Mark I wanted to go to counseling with him because I wondered if I might be contributing to the cycles although I had no idea how. On December 27, as we rode the elevator up to counseling, he told me that he had never really been faithful during our married life. I really had to fight not to pass out right there in the elevator. Mark helped me out of the elevator and then everything went numb. My whole world came crashing down around me. Nothing made sense. I put my life into auto pilot. I was the primary president and my four children needed me. The youngest was barely six months old.

After the numbness came the anger. It came in waves. I tried to hold it back because I thought anger was wrong. Since then, I have discovered that there is such a thing as righteous anger and that it's important to let the anger out. I was angry at everyone: at myself for being so stupid, at God for letting this happen to me, at the Church for misguided counsel, and at Mark for not loving me enough if he ever really had. I felt used as a front for his perverted lifestyle. I started wondering if Mark had HIV, or if I or even my baby had it. The list of things to worry about went on and on.

Slowly over the next few days and weeks the question of "How could Mark do this to me?" changed to "How could Mark do this to himself?" Mark was my light, my love, a righteous and valiant spirit, I was sure. How could things have gone so terribly wrong? That's when Mark and I started talking—really talking for the first time. I wanted to know everything from the beginning. As the story unfolded, there were two things that stayed in my mind. First, he had been sexually abused. Mark was told he had the problem and he needed to repent. Secondly, my husband had contemplated suicide. This was incredible to me—suicide! These two things helped me stay and fight for a thirteen-year-old boy who was robbed of his innocence, whose cries for help went unanswered. I felt I had been given a second chance with Mark and my family. It would be awful to have Mark kill himself and never really understand why. I wanted to understand now and was willing to try as hard as I could. If there was a chance, no matter how small, I felt I had to try to save my marriage. I truly loved my husband.

Mark's disfellowshipment was actually a very spiritual experience filled with love and acceptance from the great men who were there. I came away with a better understanding of the Savior's atonement and had a true testimony that Mark could become clean again.

Our progress has been slow at times and faster at others. We've had many set backs. We were blessed to find Evergreen, which was wonderful for Mark. It provided me with a lot of books to read that gave me a base for understanding same-sex attraction. I feel Mark is a textbook case. After struggling with ups and downs for a year, things looked pretty bleak. For the first time, I considered divorce as a real option. Mark and I often fought about honesty. Mark's definition and mine were very different. This brought great discouragement to me and Satan took advantage of it. Every day it was like I had a neon sign blinking on and off in my head: "Homosexual. Homosexual. That's what Mark is and he won't ever change." At the time, I didn't realize that because of the abuse Mark didn't really have a true concept of honesty. It was a relief when I finally learned that honesty was something same-sex attraction strugglers and abuse victims have a hard time with. I also wondered if I could ever trust him again. I started to feel I had lost the love I felt for him in the past and didn't know if I could ever feel the same way about him again. Too much had happened.

I decided that I was in no shape mentally to make such a decision. I went to the temple to ask my Father in Heaven what I should do. In the celestial room, I poured out my heart to God. I was told that I was loved, and if I couldn't take anymore, it was ok. If divorce was my choice, He would understand and be with me and help me. This was the most amazing thing to me. He would always love me and help me no matter my choices or mistakes. All I had to do was ask. I learned more. He told me that if I did stay with Mark, he would make progress and that my love for him would grow stronger and bring me more joy than I could ever imagine. He told me to ask Mark to seek a new counselor just for him, one that had experience and success in treating people with same-sex attraction. He told me that Mark should ask the bishop for a priesthood blessing requesting that his burdens would be lightened. I also felt I should pray that he would not be tempted above that which he could handle.

I went home feeling somewhat better, but I didn't fully understanding the significance of what had just happened. Mark received the blessing within the week. I prayed every day that he would not be tempted beyond his capacity and that his burdens would be lightened. Mark also found a new counselor through Evergreen. I soon forgot about the things that happened in the temple that night, although I continued to pray for him.

Mark also asked that I seek some counseling for myself. He asked me to commit to go to the friends and family support group sponsored by Evergreen. I wasn't thrilled about doing either of these things but didn't know how to get out of them. Surprisingly, I really enjoyed counseling. It wasn't the painful experience it had been in the past. This time, most of the focus wasn't on Mark. She cared about me and how I was doing. It was also nice to know that my feelings were normal for a person going through this situation. The support group was even better than counseling. The people there were great. I felt loved and cared about as soon as I walked in the door. I knew that I, too, loved and cared about those who were there trying to understand and help the struggler in their lives. I wasn't alone anymore!

Several months later, we were sitting in Mark's second Church council and I listened to Mark tell about the things he had learned and how his testimony had grown. Someone asked how he had learned to trust the Savior and believe in the atonement of Jesus Christ? His answer amazed me. He had learned to trust God from me. As we prayed together, I would ask that his burdens be lightened and that he would not be tempted above that which he could bear. I had no idea that these prayers had any impact. Suddenly, I remembered that night in the temple, and the promises the Lord made to me. I was humbled and thankful that I had listened and obeyed. All the promises that were made to me in the temple that night have come true.

Mark has made great progress. My love for him is the brightest light in my life next to my love for my Heavenly Father. I know He made all of this possible. My marriage is blessed with a worthy priesthood holder at the helm and my dreams really are coming true. All aspects of my marriage, the physical, emotional and spiritual are all better than I could have ever imagined. I am so proud of Mark and his righteous desires. I am proud of the fact that he has never given up. I'm grateful for a loving bishop who also never gave up and taught me through his example about the Savior's unconditional love. He taught me how to use the atonement and place my pain and burdens on the Savior's shoulders. I am grateful for a loving Father in Heaven who is always with me, who knows me, and understands me. Mark and I have come a long way. Things are good. Mark still has times of struggle and so do I, but we will always strive to keep a balance. We will help each other grow and progress and we will endure to the end. I am grateful for our four beautiful children. They have seen us struggle and grow together. I hope that they know and feel the love their parents have for one another. I hope we can effectively teach them of their Father in Heaven's love for them and the great gift of the atonement that Jesus gave to them.

This is my story. I could not survive these painful times without the love and support of great people: my bishop, stake president, husband, Evergreen and great counselors. Even many who do not know of our struggle but seem to be there when I need them. As the events unfolded, there were many parts of the story that I couldn't understand myself. I was too involved with day-to-day survival to see that each step I take is guided and made possible by a loving Father in Heaven. He never left me alone and somehow endowed me with the strength to keep going.

May He bless you and those you love as you work together to learn and grow.

Love, Becky

Please Don't Let Me Grow Up Gay
Brad Anderson

The best times I can remember were when I was four years old. It was the summer of 1959, and I was growing up in a small town in Upper Michigan. I remember warm summer days of fun and happiness, the eager anticipation of beginning school. After I started school, I found that my anticipation was only answered by rejection and ridicule. Because of the jeers of "sissy," "fag," and "queer," I inverted my energies to self-preservation and I journeyed through grade school and junior high with the girls, which only solidified the jeers I endured.

In an eighth-grade sex education class, I heard how some boys would look up to an older man or a peer as a role model and that this was not to be confused with homosexual tendencies because it would pass. For myself, I knew that my attraction for other males was so intense that it would not pass. At that young, tender age, I knelt by my bedside and cried, begging God that what was happening to me wasn't really happening. I cried and begged, "Please God, don't let me grow up gay!"

In the ninth grade, my friend Valarie joined the Mormon Church and she gave me a copy of The Book of Mormon. I read and prayed and, unknown to me, received a testimony. The Church was much different from the Catholic upbringing I had and things did not work out for me to continue attending Church and I soon headed in a far different direction.

At school, I began to hang around with a new group—the hippies of the early 1970s. By age sixteen, I had become involved in the gay lifestyle, had run away from home, and spent the next year and a half bouncing through foster homes. At age seventeen, having graduated from high school, I moved out on my own. During that summer, I hitch hiked to California to "find myself." During that trip, a Latter-Day Saint couple attending BYU picked me up south of the Tetons and, by the time we reached Salt Lake City, invited me to stay at their house in Provo. I ended up spending a week with them. The Savior whispered, "Come Follow Me."

Not long after returning to Michigan, two missionaries showed up at my door. I wanted to join the Church, but how could I be both gay and a Mormon? I spoke to the branch president before baptism and shared with him my concerns. He counseled me to go ahead and be baptized, that there was help available to me, and he would locate it. I was baptized and within six months was inactive and back living the lifestyle, believing that there was no help for me.

I later became active in the Church again and began counseling to deal with my homosexual desires and tried to make headway in overcoming this condition. I did all I could to prepare myself to serve a mission. This was during the time President Kimball had issued the great call for young men to serve a mission. I wanted to be like the other guys and serve a mission and bring people to the Savior. After much preparation, and an interview with an Apostle, I was given permission to serve. What a joyous opportunity had been laid before me! What I didn't realize was that the jeering would begin again as early as my first weeks in the Missionary Training Center. My world came crashing down around me. How could I be in Zion and endure such rejection? I thought it would be better to cease to exist, to just never have been. I struggled through the two years and returned home disillusioned, angry, frustrated, and experiencing homosexual desires as intense as before joining the Church, despite six years of counseling. Why had God abandoned me?

I separated myself from the Church and plunged into the gay lifestyle. Throughout this time, the Holy Spirit continually prompted me with the feeling of knowing where I should be—back with the Saints. But how would it ever happen? I was so entangled in the gay lifestyle that my only reply was, "Ok, then you'll have to do it for me." That summer brought a foreboding spirit. I began to feel as though I would not live to see Christmas. I was scared, and in August went to the Catholic Church where I had served as an altar boy, and kneeling, pled for my life. On the twelfth of December I was assaulted on the street, developed a blood clot on the brain, and was given a one percent chance to live. But I did live, and during the ensuing years regained the ability to talk and function normally. During that time, all my entanglements in the gay lifestyle became unraveled and I knew that God had spared my life.

I came in contact with another member of my ward who was also suffering from homosexual desires and we talked about our feelings. One day we read about a conference that had been held in Utah by a group of Mormons who were overcoming same-sex attraction. The Spirit moved upon me and I knew I had to investigate. It had been twenty-three years since that thirteen-year-old boy had knelt by his bedside and pled to God for help. I contacted Evergreen and we started the Evergreen Midwest Chapter with two participants and a facilitator. We met for many months, knowing that if we would press forward, this chapter would work.

After waiting so many years, I cannot tell you what it is like to finally be progressing! I am coming out of my shell! I have found that there really is a good person underneath all the years of jeering and rejection and I am discovering myself. It is taking time to repair the many years of damage, but what a relief to finally be able to feel at ease with myself, to no longer have to footnote all my accomplishments with "But you're still a fag." It is especially fulfilling for me to see the men in our chapter grow, gain self acceptance, and progress toward the men we are underneath all the garbage heaped upon us for so many years.

The world has a different voice than the one Evergreen puts forth. As Captain Moroni held aloft the Title of Liberty which read, "In memory of our God, our religion, and freedom, and our peace, our wives, and our children," might we continue to hold this title of liberty as a testimony to the world of what God can do through grace as we resolve our problems. I am thankful I no longer need to look at the best days of my life being in 1959 when I was four. I can now look to today! I am within two credit hours of completing my bachelor's degree, and this fall start work on my master's degree in guidance and counseling. I am employed by the University. As a high priest, I serve as the second counselor in the bishopric of my ward, and this morning, attended the temple. I know that, with God, I will one day find my Eve and as my patriarchal blessing promises: "We bless you to know that you and the bride that the Lord will prepare for you will work your lives together in the spirit of harmony and love."

I testify that as God has helped me to this point, He will do the same for you.

It Works!
Buzz Jackson

I have watched Jason Park (the author of this book), over the past seven years, go through a remarkable transformation. He has grown out of his homosexual problems and in the process become a better husband, father, and spiritual leader. Though each person must find his or her unique pathway out of this challenge, following the steps outlined in this book will help. I have seen them work firsthand, in Jason's life and in my own.

Selected Readings

If you can't find these books at your local bookstore, you can order them conveniently and confidentially through the mail from Evergreen International or from Regeneration Books (se the Organizations section in this book).

Desires in Conflict: Answering the Struggle for Sexual Identity, by Joe Dallas (Harvest House Publishers, Eugene, OR, 1991). This Christian book provides practical, effective help for restoring sexual wholeness. It also provides information for family members and friends on how to give loving support and explains the rage felt by gay activists. The appendix gives answers to the pro-gay theology. Two chapters address lesbian concerns.

A Place in the Kingdom: Spiritual Insights from Latter-day Saints about Same-Sex Attraction, edited by Garrick Hyde and Ginger Hyde (Century Publishing, Salt Lake City, UT, 1997). This book is a collection of life-story essays of men and women struggling with same-sex attraction, as well as spouses and parents. It provides both hope and perspective.

Resolving Homosexual Problems: A Guide for LDS Men, by Jason Park (Century Publishing, Salt Lake City, UT, 1997). This book explains same-sex attractions from an LDS perspective and gives practical suggestions on how to resolve your homosexual problems. The companion book *Helping LDS Men Resolve their Homosexual Problems* is written to suggest to others how they may help the LDS man as he struggles with these issues.

Helping LDS Men Resolve their Homosexual Problems: A Guide for Family, Friends, and Church Leaders, by Jason Park (Century Publishing, Salt Lake City, UT, 1997). This book explains same-sex attractions from an LDS context and suggests how to help a man who is struggling to resolve his homosexual problems. It is written as a companion to *Resolving Homosexual Problems: A Guide for LDS Men*, which is written to the LDS man.

Understanding Male Homosexual Problems: An Introduction for

Latter-day Saints by Jason Park (Century Publishing, Salt Lake City, UT, 1997). This short booklet gives a brief overview of the causes, challenges, and solutions to homosexual problems from an LDS perspective.

You Don't Have to be Gay, by J. A. Konrad (Pacific House Publishing, Newport Beach, CA, 1987). This easy-to-read book is written as a series of letters to a young man unfulfilled in his homosexuality. It teaches from a Christian perspective that people are not "born that way," that homosexuality is not a problem in relating to members of the opposite sex, and that homosexuality can be changed.

AMCAP Journal, vol. 19, no. 1–1993 (Association of Mormon Counselors and Psychotherapists, Salt Lake City, UT, 1993). This issue of the journal is devoted to the topic of homosexuality and contains articles, interviews and book reviews on homosexuality. It gives pertinent information about homosexuality from an LDS perspective.

Homosexuality: A New Christian Ethic, by Elizabeth R. Moberly (James Clarke & Co., Cambridge, England, 1983). A short, scholarly book on the root causes of homosexuality. Although hard for some to understand, this enlightening book states that the homosexual condition is an emotional and social problem, not just a sexual problem. It explains that the homosexual condition is a misguided attempt to fulfil normal developmental needs which for some reason were not fulfilled earlier. It distinguishes between the homosexual condition and its expression in homosexual activity.

Coming Out of Homosexuality: New Freedom for Men & Women, by Bob Davies and Lori Rentzel (Inter Varsity Press, Downers Grove, IL, 1993). This Christian book is written to people struggling with same-sex attractions. It provides straightforward ideas and helps.

Homosexual No More: Practical Strategies for Christians Overcoming Homosexuality, by Dr. William Consiglio (Victor Books, Wheaton, IL, 1991). Based on teachings developed for Christian ex-gay group meetings, this book identifies six stages of homosexual development and gives practical strategies for change, including principles of daily self-therapy.

Reparative Therapy of Male Homosexuality: A New Clinical Approach, by Joseph Nicolosi, Ph.D. (Jason Aronson, Inc, Northvale,

NJ, 1991). Although written as a resource for therapists, this book can give insights and practical helps to those who struggle with homosexuality themselves. The book is helpful, readable, and consistent with general Christian teaching.

Born That Way? by Erin Eldridge (Deseret Book Company, Salt Lake City, UT, 1994). This LDS book describes a woman's personal struggle with same-sex feelings and how she overcame them through the power of Jesus Christ and by applying gospel principles.

Understanding and Helping Those Who Have Homosexual Problems: Suggestions for Ecclesiastical Leaders (Church of Jesus Christ of Latter-day Saints, 1992, item number 32250). This booklet gives information to Church leaders on how to counsel and help.

A Letter to a Friend, by Spencer W. Kimball (Church of Jesus Christ of Latter-day Saints, 1978, item number 30941). This pamphlet is written as a letter to a person with homosexual desires inviting him to come to Christ.

To the One, by Boyd K. Packer (Church of Jesus Christ of Latter-day Saints, 1978, item number 30942). This pamphlet discusses the temporary condition of homosexuality.

Healing Homosexuality: Case Stories of Reparative Therapy, by Joseph Nicolosi, Ph.D (Jason Aronson, Inc., Northvale, NJ, 1993). Personal testimonies from homosexual men who tried to accept a gay identity but were dissatisfied and then benefitted from psychotherapy to help free them from homosexuality. Offers insight to both therapists and patients who see homosexuality as a treatable condition. Discusses how group therapy heals and how reparative therapy works.

"Understanding Homosexuality and the Reality of Change" (Impact Resources, P.O. Box 1169, Murrieta CA 92564–1169, phone 800/333–6475). This sixty–minute video suitable for family viewing contains interviews with two men and two women on the roots of homosexual orientation and the change process, as well as interviews with therapists Joe Dallas and Joseph Nicolosi. This professional video is a valuable resource.

"Homosexuality: Hot Topics for Teens" (Media International, 313 E. Broadway, Suite 202, Glendale CA 91209, phone 800/477–7575). This is a fast-paced video is geared for teenagers. It is a shortened, sixteen-minute version of the video "Understanding Homosexuality and the Reality of Change." It includes a leader's study guide.

Homosexuality & Hope: A Psychologist Talks About Treatment and Change, by Gerard van den Aardweg (Servant Books, Ann Arbor, MI, 1985). This book states that homosexuality is a psychological problem that can be successfully treated. It discusses self-pity, inferiority complex, self-centeredness, and the value of humor. It states that homosexuality is not genetically based.

Organizations

Evergreen International, P.O. Box 3, Salt Lake City, UT 84110, phone 800/391–1000, internet home page: http://www.members.aol. com/evergrn999, e-mail: evergrn999@aol.com. This nonprofit organization provides direction and support to LDS men and women who want to diminish their same-sex attraction and free themselves from homosexual behavior. It is also a resource to family and friends, professional counselors, religious leaders, and all others who wish to help individuals who desire to change. The organization refers people to affiliated support groups and therapists, publishes manuals and newsletters, sells books by mail, and sponsors conferences. Call or write for a list of publications or information on a support group near you.

Regeneration Books, P. O. Box 9830, Baltimore, MD 21284–9830, 410/661–4337 or 410/661–0284. This mail-order organization sells many books written to a Christian audience. Call or write for a catalog.

Exodus International, P.O. Box 77652, Seattle, WA 98177-0652, phone 206/784–7799.This network of interdenominational Christian ministries offers support to men and women seeking to overcome homosexuality. Exodus maintains a referral list of ministries, churches, and individuals. It also publishes a newsletter and sponsors conferences. Call or write for an introductory packet of information.

Homosexuals Anonymous, P. O. Box 7881, Reading, PA 19603, phone 800/253-3000 or 610/376–1146. A nondenominational Christian organization that uses a modified twelve–step program modeled on that of Alcoholics Anonymous. The organization publishes a newsletter and other publications.

Sexaholics Anonymous, P. O. Box 111910, Nashville, TN 37222, phone 615/331–6230. A fellowship of men and women who want to stop their sexually self-destructive thinking and behavior. The philosophy and program are taken directly from the twelve steps and twelve traditions of Alcoholics Anonymous.

Family Research Council, 700 13th Street NW, Suite 500, Washington, DC 20005, phone 202/393–2100. The council is a research, resource, and educational organization that promotes the traditional family. It opposes gay marriage and adoption rights. It publishes numerous reports and newsletters from a conservative perspective on issues affecting the family.

Focus on the Family, 420 N. Cascade Avenue, Colorado Springs, CO 80903, phone 719/531–3400. A Christian organization that seeks to strengthen the traditional family. It has done research on homosexuality and school programs, civil rights laws, and other public policy questions. They publish numerous books and a monthly magazine.

NGO Family Voice, 524 JRCB, Brigham Young University, Provo, UT 84604. A pro-family organization jointly sponsored by the BYU Law School and the David M. Kennedy Center for International Studies. It actively supports the policies and principles stated in "The Family: A Proclamation to the World" issued by the First Presidency of The Church of Jesus Christ of Latter-day Saints and has information and programs designed to help men and women improve their parenting skills. Through its university network, it has access to information and expertise related to overcoming homosexual problems.

National Association of Research and Therapy of Homosexuality (NARTH), 16542 Ventura Blvd., Suite 416, Encino, CA 91436, phone 818/789–4440.

Lambda Report, Peter LaBarbara, Accuracy in Academia, 4455 Connecticut Ave. N. W., Suite 330, Washington, DC 20008, phone 202/364–3085.

Notes

1   "Standards of Morality and Fidelity," letter from the First Presidency of the Church of Jesus Christ of Latter-day Saints, 14 Nov. 1991, numbering added.

2   "Standards of Morality and Fidelity," letter from the First Presidency of the Church of Jesus Christ of Latter-day Saints, 14 Nov. 1991.

3   "Same-Gender Attraction," Dallin H. Oaks, *Ensign*, Oct. 1995, p. 8.

4   "Reverence and Morality," Gordon B. Hinckley, *Ensign*, May 1987, p. 47.

5   "Standards of Morality and Fidelity," letter from the First Presidency of the Church of Jesus Christ of Latter-day Saints, 14 Nov. 1991.

6   "Standards of Morality and Fidelity," letter from the First Presidency of the Church of Jesus Christ of Latter-day Saints, 14 Nov. 1991.

7   "Stand Strong Against the Wiles of the World", Gordon B. Hinckley, *Ensign*, Nov. 1995, p. 99.

8   "Same-Gender Attraction," Dallin H. Oaks, *Ensign*, Oct. 1995, p. 13.

9   "Same-Gender Attraction," Dallin H. Oaks, *Ensign*, Oct. 1995, p. 13.

10 "Same-Gender Attraction," Dallin H. Oaks, *Ensign*, Oct. 1995, p. 14.

11 Alfred C. Kinsey, et. al., *Sexual Behavior in the Human Male*, W. B. Saunders Company, Philadelphia, 1948.

12 *Sexual Behavior in the Human Female*, 1953.

13 *Sexual Behavior in the Human Male*, Alfred C. Kinsey, et. al., W. B. Saunders Company, Philadelphia, 1948, p. 638.

14 *Sexual Behavior in the Human Male*, Alfred C. Kinsey, et. al., W. B. Saunders Company, Philadelphia, 1948, p. 651.

15 *Sexual Behavior in the Human Male*, Alfred C. Kinsey, et. al., W. B. Saunders Company, Philadelphia, 1948, p. 651

16 *Homosexuality in America: Exposing the Myths*, American Family Association, Tupelo, MS, 1994, pp. 9–10.

17 See *Setting the Record Straight: What Research Really Says About the Social Consequences of Homosexuality*, Larry Burtoft, Ph.D., Focus on the Family, Colorado Springs, Colorado, 1995, p. 23.

18 See "Homosexuality and Bisexuality in Different Populations," Milton Diamond, *Archives of Sexual Behavior*, 1993, vol. 22, no. 4, p. 303.

19 "The Sexual Behavior of Men in the United States," John O. G. Billy et. al., *Family Planning Perspectives*, March/April 1993, vol. 25, no. 2, pp. 52–60.

20 See "Sex in America," U.S. News & World Report, Oct. 17, 1994, pp. 74–81, and "Now for the Truth About Americans and Sex," Time, 17 Oct. 1994, pp. 62–71.

21 *The Social Organization of Sexuality*, University of Chicago, Chicago, IL, 1994. A smaller companion volume is published as *Sex in America: A Definitive Survey*, Gina Kolata, Little, Brown and Company, Boston, MA, 1994.

22 Figures used in this estimate: 5% of 10 million members of the Church equals 500,000 who struggle with homosexual problems; 200,000 spouses (about 40% are or have been married according to NARTH survey results); 1,000,000 parents; 1,150,000 siblings (average 2.3 siblings per family in the Church according to a 1981 survey by the Church's Correlation Research Division); giving a total of 2.85 million. The figures for the United States would be 5% of 270 million equals 13.5 million; 5.4 million spouses; 27 million parents; 14.85 million siblings (average 1.1 per family according to "Family Life: Holding Together Better Than Most," *The Economist*, vol. 22, Feb. 97, pp. 28–29.); giving a total of 60.75 million in the USA.

23 *Homosexuality: A New Christian Ethic*, Elizabeth R. Moberly, James Clarke and Company, Cambridge, England, 1983, p. 3.

24 "Theories of Origins of Male Homosexuality: A Cross-Cultural Look," *Archives of General Psychiatry* 42, pp. 399–404.

25 "Same-gender Attraction," Dallin H. Oaks, *Ensign*, Salt Lake City, Utah, Oct. 95, p. 9.

26 "Neurobiology and Sexual Orientation: Current Relationships," R. C. Friedman and J. Downey, *Journal of Neuropsychiatry* 5, 1993, p. 149.

27 "Neurobiology and Sexual Orientation: Current Relationships," R. C. Friedman and J. Downey, *Journal of Neuropsychiatry* 5, 1993, p. 149.

28 *Not in Our Genes*, R. C. Lewontin, et. al., Pantheon Books, New York, 1984 and *Exploding the Gene Myth*, R. Hubbard and E. Wald, Beacon Press, Boston, 1993.

29 "A Genetic Study of Male Sexual Orientation," J. M. Bailey and R. C. Pillard, *Archives of General Psychiatry* 48, 1991, pp. 1089–96.

30 "A Genetic Study of Male Sexual Orientation," J. M. Bailey and R. C. Pillard, *Archives of General Psychiatry* 48, 1991, p. 1094.

31 *British Journal of Psychiatry*, vol. 160, March 1992, pp. 407–409.

32 "A Difference in Hypothalamic Structure Between Heterosexual and Homosexual Men," Simon LeVay, *Science*, vol. 253, pp. 1034–37.

33 "Human Sexual Orientation: The Biologic Theories Reappraised," William Byne and Bruce Parsons, *Archives of General Psychiatry* 50, Mar. 1993, pp. 228–39.

34 "Human Sexual Orientation: The Biologic Theories Reappraised," William Byne and Bruce Parsons, *Archives of General Psychiatry* 50, Mar. 1993, pp. 234–35.

35 There is also the possibility of research bias. Dr. LeVay told *Newsweek* that his lover's death from AIDS prompted him to find an inborn cause for homosexuality, a quest so important that he would give up his scientific career if he did not find it.

36 Paul Cameron in *Gay Rights: A Public Health Disaster and Civil Wrong*, Tony Marco, Coral Ridge Ministries, Ft. Lauderdale, FL, 1992, p. 45.

37 "A Difference in Hypothalamic Structure Between Heterosexual and Homosexual Men," *Science*, vol. 253, p. 1036.

38 "Are Gay Men Born That Way?," C. Gorman, *Time*, 9 Sep. 1991, p. 61.

39 "A Linkage Between DNA Markers on the X Chromosome and Male Sexual Orientation," Dean Hamer, et. al., *Science* 261, 16 Jul. 1993, pp. 325.

40 *The Science of Desire*, Dean Hamer and P. Copeland, Simon & Schuster, New York, 1994, pp. 145–46.

41 "The Biological Evidence Challenged," *Scientific American*, May 1994, pp. 50–55.

42 "Gay Genes, Revisited," *Scientific American*, Nov. 1995, p. 26.

43 *Washington Post*, 31 Oct. 1994, pp. 5–6.

44 "Effects of Prenatal Hormones on Gender-Related Behavior," A.A. Ehrhardt and H.F.L. Meyer-Bahlburg, *Science*, vol. 211, 20 Mar. 1981, p. 1316.

45 "Sin, Sickness or Status? Homosexual Gender Identity and Psychoneuroendocrinology," John Money, *American Psychologist* 42, no. 4, Apr. 1987, p. 398.

46 *The Homosexual Matrix*, C. A. Tripp, McGraw-Hill, New York, 1975, p. 12.

47 "Human Sexual Orientation: The Biologic Theories Reappraised," William Byne and Bruce Parsons, *Archives of General Psychiatry* 50, Mar. 1993, p. 228.

48 See *Exploding the Gene Myth*, Ruth Hubbard and Elijah Wald, Beacon Press, Boston, 1993 and "Human Sexual Orientation: The Biologic Theories Reappraised," William Byne and Bruce Parsons, *Archives of General Psychiatry* 50, Mar. 1993, p. 228.

49 *Counseling and Homosexuality*, Earl D. Wilson, Word Books, Waco, TX, 1988, p. 76.

50 "Born Gay? How Politics Have Skewed the Debate Over the Biological Causes of Homosexuality," Joe Dallas, *Christianity Today*, 22 Jun. 1992, pp. 20–23.

51 *Homosexual No More: Practical Strategies for Christians Overcoming Homosexuality*, Dr. William Consiglio, Victor Books, Wheaton, IL, 1991, p. 59.

52 *Homosexuality: A New Christian Ethic*, Elizabeth R. Moberly, James Clark & Co., Cambridge, England, 1983, p. 6

53 For more information on these disordered relationships, you may refer to chapter four of *The Wonder of Boys* by Michael Gurian, audio book, Audio Partners Publishing Corp., Auburn, CA, 1996.

54 "Sexual Orientation and Boyhood Gender Conformity: Development of the Boyhood Gender Conformity Scale (BGCS)," S. L. Hockenberry and R. C. Billingham, *Archives of Sexual Behavior*, vol. 16, 1987, pp 475–87.

55 "Homosexuality: Nature vs. Nurture," Judd Marmor, *The Harvard Mental Health Letter*, Oct. 1985, p. 6.

56 *Reparative Therapy of Male Homosexuality: A New Clinical Approach*, Joseph Nicolosi, Jason Aaronson, Inc, Northvale, NJ, 1991, p. 213.

57 See "The Transition from Homosexuality: Balancing Belief System, Sexuality, and Homo-Emotional Needs," unpublished paper by David Matheson, Executive Director, Evergreen International, Salt Lake City, UT, 1993, p. 2.

58 See "The Transition from Homosexuality: Balancing Belief System, Sexuality, and Homo-Emotional Needs," unpublished paper by David Matheson, Executive Director, Evergreen International, Salt Lake City, UT, 1993, pp. 3–4.

59 "Homosexuality: Getting Beyond the Therapeutic Impasse," Thomas E. Pritt, Ph.D. and Ann F. Pritt, M.S., *AMCAP Journal*, vol. 13, no. 1, 1987, p. 55.

60 See *Homosexuality: A New Christian Ethic*, Elizabeth R. Moberly, James Clarke & Co., Cambridge, England, SC, 1983.

61 *Males at Risk: The Other Side of Child Sexual Abuse*, F. G. Bolton, L. A. Morris, and A. E. MacEachron, Sage Publications, Newbury Park, CA, 1989, p. 86 and "Victimization of Boys," *Journal of Adolescent Health Care*, vol. 6, pp. 372–376.

62 *Gay, Straight, and In-Between*, John Money, Oxford University Press, New York, NY, 1988, p. 124.

63 *Homosexual No More: Practical Strategies for Christians Overcoming Homosexuality*, Dr. William Consiglio, Victor Books, Wheaton, IL, 1991, p. 22.

64 *Homosexual No More: Practical Strategies for Christians Overcoming Homosexuality*, Dr. William Consiglio, Victor Books, Wheaton, IL, 1991, p. 22.

65 See *Homosexuality: A New Christian Ethic*, Elizabeth R. Moberly, James Clarke & Co., Cambridge, England, SC, 1983, chapter two.

66 "Human Sexual Orientation: The Biologic Theories Reappraised," William Byne and Bruce Parsons, *Archives of General Psychiatry* 50, Mar. 1993, pp. 236–37.

67 *Gay, Straight, and In-Between*, John Money, Oxford University Press, New York, NY, 1988, p. 123.

68 "Freedom from Cross-Dressing," *Harvest News*, Spring 1995, Harvest USA, Philadelphia, PA, p. 3

69 "Same-Gender Attraction," Dallin H. Oaks, *Ensign*, Salt Lake City, Utah, Oct. 1995, p. 10.

70 "Homosexuality", Charles W. Socarides, in *American Handbook of Psychiatry*, second edition, vol. 3, p. 309.

71 *The Miracle of Forgiveness*, Spencer W. Kimball, Bookcraft, Salt Lake City, UT, 1969, p. 82.

72 *Desires in Conflict: Answering the Struggle for Sexual Identity*, Joe Dallas, Harvest House Publishers, Eugene, OR, 1991, p. 47.

73 "Counseling Overcomers: A Four-Focus Framework," an address by Dr. William Consiglio at the 18th Annual Exodus Conference. Also quoted by Bob Davies in "Mainstreamed Homosexuality," *Leadership*, Summer 1995, p. 82.

74 *Homosexual No More: Practical Strategies for Christians Overcoming Homosexuality*, Dr. William Consiglio, Victor Books, Wheaton, IL, 1991, p. 13.

75 "Psychological Theory," Reuben Fine, in *Male and Female Homosexuality: Psychological Approaches*, ed. Louis Diamant, Hemisphere, New York, 1987, p. 84.

76 "Psychological Theory," Reuben Fine, in *Male and Female Homosexuality: Psychological Approaches*, ed. Louis Diamant, Hemisphere, New York, 1987, pp. 84–86.

77 "Attitudes and Experiences of Psychoanalysts in Analyzing Homosexual Patients," Dr. Houston MacIntosh, M.D., *Journal of the American Psychoanalytic Association*, vol. 42, no. 4, pp. 1183–1207.

78 Reported in NARTH Bulletin, National Association of Research and Therapy of Homosexuality, Encino, CA, Dec. 1994, p. 14.

79 William H. Masters and Virginia E. Johnson, *Homosexuality in Perspective*, Bantam, New York, 1979, p. 400

80 *Homosexuality: A Psychoanalytic Study*, Irving Bieber, Basic Books, New York, 1962, pp. 318–19

81 "Male Homosexuality," Irving Bieber and Toby Bieber, in *Canadian Journal of Psychiatry*, no. 5, 1979, p. 416.

82 *Homosexuality and Hope: A Psychologist Talks About Treatment and Change*, Gerard van den Aardweg, Servant Books, Ann Arbor, MI, 1985, p. 105–6.

83 *Treatment of Homosexuality: A Reanalysis and Synthesis of Outcome Studies*, Elizabeth C. James, doctoral dissertation, Brigham Young University, Provo, UT, 1978, p. 183.

84 *Treatment of Homosexuality: A Reanalysis and Synthesis of Outcome Studies*, Elizabeth C. James, doctoral dissertation, Brigham Young University, Provo, UT, 1978, p. 99.

85 "Homosexuality: Getting Beyond the Therapeutic Impasse," Thomas E. Pritt, Ph.D. and Ann F. Pritt, M.S., *AMCAP Journal*, vol. 13, no. 1, 1987, p. 55–56.

86 *Homosexuality and Hope: A Psychologist Talks About Treatment and Change*, Gerard van den Aardweg, Servant Books, Ann Arbor, MI, 1985, p. 96.

87 Address by Garrick Hyde at the Annual Evergreen International Conference, Salt Lake City, UT, 1996.

88 *Desires in Conflict: Answering the Struggle for Sexual Identity*, Joe Dallas, Harvest House Publishers, Eugene, OR, 1991, p. 46.

89 "Interview: An LDS Reparative Therapy Approach for Male Homosexuality," A. Dean Byrd, *AMCAP Journal*, vol. 19, no. 1, Association of Mormon Counselors and Psychotherapists, Salt Lake City, UT, 1993, p. 93.

90 *Desires in Conflict: Answering the Struggle for Sexual Identity*, Joe Dallas, Harvest House Publishers, Eugene, OR, 1991, p. 28.

91 "Life Is Good and Getting Better," Leo Hall, in *A Place in the Kingdom: Spiritual Insights from Latter-day Saints about Same-sex Attraction*, eds. Garrick Hyde and Ginger Hyde, Century Publishing, Salt Lake City, UT, 1997, p. 84, emphasis in original.

92 *Homosexuality: A New Christian Ethic*, Elizabeth R. Moberly, James Clarke and Company, Cambridge, England, 1983, p. 41.

93 Many of the ideas in the following paragraphs are taken from a talk titled "Free Agency and Freedom," by Dallin H. Oaks, *Brigham Young University 1987–88 Devotional and Fireside Speeches*, BYU Publications, Provo, UT, 1988, pp. 46–47. An edited version is also found in *The Book of Mormon: Second Nephi, The Doctrinal Structure*, Papers from the Third Annual Book of Mormon Symposium, edited by Monte S. Nyman and Charles D. Tate, Jr., Religious Studies Center, Brigham Young University, Provo, Utah, 1989, pp. 1–17.

94 "Free Agency and Freedom," by Dallin H. Oaks, *The Book of Mormon: Second Nephi, The Doctrinal Structure*, Papers from the Third Annual Book of Mormon Symposium, edited by Monte S. Nyman and Charles D. Tate, Jr., Religious Studies Center, Brigham Young University, Provo, Utah, 1989, p. 10.

95 "Free Agency and Freedom," by Dallin H. Oaks, *The Book of Mormon: Second Nephi, The Doctrinal Structure*, Papers from the Third Annual Book of Mormon Symposium, edited by Monte S. Nyman and Charles D. Tate, Jr., Religious Studies Center, Brigham Young University, Provo, Utah, 1989, p. 11.

96 "Reverence and Morality," Gordon B. Hinckley, *Ensign*, May 1987, p. 47.

97 Some ideas in the section are taken from an article entitled "Advice to the Married Man Struggling with Homosexuality," by Alan Medinger, available through Love In Action, San Rafael, CA.

98 "Jesus, the Very Thought of Thee," Howard W. Hunter, *Ensign*, May 1993, pp. 64–65.

99 "Answers to Life's Questions," M. Russell Ballard, *Ensign*, May 1995, p. 24.

100 "The Gift of the Holy Ghost—A Sure Compass," James E. Faust, *Ensign*, May 1989, p. 31.

101 The Seven Habits of Highly Effective People Calendar, Stephen R. Covey, 8 Feb. 1996.

102 The Seven Habits of Highly Effective People Calendar, Stephen R. Covey, 25 Mar. 1996.

103 Many of the ideas in this section come from a talk given by Melanie Geyer entitled "Boundaries" at the 18th Exodus International Conference.

104 *Homosexuality and Hope: A Psychologist Talks About Treatment and Change*, Gerard van den Aardweg, Servant Books, Ann Arbor, MI, 1985, p. 89.

105 The Seven Habits of Highly Effective People Calendar, Stephen R. Covey, 12 Mar. 1996.

106 "We Are the Clay and Thou Our Potter," Ginger Hyde, in *A Place in the Kingdom: Spiritual Insights from Latter-day Saints about Same-Sex Attraction*, eds. Garrick Hyde and Ginger Hyde, Century Publishing, Salt Lake City, UT, 1997, p. 13.

107 "We Have a Work to Do," Gordon B. Hinckley, *Ensign*, May 1995, p. 88.

108 "Dealing with Issues of Homosexuality: A Qualitative Study of Six Mormons," A. Dean Byrd, Ph.D. and Mark D. Chamberlain, *AMCAP Journal*, vol. 19, no. 1, Association of Mormon Counselors and Psychotherapists, Salt Lake City, UT, 1993, p. 73.

109 "Dealing with Issues of Homosexuality: A Qualitative Study of Six Mormons," A. Dean Byrd, Ph.D. and Mark D. Chamberlain, *AMCAP Journal*, vol. 19, no. 1, Association of Mormon Counselors and Psychotherapists, Salt Lake City, UT, 1993, p. 76.

110 Book review by Scott R. Peterson on *Peculiar People: Mormons and Same-Sex Orientation*, found in the *AMCAP Journal, vol. 19, no. 1–1993*, The Association of Mormon Counselors and Psychotherapists, Salt Lake City, UT, p. 121.

111 *Desires in Conflict: Answering the Struggle for Sexual Identity*, Joe Dallas, Harvest House Publishers, Eugene, OR, 1991, pp. 262–63.

112 "Covenants," Boyd K. Packer, *Ensign*, Nov. 1990, p. 86.

113 For more information on these Christian groups, see the Organizations section in this book. For an objective review of Christian ministries, see "Coming Out," Tim Stafford, *Christianity Today*, 18 Aug. 1989, pp. 16–21.

114 *Homosexuality: Opposing Viewpoints*, William Dudley, editor, Greenhaven Press, San Diego, CA, 1993, p. 125.

115 *Reparative Therapy of Male Homosexuality: A New Clinical Approach*, Joseph Nicolosi, Jason Aronson, Northvale, NJ, 1991, dust jacket.

116 *Reparative Therapy of Male Homosexuality: A New Clinical Approach*, Joseph Nicolosi, Jason Aronson, Northvale, NJ, 1991, dust jacket.

117 *Desires in Conflict: Answering the Struggle for Sexual Identity*, Joe Dallas, Harvest House Publishers, Eugene, OR, 1991, p. 87.

118 "Where Much is Given, Much is Required", Boyd K. Packer, *Ensign*, Nov. 1974, p. 90.

119 "When Christians Struggle with Sexual Sin," Barney Swihart, *Harvest News*, Philadelphia, PA, Fall/Winter 1995, p. 2.

120 *A Letter to a Friend*, Spencer W. Kimball, The Church of Jesus Christ of Latter-day Saints, Salt Lake City, UT, 1978, item number 30941, p. 8.

121 "Unclutter Your Life," William R. Bradford, *Ensign*, May 1992, p. 28.

122 The Seven Habits of Highly Effective People Calendar, Stephen R. Covey, 15 Jan. 1996.

123 "Using Our Free Agency," Delbert L. Stapley, *Ensign*, May 1975, p. 2

124 "Covenants," Boyd K. Packer, *Ensign*, Nov. 1990, p. 86.

125 "Reverence and Morality," Gordon B. Hinckley, *Ensign*, May 1987, pp. 47–48.

126 "We're Dealing With a Crisis of Truth," Bob Ragan, in *Nexus* newsletter, Metanoia Ministries, Seattle, WA, Nov. 1996, p. 2.

127 This paragraph includes some ideas from the article "Justifying Our Sin: A Subtle Trap," Alan P. Medinger, *Regeneration News*, Baltimore, MD, Oct. 1996.

128 "Life Is Good and Getting Better," Leo Hall, in *A Place in the Kingdom: Spiritual Insights from Latter-day Saints about Same-Sex Attraction*, eds. Garrick Hyde and Ginger Hyde, Century Publishing, Salt Lake City, UT, 1997, p. 83.

129 "Addiction or Freedom", Russell M. Nelson, *Ensign*, Nov. 1988, p. 6.

130 "Free Agency and Freedom," Dallin H. Oaks, *The Book of Mormon: Second Nephi, The Doctrinal Structure*, Papers from the Third Annual Book of Mormon Symposium, edited by Monte S. Nyman and Charles D. Tate, Jr., Religious Studies Center, Brigham Young University, Provo, Utah, 1989, p. 14.

131 "Addiction or Freedom," Russell M. Nelson, *Ensign*, Nov. 1988, p. 7.

132 *Desires in Conflict: Answering the Struggle for Sexual Identify*, Joe Dallas, Harvest House Publishers, Eugene, OR, 1991, pp. 127–28.

133 *Desires in Conflict: Answering the Struggle for Sexual Identify*, Joe Dallas, Harvest House Publishers, Eugene, OR, 1991, p. 63.

134 "Addiction or Freedom," Russell M. Nelson, *Ensign*, Nov. 1988, p. 8.

135 "Inspiring Music—Worthy Thoughts," Boyd K. Packer, *Ensign*, Jan. 1974, p. 28.

136 "Passion: How Much Will We Pay?," Jack Hickey, *Victory Notes*, 1986.

137 *Coming Our of Homosexuality: New Freedom for Men & Women*, Bob Davies & Lori Rentzel, InterVarsity Press, Downers Grove, IL, 1993, pp. 85–86.

138 *Desires in Conflict: Answering the Struggle for Sexual Identity*, Joe Dallas, Harvest House Publishers, Eugene, OR, 1991, p. 137.

139 "Standards of Morality and Fidelity," letter from the First Presidency of the Church of Jesus Christ of Latter-day Saints, 14 Nov. 1991.

140 "Covenants," Boyd K. Packer, *Ensign*, Nov. 1990, p. 86.

141 *The Miracle of Forgiveness*, Spencer W. Kimball, Bookcraft, Salt Lake City, UT, 1969, p. 79.

142 "Justifying Our Sin: A Subtle Trap," Alan P. Medinger, in *Regeneration News*, Baltimore, MD, Oct. 1996, pp. 1–2.

143 Several ideas in this section are taken from the pamphlet "An Honest Look at Temptation," Jack Hickey, Reconciliation Ministries, 1989.

144 *Homosexual No More: Practical Strategies for Christians Overcoming Homosexuality*, Dr. William Consiglio, Victor Books, Wheaton, IL, 1991, p. 36.

145 *Saturday Night Thoughts*, Orson F. Whitney, p. 239.

146 *Desires in Conflict: Answering the Struggle for Sexual Identity*, Joe Dallas, Harvest House Publishers, Eugene, OR, 1991, p. 24.

147 "Reverence and Morality," Gordon B. Hinckley, *Ensign*, May 1987, p. 47.

148 "Preparing Yourselves For Missionary Service," Ezra Taft Benson, *Ensign*, May 1985, p. 36.

149 *Homosexual No More: Practical Strategies for Christians Overcoming Homosexuality*, Dr. William Consiglio, Victor Books, Wheaton, IL, 1991, pp. 91–92.

150 *Homosexual No More: Practical Strategies for Christians Overcoming Homosexuality*, Dr. William Consiglio, Victor Books, Wheaton, IL, 1991, p. 90.

151 *Homosexual No More: Practical Strategies for Christians Overcoming Homosexuality*, Dr. William Consiglio, Victor Books, Wheaton, IL, 1991, pp. 90–91.

152 *Homosexuality and Hope: A Psychologist Talks About Treatment and Change*, Gerard van den Aardweg, Servant Books, Ann Arbor, MI, 1985, pp. 84–5, 87, 113.

153 "Reverence and Morality," Gordon B. Hinckley, *Ensign*, May 1987, p. 47.

154 "Emotional Maturity," David O. McKay, *Instructor*, Sep. 1959, p. 281.

155 *Hymns*, The Church of Jesus Christ of Latter-day Saints, Salt Lake City, Utah, 1985, p. x.

156 "De-Sexualizing the Deeper Need," Alan Medinger, *Regeneration News*, Baltimore, MD, Sep. 1994, p. 2.

157 "Like All the Nations," Spencer W. Kimball, *Church News*, Deseret News, Salt Lake City, UT, 15 Oct. 1960, p. 14.

158 *To the One*, Boyd K. Packer, The Church of Jesus Christ of Latter-day Saints, 1978, p. 16.

159 *The Miracle of Forgiveness*, Spencer W. Kimball, Bookcraft, Salt Lake City, UT, 1969, p. 83.

160 "Homosexual Lifestyle Still an Unhealthy One," Col. Gary Stephens, *The Ogden Standard Examiner*, Ogden, UT, 23 Feb. 1996.

161 *Medical Consequences of What Homosexuals Do*, Paul Cameron, Family Research Institute, Washington, DC, 1993 and "The Longevity of Homosexuals: Before and After the AIDS Epidemic," Paul Cameron, William Playfair, and Stephen Wellum, *Omega Journal of Death and Dying*, vol. 29, no. 3, 1994, Baywood Publishing, Amityville, NY.

162 USA Today, 17 Apr. 1995, p. D-1.

163 "The AIDS Exception: Privacy vs. Public Health," Chandler Burr, *The Atlantic Monthly*, Jun. 1997, p. 61 and *Surgeon General's Report to the American Public on HIV Infection and AIDS*, Centers for Disease Control and Prevention, Health Resources and Services Administration, National Institutes of Health, 1992, p. 1.

164 *Surgeon General's Report to the American Public on HIV Infection and AIDS*, Centers for Disease Control and Prevention, Health Resources and Services Administration, National Institutes of Health, 1992, p. 1.

165 *Condoms and Sexually-transmitted Diseases . . . Especially AIDS*, pamphlet by the Department of Health and Human Services, HHS Publication FDA 90–4239, p. 7.

166 *Surgeon General's Report to the American Public on HIV Infection and AIDS*, Centers for Disease Control and Prevention, Health Resources and Services Administration, National Institutes of Health, 1992, p. 6.

167 According to the March 1993 Journal of AIDS, as reported in "Positively Aware On-Line," Test Positive Aware Network, Chicago, IL, Jun. 1993.

168 "The 1994 Advocate Survey of Sexuality and Relationships: The Men," Janet Lever, *The Advocate*, August 23, 1994, p. 23.

169 "Predictors of Unprotected Intercourse Among Gay and Bisexual Youth: Knowledge, Beliefs, and Behavior," Gary Remafedi, *Pediatrics*, August 1994, vol. 94, no. 2, pp. 163–168. See also "Seroprevalence of HIV and Risk Behaviors Among Young Homosexual and Bisexual Men—The San Francisco/Berkeley Young Men's Survey," George F. Lemp, et. al., *Journal of the American Medical Association*, August 10, 1994, vol. 272, no. 6, pp. 449–54.

170 "The 1994 Advocate Survey of Sexuality and Relationships: The Men," Janet Lever, *The Advocate*, 23 Aug. 1994, p. 23.

171 "Predictors of Unprotected Intercourse Among Gay and Bisexual Youth: Knowledge, Beliefs, and Behavior," Gary Remafedi, *Pediatrics*, August 1994, vol. 94, no. 2, pp. 163–68. See also "Seroprevalence of HIV and Risk Behaviors Among Young Homosexual and Bisexual Men—The San Francisco/Berkeley Young Men's Survey," George F. Lemp, et. al., *Journal of the American Medical Association*, 10 Aug. 1994, vol. 272, no. 6, pp. 449–54.

172 "The 1994 Advocate Survey of Sexuality and Relationships: The Men," Janet Lever, *The Advocate*, 23 Aug. 1994, p. 23.

173 "The 1994 Advocate Survey of Sexuality and Relationships: The Men," Janet Lever, *The Advocate*, 23 Aug. 1994, p. 22.

174 See "News of the Church," *Ensign*, Jul. 1988, p. 79.

175 A 1988 study by the U.S. Department of Health and Human Services showed that gay teens commit suicide at two to three times the rate of other teens and some studies show that 40% of all gay people make attempts on their lives when they are young (as reported in *Is it a Choice?: Answers to 300 of the Most Frequently Asked Questions About Gays and Lesbians*, Eric Marcus, Harper Collins Publishers, New York, 1993, p. 29).

176 *The Secret Sin: Healing the Wounds of Sexual Addiction*, Mark Laaser, Zondervan Publishing House, Grand Rapids, ND, 1992, p. 29.

177 "Personal Morality," David B. Haight, *Ensign*, Nov. 1984, pp. 70–73.

178 Kevin Jacobson, reported in *Reconciliation's Victory News*, Winter 1996, Reconciliation Ministries, Detroit, MI, p. 4.

179 "Preserving the Past—Hormonal Influences on Memory Storage," James L. McGaugh, *American Psychologist*, Feb. 1983, pp. 161-74.

180 "Personal Morality," David B. Haight, *Ensign*, Nov. 1984, p. 70.

181 *Coming Out of Homosexuality: New Freedom for Men & Women*, Bob Davies & Lori Rentzel, Inter Varsity Press, Downers Grove, IL, 1993, p. 153.

182 "The Effect of Pornography on Male Homosexuals," Andrew Comiskey, Hot Thoughts, Desert Stream Ministries, Anaheim, CA, 1996.

183 "The Effect of Pornography on Male Homosexuals," Andrew Comiskey, Hot Thoughts, Desert Stream Ministries, Anaheim, CA, 1996.

184 *Homosexual No More: Practical Strategies for Christians Overcoming Homosexuality*, Dr. William Consiglio, Victor Books, Wheaton, IL, 1991, p. 88.

185 *The Miracle of Forgiveness*, Spencer W. Kimball, Bookcraft, Salt Lake City, UT, 1969, p. 77.

186 *Homosexual No More: Practical Strategies for Christians Overcoming Homosexuality*, Dr. William Consiglio, Victor Books, Wheaton, IL, 1991, p. 93.

187 *Homosexual No More: Practical Strategies for Christians Overcoming Homosexuality*, Dr. William Consiglio, Victor Books, Wheaton, IL, 1991, pp. 93–94.

188 *The Miracle of Forgiveness*, Spencer W. Kimball, Bookcraft, Salt Lake City, UT, 1969, p. 77–78.

189 *The Littlest Angel*, Charles Tazewell, Ideals Publishing Corporation, Nashville, TN, 1974.

190 "The 1994 Advocate Survey of Sexuality and Relationships: The Men," Janet Lever, *The Advocate*, 23 Aug. 1994, p. 23.

191 "The 1994 Advocate Survey of Sexuality and Relationships: The Men," Janet Lever, *The Advocate*, 23 Aug. 1994, p. 24.

192 "The 1994 Advocate Survey of Sexuality and Relationships: The Men," Janet Lever, *The Advocate*, 23 Aug. 1994, p. 24.

193 This study was undertaken by a homosexual couple (a psychiatrist and a psychologist) to disprove the reputation that gay male relationships don't last. They identified 156 couples in relationships from one to thirty-seven years, two thirds of which had entered the relationship with the expectation of sexual fidelity. Of the hundred couples who had been together more than five years, none had been able to maintain sexual fidelity. Of the fifty-six couples who had been together less than five years, only seven had maintained sexual fidelity. (See *The Male Couple: How Relationships Develop*, D. McWhirter and A. Mattison, Prentice-Hall, Englewood Cliffs, NJ, 1984.) Evelyn Hooker's study of thirty couples showed only one was faithful. (See *Reparative Therapy of Male Homosexuality: A New Clinical Approach*, Joseph Nicolosi, Jason Aronson, Inc, Northvale, NJ, 1991, pp. 111–12.)

194 See "Come unto Christ Through Your Trials," H. Burke Peterson, *Brigham Young University 1995-96 Speeches*, Brigham Young University Publications & Graphics, Provo, UT, 1996, p. 155.

195 The Seven Habits of Highly Effective People Calendar 1996, Stephen R. Covey, 4/5 May 1996.

196 As quoted in *The Seven Habits of Highly Effective People*, Stephen R. Covey, Simon and Schuster, New York, 1989, p. 42.

197 The Seven Habits of Highly Effective People Calendar, Stephen R. Covey, 10 Jul. 1996.

198 *The Road Less Traveled*, M. Scott Peck, M.D., Simon & Schuster, New York, 1978, p. 44.

199 The Seven Habits of Highly Effective People Calendar, Stephen R. Covey, 23 Feb. 1996.

200 The Seven Habits of Highly Effective People Calendar, Stephen R. Covey, 31 Dec. 1996.

201 The Seven Habits of Highly Effective People Calendar, Stephen R. Covey, 6 Aug. 1996.

202 *The Teachings of Spencer W. Kimball*, ed. Edward L. Kimball, Bookcraft, Salt Lake City, UT, 1982, pp. 38–39.

203 *Coming Out of Homosexuality: New Freedom for Men & Women*, Bob Davies and Lori Rentzel, Inter Varsity Press, Downers Grove, IL, 1993, p. 95.

204 "The Gift of the Holy Ghost—A Sure Compass," James E. Faust, *Ensign*, May 1989, p. 33.

205 *The Seven Habits of Highly Effective People*, Stephen R. Covey, Simon and Schuster, New York, 1989, pp. 66–67.

206 *Reparative Therapy of Male Homosexuality: A New Clinical Approach*, Joseph Nicolosi, Jason Aronson, Inc., Northvale, NJ, 1991, p. 165.

207 "An Ephah of Fine Flour", Randy Walters, in *A Place in the Kingdom: Spiritual Insights from Latter-day Saints about Same-Sex Attraction*, eds. Garrick Hyde and Ginger Hyde, Century Publishing, Salt Lake City, UT, 1997, p. 60.

208 The Serenity Prayer, Reinhold Niebuhr, 1943, as quoted in *Familiar Quotations*, John Bartlett, Little, Brown and Company, Boston, MA, 1980, p. 823.

209 "The Rewards of Correct Choices," Camila E. Kimball, *Ye Are Free To Choose: Agency and the Latter-day Saint Woman*, ed. Maren M. Mouritsen, Brigham Young University Publications, Provo, UT, 1981, p. 18.

210 See *Learned Helplessness: A Theory for the Age of Personal Control*, Christopher Peterson, et. al., Oxford University Press, New York, 1993.

211 "Finding Joy in Life," Richard G. Scott, *Ensign*, May 1996, p. 24.

212 Branden Institute for Self-Esteem, Box 2609, Beverly Hills, CA 90213.

213 "To Succeed at Anything in Life You Must Know How and When to be Assertive," Nathaniel Branden, *Bottom Line Personal* newsletter, 1 May 1995, Boardroom, Inc, Greenwich, Conn., 1995, pp. 1–2.

214 "To Succeed at Anything in Life You Must Know How and When to be Assertive," Nathaniel Branden, *Bottom Line Personal* newsletter, 1 May 1995, Boardroom, Inc, Greenwich, Conn., 1995, pp. 1–2.

215 "The Family: A Proclamation to the World," The First Presidency of the Church of Jesus Christ of Latter-day Saints, Salt Lake City, UT, 1995, item number 35602.

216 "Contempt for the Man," Alan Medinger, *Regeneration News*, Baltimore, MD, Apr. 1996, p. 1.

217 *Reparative Therapy of Male Homosexuality*, Joseph Nicolosi, Jason Aronson, Northvale, NJ, 1991, p. 84.

218 *The Hazards of Being Male: Surviving the Myth of Masculine Privilege*, Herb Goldberg, Signet, New York, 1976, pp. 174–75.

219 *The Hazards of Being Male: Surviving the Myth of Masculine Privilege*, Herb Goldberg, Signet, New York, 1976, p. 175.

220 *The Hazards of Being Male: Surviving the Myth of Masculine Privilege*, Herb Goldberg, Signet, New York, 1976, p. 176.

221 "Churches, Synagogues Adopting and Adapting Rites of Passage," *Religion Watch*, Mar. 1996, pp. 1–2.

222 "A Happy Life", Garrick Hyde in *A Place in the Kingdom: Spiritual Insights from Latter-day Saints about Same-Sex Attraction*, eds. Garrick Hyde and Ginger Hyde, Century Publishing, Salt Lake City, UT, 1997, p. 2.

223 *Reparative Therapy of Male Homosexuality*, Joseph Nicolosi, Jason Aronson, Inc, Northvale, NJ, 1991, p. 280.

224 *Homosexuality and Hope: A Psychologist Talks About Treatment and Change*, Gerard van den Aardweg, Servant Books, Ann Arbor, MI, 1985, p. 68.

225 *You Don't Have To Be Gay*, J. A. Konrad, Pacific Publishing House, Newport Beach, CA, 1987, pp. 237–38.

226 "Emotions: How Do We Handle Our Feelings?" by Lori Rentzel, handout published by Love In Action, San Rafael, CA, 1981.

227 "Emotions: How Do We Handle Our Feelings?" by Lori Rentzel, handout published by Love In Action, San Rafael, CA, 1981.

228 "Emotions: How Do We Handle Our Feelings?" by Lori Rentzel, handout published by Love In Action, San Rafael, CA, 1981.

229 *When Bad Things Happen to Good People*, Harold S. Kushner, Avon Books, New York, 1981, p. 109.

230 *Parade* magazine, 13 Aug. 1989, p. 6

231 *Coming Out of Homosexuality: New Freedom for Men & Women*, Bob Davies & Lori Rentzel, InterVarsity Press, Downers Grove, IL, 1993, p. 119.

232 "What About the Next Step?," Alan P. Medinger, *Regeneration News*, Baltimore, MD, Jan. 95, p. 3.

233 "What About the Next Step?," Alan P. Medinger, *Regeneration News*, Baltimore, MD, Jan. 95, p. 3.

234 *The Road Less Traveled*, M. Scott Peck, Simon & Schuster, New York, 1978, p. 131.

235 "Small Acts of Service," Spencer W. Kimball, *Ensign*, Dec. 1974, p. 5.

236 "Organizational Accountability in Ministry," Kathy Koch, address given at the 19th Annual Exodus International Conference.

237 "The Ultimate Friend," by Ed Hurst, *Outpost News*, vol. 18, no. 4, Jul. 1994, p. 1.

238 "The Ultimate Friend," by Ed Hurst, *Outpost News*, vol. 18, no. 4, Jul. 1994, p. 1.

239 "The Ultimate Friend," by Ed Hurst, *Outpost News*, vol. 18, no. 4, Jul. 1994, p. 3.

240 "Emotional Dependency and Lesbianism," by Dr. Carol Ahrens, in *Desires in Conflict: Answering the Struggle for Sexual Identity*, Joe Dallas, Harvest House Publishers, Eugene, OR, 1991, p. 204.

241 *The Road Less Traveled*, M. Scott Peck, Simon & Schuster, New York, 1978, p. 99.

242 *The Road Less Traveled*, M. Scott Peck, Simon & Schuster, New York, 1978, p. 98.

243 *Codependent No More: How to Stop Controlling Others and Start Caring for Yourself*, Melody Beattie, Harper and Row, San Francisco, CA, 1987, p. 31.

244 This thought ws taken from "The Ultimate Friend," by Ed Hurst, *Outpost News*, vol. 18, no. 4, Jul. 1994, pp. 1–4.

245 "Trust in the Lord," Richard G. Scott, *Ensign*, Nov. 1995, p. 17.

246 "Hallowed Be Thy Name," Howard W. Hunter, *Ensign*, Nov. 1977, p. 52.

247 *Treasures of Life*, comp. Clare Middlemiss, Deseret Book, Salt Lake City, UT, 1962, p. 302.

248 "Reverence and Morality," Gordon B. Hinckley, *Ensign*, May 1987, p. 47.

249 Address by Brad Anderson at the Annual Evergreen International Conference, Salt Lake City, UT, 1995.

250 *Homosexuality: A New Christian Ethic*, Elizabeth Moberly, James Clarke & Co., Cambridge, England, 1983, p. 42.

251 *Desires in Conflict: Answering the Struggle for Sexual Identity*, Joe Dallas, Harvest House Publishers, Eugene, OR, 1991, p. 80.

252 *The Hazards of Being Male: Surviving the Myth of Masculine Privilege*, Herb Goldberg, Signet, New York, 1976, p. 131.

253 *The Hazards of Being Male: Surviving the Myth of Masculine Privilege*, Herb Goldberg, Signet, New York, 1976, p. 133.

254 *Reparative Therapy of Male Homosexuality: A New Clinical Approach*, Joseph Nicolosi, Jason Aronson, Inc, Northvale, NJ, 1991, p. 200.

255 *Coming Out of Homosexuality: New Freedom for Men & Women*, Bob Davies & Lori Rentzel, InterVarsity Press, Downers Grove, IL, 1993, p. 29.

256 "A Mighty Change of Heart," Ezra Taft Benson, *Ensign*, Oct. 1989, p. 4.

257 "Trust in the Lord," Richard G. Scott, *Ensign*, Nov. 1995, p. 16.

258 "Peace," Robert E. Wells, *Ensign*, May 1991, p. 87.

259 *The Holy Bible*, Appendix, Bible Dictionary, The Church of Jesus Christ of Latter-day Saints, Salt Lake City, UT, 1986, p. 617.

260 *Gospel Principles*, The Church of Jesus Christ of Latter-day Saints, Salt Lake City, UT, 1992, item number 31110, p. 71.

261 *The Holy Bible*, Appendix, Bible Dictionary, The Church of Jesus Christ of Latter-day Saints, Salt Lake City, UT, 1986, p. 760-61.

262 "A Mighty Change of Heart," Ezra Taft Benson, *Ensign*, Oct. 89, p. 2.

263 *Desires in Conflict: Answering the Struggle for Sexual Identity*, Joe Dallas, Harvest House Publishers, Eugene, OR, 1991, p. 86.

264 *Gospel Principles*, The Church of Jesus Christ of Latter-day Saints, Salt Lake City, UT, 1992, item number 31110, pp. 124–26.

265 "A Mighty Change of Heart," Ezra Taft Benson, *Ensign*, Oct. 1989, p. 4.

266 "Stand Ye In Holy Places," Harold B. Lee, *Ensign*, Jul. 1973, p. 122.

267 "The Forgiving Heart," Roderick J. Linton, *Ensign*, Apr. 1993, p. 15.

268 As quoted by Spencer W. Kimball, *The Miracle of Forgiveness*, Bookcraft, Salt Lake City, UT, 1969, p. 283.

269 *The Miracle of Forgiveness*, Spencer W. Kimball, Bookcraft, Salt Lake City, 1969, p. 179.

270 "Same-Gender Attraction," Dallin H. Oaks, *Ensign*, Oct. 1995, p. 8.

271 "Constancy Amid Change," Russell M. Nelson, *Ensign*, Nov. 1993, p. 34.

272 *Teachings of the Prophet Joseph Smith*, compiled by Joseph Fielding Smith, Deseret Book, Salt Lake City, Utah, 1965, p. 181.

273 "The Great Imitator", James E. Faust, *Ensign*, Nov. 1987, p. 35.

274 "The Gift of the Holy Ghost—A Sure Compass," James E. Faust, *Ensign*, May 1989, p. 31.

275 *A Letter to a Friend*, Spencer W. Kimball, The Church of Jesus Christ of Latter-day Saints, Salt Lake City, Utah, 1978, item number 30941, pp. 3–4.

276 *A Letter to a Friend*, Spencer W. Kimball, The Church of Jesus Christ of Latter-day Saints, Salt Lake City, Utah, 1978, item number 30941, p. 8.

277 *Marriage and Divorce: Brigham Young University Devotional September 7, 1976*, Spencer W. Kimball, Brigham Young University Publications, Provo, UT, 1976, p. 8.

278 "Addiction or Freedom," Russell M. Nelson, *Ensign*, Nov. 1988, p. 7.

279 *Mere Christianity*, C. S. Lewis, MacMillian Publishing Co., New York, 1952, p. 87.

280 "The Reality of the Resurrection," David O. McKay, *Improvement Era*, Jun. 1966, p. 493, emphasis added.

281 "Born of God," Ezra Taft Benson, *Ensign*, Nov. 1985, p. 6.

282 *Following Christ*, Stephen E. Robinson, Deseret Book Company, Salt Lake City, UT, 1995, p. 42.

283 "Come unto Christ Through Your Trials," H. Burke Peterson, *Brigham Young University 1995-96 Speeches*, Brigham Young University Publications & Graphics, Provo, UT, 1996, p. 156.

284 "Beware of Pride," Ezra Taft Benson, *Ensign*, May 1989, p. 4.

285 "Beware of Pride," Ezra Taft Benson, *Ensign*, May 1989, pp. 5–6.

286 "Jesus Christ—Gifts and Expectations," Ezra Taft Benson, Christmas Devotional, Salt Lake City, UT, 7 Dec. 1986, quoted in *Teachings of Ezra Taft Benson*, Ezra Taft Benson, Bookcraft, Salt Lake City, UT, 1988, p. 361.

287 *That We Might Have Joy*, Howard W. Hunter, Deseret Book Company, Salt Lake City, UT, 1994, p. 30.

288 "An Ephah of Fine Flour," Randy Walters, in *A Place in the Kingdom: Spiritual Insights from Latter-day Saints about Same-Sex Attraction*, eds., Garrick Hyde and Ginger Hyde, Century Publishing, Salt Lake City, UT, 1997, p. 61.

289 *Following Christ*, Stephen E. Robinson, Deseret Book Company, Salt Lake City UT, 1995, p. 34.

290 *Following Christ*, Stephen E. Robinson, Deseret Book Company, Salt Lake City UT, 1995, pp. 34–38.

291 "Come unto Christ Through Your Trials," H. Burke Peterson, *Brigham Young University 1995-96 Speeches*, Brigham Young University Publications & Graphics, Provo, UT, 1996, p. 152.

292 "Come unto Christ Through Your Trials," H. Burke Peterson, *Brigham Young University 1995-96 Speeches*, Brigham Young University Publications & Graphics, Provo, UT, 1996, p. 152.

293 "Answers to Life's Questions," M. Russell Ballard, *Ensign*, May 1995, p. 22.

294 "Answers to Life's Questions," M. Russell Ballard, *Ensign*, May 1995, p. 24.

295 "Spirituality," Dallin H. Oaks, *Ensign*, Nov. 1985, p. 61.

296 *Following Christ*, Stephen E. Robinson, Deseret Book Company, Salt Lake City UT, 1995, p. 65.

297 "Making the Right Decisions," Richard G. Scott, *Ensign*, May 1991, p. 36.

298 Address by Garrick Hyde at the Annual Evergreen International Conference, Salt Lake City, UT, 1996.

299 "Come unto Christ Through Your Trials," H. Burke Peterson, *Brigham Young University 1995-96 Speeches*, Brigham Young University Publications & Graphics, Provo, UT, 1996, p. 154.

300 *Teachings of the New Testament*, Lowell Bennion, Deseret Sunday School Union Board, Salt Lake City, 1953, pp. 178–80.

301 *When a Child Wanders*, Robert L. Millet, Deseret Book, Salt Lake City, Utah, 1996, p. 58.

302 *When Bad Things Happen to Good People*, Harold S. Kushner, Avon Books, New York, 1981, p. 94.

303 "Beauty for Ashes: The Atonement of Jesus Christ," Bruce C. Hafen, *Ensign*, Apr. 1990, p. 10.

304 "Answers to Life's Questions," M. Russell Ballard, *Ensign*, May 1995, p. 23.

305 "Answers to Life's Questions," M. Russell Ballard, *Ensign*, May 1995, p. 23

306 "Answers to Life's Questions," M. Russell Ballard, *Ensign*, May 1995, p. 23.

307 See "Beauty for Ashes: The Atonement of Jesus Christ," Bruce C. Hafen, *Ensign*, Apr. 1990.

308 As related by David O. McKay, *Relief Society Magazine*, January 1948, pp. 5–9. See also James E. Faust, *Ensign*, May 1979, p. 53.

309 Cited in *Faith Precedes the Miracle*, Spencer W. Kimball, Deseret Book Company, Salt Lake City, UT, 1972, p. 98.

310 "Jesus Christ—Gifts and Expectations," Ezra Taft Benson, Christmas Devotional, 7 Dec. 1986.

311 "Trust in the Lord," Richard G. Scott, *Ensign*, Nov. 1995, p. 16.

312 "Lessons from the Potter and the Clay," Camille Fronk, unpublished manuscript of a devotional address at Brigham Young University, Provo, UT, 7 Mar. 1995, pp. 8–9.

313 "Trust in the Lord," Richard G. Scott, *Ensign*, Nov. 1995, p. 17.

314 "Finding Joy in Life," Richard G. Scott, *Ensign*, May 1996, p. 25.

315 *The Road Less Traveled*, M. Scott Peck, M.D., Simon & Schuster, New York, 1978, p. 15.

316 *The Road Less Traveled*, M. Scott Peck, M.D., Simon & Schuster, New York, 1978, p. 16.

317 See "Annette's Halo," *Ensign*, September 1991, pp. 71–73.

318 *When Bad Things Happen to Good People*, Harold S. Kushner, Avon Books, New York, 1981, p. 64.

319 "Endurance," Dean Conlee, unpublished devotional address, Brigham Young University, 16 May 1995, p. 7.

320 "Endurance," Dean Conlee, unpublished devotional address, Brigham Young University, 16 May 1995, p. 8.

321 "Solving Emotional Problems in the Lord's Own Way," *Ensign*, May 1978, p. 83.

322 *When Bad Things Happen to Good People*, Harold S. Kushner, Avon Books, New York, 1981, pp. 138–39.

323 *When Bad Things Happen to Good People*, Harold S. Kushner, Avon Books, New York, 1981, pp. 110–11.

324 "For Times of Trouble," Jeffrey R. Holland, *New Era*, Oct. 1980, p. 10.

325 "Keep the Faith," Richard C. Edgley, *Ensign*, May 1993, p. 11.

326 *Teachings of the New Testament*, Lowell Bennion, Deseret Sunday School Union Board, Salt Lake City, 1953, pp. 178–80.

327 *Faith Precedes the Miracle*, Spencer W. Kimball, Deseret Book Company, Salt Lake City, UT, 1972, p. 97.

328 "Gay bashing" is usually by white, straight males in their late teens or early twenties, but it occurs at all ages.

329 A 1988 study by the U.S. Department of Health and Human Services showed that gay teens commit suicide at two to three times the rate of other teens and some studies show that 40% of all gay people make attempts on their lives when they are young (as reported in *Is it a Choice?: Answers to 300 of the Most Frequently Asked Questions About Gays and Lesbians,* Eric Marcus, Harper Collins Publishers, New York, 1993, p. 29).

330 Less than 2% survive to age sixty-five. For those who contract AIDS, the median age of death is thirty-nine. For those whose death is from other factors besides AIDS, the median age of death is forty-two. (See *Medical Consequences of What Homosexuals Do,* Paul Cameron, Family Research Institute, Washington, DC, 1993 and "The Longevity of Homosexuals: Before and After the AIDS Epidemic," Paul Cameron, William Playfair, and Stephen Wellum, *Omega Journal of Death and Dying,* vol. 29, no. 3, 1994, Baywood Publishing, Amityville, NY.)

331 "Same-Gender Attraction," Dallin H. Oaks, *Ensign,* Oct. 1995, p. 9.

332 See "The Greeks Had No Word For It," Marjorie Rosenberg, *The Partisan Review,* Spring 1993, vol. 60, no. 2.

333 "Parents and Loved Ones: Is There Hope?," Alan Medinger, *Regeneration News,* Sep. 1995, p. 2.

334 "Record Number of Foundations & Corporations Funding Gay & Lesbian Causes," John Freeman, *Harvest News,* summer 1997, Harvest USA, Philadelphia, PA, p. 8.

335 Figures confirmed by telephone with the organizations' development offices in June 1997.

336 These concepts were formally prepared for the United Nations Fourth World Conference on Women in Beijing, China, 30 Aug. to 15 Sep. 1995. See "Gender: The Deconstruction of Women: Analysis of the Gender Perspective in Preparation for the Fourth World Conference on Women in Beijing, China," 1995, p. 21.

337 "Covenants," Boyd K. Packer, *Ensign,* Nov. 1990, pp. 84–86.

338 "Same Gender Marriages," letter from the First Presidency dated 1 Feb. 1994.

339 *The New American,* 25 Jan. 1993.

340 *Intercessor's for America Newsletter,* Apr. 1988.

341 *Homosexuality and the Politics of Truth,* Jeffrey Satinover, Baker Books, Grand Rapids, MI, 1966, chapter thirteen.

342 In 1977, for example, a poll was sent to psychiatrists in the USA. 69% of those responding said they considered homosexuality to be the result of psychological maladaption.

343 *Diagnostic and Statistical Manual of Mental Disorders (Fourth Edition),* American Psychiatric Association, Washington, DC, 1994, p. 528.

344 *Is it a Choice?: Answers to 300 of the Most Frequently Asked Questions About Gays and Lesbians,* Eric Marcus, Harper Collins Publishers, New York, 1993, p. 184.

345 Cited in Spencer W. Kimball, Faith Precedes the Miracle, Deseret Book Company, Salt Lake City, UT, 1972, p. 98.

Index